While discipling others who will then disci
defining maturity is sometimes tricky. I'm
research-based, yet practical way, to under
Christlikeness. Don't miss this.

Robert E. Coleman, distinguished senior professor of Evangelism
and Discipleship, Gordon-Conwell Theological Seminary

Daniel Im is a brilliant young thought leader who in *No Silver Bullets* offers
hope to every leader by showing us five micro shifts that can bring macro
changes in our churches. This book is a reality check reminding us quick
fixes will not bring lasting change; but a change in perspective can usher in
a new day. If you are done with easy solutions and ready for a clear path to
lasting change this is the book for you!

Dave Ferguson, lead pastor of Community Christian Church and
author of *Finding Your Way Back to God* and *Starting Over*

No Silver Bullets is as good a read as the title is honest. Finally a new, young
voice enters the fray with clear thinking, rational conclusions, and a radical
call. I felt lit up, called out, and calmed down all at the same time.

Hugh Halter, US Director of Forge America and
author of *The Tangible Kingdom* and *Flesh*

While God will complete in us the good work that He began, there are no
silver bullets in our spiritual growth. And there are no silver bullets in discipling and shepherding a church. There are, however, important perspectives we may adopt that will greatly impact how we lead and the direction
and development of those we lead. I am grateful for Daniel's work and
believe this book will challenge and encourage you.

Eric Geiger, vice president of LifeWay Christian Resources

I've often said that the quality of a church's leadership is directly propor-
tional to the quality of discipleship. If you fail in the area of making disciples, you will fail in the area of leadership development. Daniel gets this as
he examines the systems and pathways for discipleship in the local church.
Don't miss out on this important work.

Alan Hirsch, author of numerous books on missional Christianity
including *The Forgotten Ways* and *5Q* and founder of
100Movements and Forge

No Silver Bullets is a refreshing effort to help church leaders guide the local church to more effective ministry. Far too many books offer over-simplified solutions and over-reaching promises. In this incredible work, Daniel reveals the necessity for church leaders to focus their efforts to faithfulness to the timeless practices of healthy churches. Every leader church should read and reread this book!

Kevin Peck, lead pastor, The Austin Stone Community Church
and coauthor of *Designed to Lead*

If the central command of the Great Commission is to make disciples, and you have a plan for marketing, facilities, and organization, but not a plan for discipleship, you have missed the point. Don't miss this important work by my friend, Daniel. In it, he will help you develop a discipleship pathway for your church by leveraging research that I was a part of.

Ed Stetzer, Billy Graham Distinguished Chair of Church,
Wheaton College

In this important book, Daniel returns discipleship to the center of the church's ministry. The discipleship process begins in evangelism and progresses all the way through healthy involvement in a local church. Daniel, who practices what he preaches, offers practical, inspiring stories and steps to guide you through every step of this process.

J.D. Greear, Ph.D., pastor of The Summit Church,
Raleigh-Durham, North Carolina and author of
Gaining by Losing: Why the Future Belongs to Churches that Send

Maybe there is a silver bullet—the understanding that small, careful, shifts in a disciplemaker's posture and direction can yield major outcomes. This book has benefitted me as a change agent.

Ralph Moore, founder, Hope Chapels

I'm so excited about Daniel Im's new book. He's honest and right—there really are no silver bullets. When we do have new ideas, they take time and don't automatically happen without a price. Daniel's book deals with something that very few people really talk about—how to effectively bring about change. This is critical for every pastor, because there are so many ideas, directions, and new ways of doing ministry that all promise to grow your church or be "the" secret—and they all leave you disappointed. But if your church has a healthy process for change, as the seasons and culture and context come and go, you can implement new ideas to be more effective. A church that cannot change will not last until the next generation!

Bob Roberts, senior pastor of Northwood Church and author of several books, most recently *Lessons from the East*

Daniel Im is a sharp thinker and keen observer. Both traits show up again and again in *No Silver Bullets*. This is a hyper-practical book that can help you and your team rethink its discipleship pathway or create one in the first place—all of which can help you prepare your church for future ministry.

Carey Nieuwhof, founding and teaching pastor, Connexus Church

In our fast-food, instant download, immediate gratification, consumer driven culture, we often fall prey to copy-cat Christianity. And yet, no matter how much we try to force it, laboring for the harvest has never been about instant gratification. Daniel Im speaks powerfully to this truth, challenging us to change the way we think about our church so that we can ultimately shift our practices to better align with an eternal Kingdom mind-set. His work is timely, practical, and a powerful application of biblical principles for our time.

Dhati Lewis, lead pastor of Blueprint Church and director of BLVD

There may not be a silver bullet when it comes to discipleship, but this book is a must-read bullet to put in the barrel of your disciple-making environments. Daniel Im has created an incredibly insightful and practically helpful work that I will read several times over both alone and with our team. If you're wondering how you or your church can become effective at the mission Jesus gave us, this book is for you.

Jeff Vanderstelt, pastor at Doxa Church, visionary leader of Saturate and The Soma Family of Churches, and author of *Saturate* and *Gospel Fluency*

We live in an age of killer apps and quick fixes for nearly every problem we run into. Is it any wonder that we look to the latest and greatest silver-bullet program or Bible study to fix the discipleship problem in our church? In this book Daniel doesn't offer a microwave approach, but five micro-shifts to break down the complex problems surrounding discipleship. He accurately diagnoses the key issues and prescribes these practical steps that help you move from great discipleship intentions to great implementation and better equipping of the saints you are called to serve.

Todd Adkins, director of leadership at LifeWay Leadership and host of the 5LQ Podcast

Daniel is one of the brightest young minds in the church. God has given him a unique discernment into the tensions and transitions facing the church. You'll be better prepared for the future if you read everything he writes. I sure do!

Shawn Lovejoy, founder and CEO, CourageToLead.com; author of *Be Mean about the Vision: Preserving & Protecting What Matters*

Leadership is more than hard work; it is habitual work. The five shifts outlined in this book will help you develop the habits required to take your church to the next level. So stop working hard and start working smart by inviting Daniel to be a guide for you and your team.

Brad Lomenick, author of *The Catalyst Leader* and *H3 Leadership* and former president of Catalyst

Even though Daniel writes about "five small shifts that will transform your ministry," there is nothing small about his book! His ideas, seasoned with years of ministry experience and theological rigor written afresh, will impact you personally and leave an imprint on your ministry. I highly recommend this much-needed book!

Derwin L. Gray, lead pastor of Transformation Church and author of *The High Definition Leader: Building Multiethnic Churches in a Multiethnic World*

While many are looking for the next BIG thing, Daniel Im shows us how small, micro-shifts can lead to macro-fruitfulness in fulfilling Jesus' co-mission. When the disciples couldn't catch any fish, Jesus told them to throw the net on the other side and they caught a boat load. One small change led to one big difference. Likewise, employing the small shifts recommended in this book can make a big difference in your ministry of multiplying missional disciples.

JR Woodward, national director of The V3 Church Planting Movement, author of *Creating a Missional Culture*, and coauthor of *The Church as Movement*

Daniel Im has captured some of the most insightful, biblically-based and well-researched ministry concepts to help both younger and older leaders guide churches toward their full kingdom potential. A must read!

Keith Taylor, lead pastor of Beulah Alliance Church

Most leaders don't have the luxury of slowing down or considering if what they are doing is truly the most effective route. Daniel Im has had the rare opportunity to observe thousands of churches and leaders and to see the small shifts that make the difference between an effective or ineffective church. While there is no simple and easy solution, small shifts and small steps can drastically change the trajectory of your church, for the glory of God.

Matt Brown, evangelist, author, and founder of Think Eternity

I like this book by Daniel. It shows his experience in Korea, Canada, and in the USA. He helps pastors to assess their disciple making systems and make changes based upon solid research. Read it, process it, and apply the insights for change.

Bobby Harrington, executive director for Discipleship.org

I am so excited about getting *No Silver Bullets* into as many pastors' hands as I can. In a day when so many leaders are looking for quick fixes and silver bullet solutions Daniel has brought a fresh shift in perspective that can free them from that chase. This book is packed full of practical advice, tips and tools that will make you a better leader and make your church more effective at making disciples.

Mac Lake, senior director of Church Planter Development,
North American Mission Board

Daniel Im is an incredibly able and astute listener. He pays attention to the changes in culture, and to the challenges of the church, and helps us consider surprising new possibilities as we forge our way forward in mission. *No Silver Bullets* is refreshing, rewarding and very much worth taking time to read and absorb.

Linda Bergquist, church planting catalyst for the North American
Mission Board, and coauthor of *Church Turned
Inside Out* and *The Wholehearted Church Planter*

Daniel Im continues to emerge as one of the sharpest minds of his generation focused on the North American Church. As a catalytic practitioner, his keen insights are rooted in experiential knowledge, thorough research, and personal interaction with pastoral leaders in a wide variety of ministry contexts. In *No Silver Bullets*, Daniel does not merely express philosophical best wishes; rather, he articulates proven and promising practices sure to assist you in establishing a dynamic local church to effectively reach an increasingly diverse and cynical society with the hope of the gospel. For these reasons and more, what Daniel writes I read, as you should, too.

Mark DeYmaz, founding pastor, Mosaic Church of Central Arkansas, president of Mosaix Global Network, and author of *Disruption, Building a Healthy Multi-ethnic Church*, and *Multiethnic Conversations*

No Silver Bullets is a treasure chest of research, strategic thinking, and practical insight for disciple-making leaders. Daniel Im fuses his heart of gold and his platinum mind to deliver a must read tool for pastors.

Will Mancini, founder of Auxano and LifeYounique.com

NO SILVER BULLETS

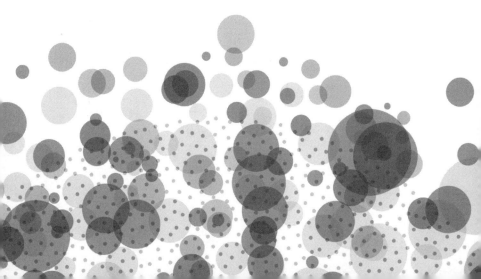

NO SILVER BULLETS

DANIEL IM

5
SMALL SHIFTS
THAT WILL
**TRANSFORM YOUR
MINISTRY**

PUBLISHING GROUP
NASHVILLE, TENNESSEE

*To pastors and church leaders everywhere. You are the true heroes.
Thanks for sticking with it. Let's finish well.*

CONTENTS

FOREWORD

I have routines. You have routines. We all have routines. Whether it's the way we start our days, commute to work, go to bed, or anything in between, we all have a certain way of doing things. In fact, a recent book on this topic outlined the fact that geniuses—both ancient and modern—tend to live and die by their routines. Charles Dickens took three-hour walks every afternoon, Mozart had a regimented daily schedule, and Charles Schultz, creator of nearly eighteen thousand Peanuts comic strips, had a ham sandwich and glass of milk almost every day.[1]

So yes, we all have routines. But why? Is it superstition? Laziness? Why is it that we do things the way that we do?

Routines exist because they are the best, most effective, and efficient way to do the things that need to get done. Well, at least, at one point in time they were the best. At one point in time they were the most efficient. And at one point in time we saw first hand just how effective they were.

The same is true for the church. At one point in time, those programs made sense, but do they still today? When's the last time you evaluated them? Or have they just become routine? How much of your church is driven by mottos like, "Well that's the way we've always done it," or, "Don't rock the boat," or "What would dear sister Sally do if you changed things? Her deceased husband basically built this church."

Change or die. This is the decision you'll have to make if you continue to let routines from yesteryear run your church. The majority of churches in the West are either declining or growing at a pace that's slower than the community they're located in. In other words, they're losing ground. Church has become a litany of activities and busyness. It's become one program or one thing after another. And there's no intentionality or movement forward in a direction that demonstrates faithfulness with what God has entrusted that church.

The solution isn't to look down the street and copy the nearby mega-church. Nor is it to blow everything up and start from scratch. And by all means, staying the same is not an option either. There is no one silver bullet to turning around a dying church or continuing the growth of a healthy one. It takes several little improvements in different areas to add up to growth. And that's precisely what this book is about.

In *No Silver Bullets*, Daniel will show you how to shift your church in a Great Commission and Great Commandment direction. He'll show you how to make small changes that will get you out of the very routines that are preventing your church from fulfilling it's God given vision. And he'll do this by helping you root it into the very fabric of your church—your discipleship pathway.

God has given you talents and God has given the body of Christ talents. So don't be like a hamster on a spinning wheel, where you are just going around and around without any productive action. Take what God has given you, and learn from what God has given Daniel, and together make something beautiful.

Quite frankly, I've seen many churches who have this wide, broad, and deep list of activities. And their people are busy. Something is always going on during the day and in the evenings. They're constantly doing things. And they go on and on. But then you look at their impact in the community, and many have never even heard of them. Very few people are being reached for Christ. They simply don't have a clear direction. They think that busyness is equivalent to obedience. But busyness without the right direction is poor stewardship.

So gather your leadership team together and work through the small shifts that are outlined in this book. Stop producing consumers and start releasing disciple makers. Your church and your neighborhood won't be the same without it. So my prayer is that as you read this book, you would become a better steward of that which God has given you.

Thom S. Rainer
President
LifeWay Christian Resources

INTRODUCTION

"By perseverance the snail reached the ark."

—Charles Spurgeon

When Hester Griggs, a small-town utilities commissioner in Pecos County, Texas, decided to add sugar to the municipal water supply, he didn't experience the sort of outcry that you might have expected. Over the previous twenty years, though the population had slowly increased, the amount of water consumed hadn't. Instead of drinking water, his residents had turned to soda, sweet tea, and energy drinks. Simply put, people weren't getting their recommended daily intake of eight glasses of water. So Griggs decided to do something about it.

Since the normal route of public service announcements, policies, and procedures was too slow, and never resulted in any lasting change, he decided to take matters into his own hands and devise a solution to get people to drink more water. His solution? Add sugar to the water supply. But it wasn't just a bit; it was enough to fill an eight-ounce cup of water with four tablespoons of sugar!

Surprisingly, this small shift made a big difference. Rather than complaining about sticky showers, the residents in the town began drinking more water than ever. When going out to restaurants, instead of drinking soda, they were now asking for tap water.

When asked whether residents were now just consuming too much sugar, Griggs responded, "I wouldn't say there's too much concern. The more important part is that our citizens are getting their eight cups of water, and in many cases more. So the upside overweighs the downside . . . unless you have diabetes."[1]

Let's play a game here. Two truths and a lie. I'll tell you two more stories about small shifts that have made a big difference, and you can be the judge. So put away your phone, don't ask Google or Siri if Pecos County is real (because it is), and keep on reading.

What do you think would happen if you set off enough explosives to blow up four hundred ten-story buildings? Two hundred tons' worth? When would you need to use this outrageous amount of dynamite? Precisely when you're building a dam along China's longest river, the Yangtze, that's been a dream since 1919. Both Sun Yat-sen, the father of modern China, and Mao Zedong, the father of China's communist revolution, imagined this dam. And lo and behold, in 2006, more than two hundred tons of explosives were set off to destroy the last barrier holding back the Yangtze River from the Three Gorges Dam.[2]

Do you think it's possible for humans to shift the earth's rotation? Well, up until the Three Gorges Dam was built, earthquakes, wind, climate change, and atmospheric pressure systems were among the only known means able to affect it.[3] The Three Gorges Dam changed everything. According to research from NASA, when this dam is filled, it's estimated to hold more than ten trillion gallons of water, which is enough to actually shift the earth, and affect its rotation.[4]

Although this dam is one of the largest in the world, it's still quite small compared to the distance between Los Angeles and Toronto, or the time it would take to go from London to Sydney. After all, the dam is only 1.4 miles (2.3 kilometers) long and 607 feet (185 meters) tall.[5] So how could such a small structure cause that big of an impact that it would affect the earth's rotation?

For the last story, let's roll back to January 28, 1986, and take a look at the tenth and final mission of NASA's space shuttle *Challenger*. What went wrong? Why did it fail and kill the lives of all seven astronauts on board, including a civilian high school teacher? Was it simply an accident caused by factors beyond human control? Or was there political pressure because of the ongoing Cold War with the Soviets? Was it preventable? Did someone know it was going to happen before it took place?

The latter half of the twentieth century was marked by a race to space. It was a competition between the Americans and Soviets to see who had more money, knowledge, and courage, to keep pushing the envelope and get there first. The Soviets managed to launch an artificial satellite and orbit a human around the earth first. So in 1961, President John F. Kennedy declared that "landing a man on the moon and returning him safely to Earth within a decade" would be the new goal for the Americans. And on July 20, 1969, the Americans did it. Neil Armstrong became the first man to take "one small step for man," and "one giant leap for mankind" on the moon.[6]

With this giant feat behind them, the seventies and eighties were marked by the normalcy of orbiting communications and navigation satellites, and a continued exploration deeper into space. As space travel became more commonplace, the Americans moved into the next wave of space travel by launching the first reusable spacecraft—the space shuttle *Columbia*—on April 12, 1981.[7]

Though each space shuttle was designed for a lifetime of one hundred flights each,[8] when the *Challenger* went down on its tenth mission, twenty-four successful launches had already taken place.[9] Launching a space shuttle into space wasn't like taking a plane from one end of the country to the other. Every mission was incredibly expensive—$450 million, to be exact. Add onto that price tag the money it cost to build one of these space shuttles—approximately $1.7 billion—the time invested in labor, and the priceless lives of humans on board, and it was in no one's best interest to take each mission lightly. So what went wrong?[10]

No, it wasn't sabotage or Cold War tactics. It was the failure of two rubber O-rings that were "designed to separate the sections of the rocket booster," that "failed due to cold temperatures on the morning of the launch."[11] Can you believe that something as small as two rubber O-rings could cause such a large disaster? Just imagine what would've happened if those rubber O-rings were replaced or the launch was delayed until it warmed up? It's amazing how big of a difference such a small shift can make.

Micro-Shifts and Macro-Changes

That's exactly what this book is about. No, I'm not talking about sugar, dams, and O-rings. I'm talking about what those three stories represent: small shifts that make a big difference.

Have you ever noticed the deep longing inside of human beings for the silver bullet? For that one quick, magical solution that will solve all of our problems? I know I have. I remember thinking to myself that this one sermon I was getting ready to preach was going to be so powerful that the chains of apathy in my church would finally be broken. The consumeristic tendencies hidden in everyone's hearts were going to be rooted out once and for all. Everyone in the church would befriend those far from God, share the gospel with them, see them experience new life in Christ, and then disciple them to do the same. People were going to move from being merely disciples to being disciple-makers. Instead of the church being a place to get their needs met, the church was going to see itself as a house of prayer for all nations, a hospital for sinners and not a hotel for saints, a disciple-making institute, and a tangible sign, instrument, and foretaste of the kingdom of God. This was going to be *the* day, *the* sermon, and *the* moment that would go down in history.

When it didn't quite happen the way I had envisioned it, I realized my mistake. Oh, how naïve I was. I thought the sermon was the silver bullet, when it was actually the discipleship model that the church down the road was using! I mean, just look at how *successful* they were.

Well, when that didn't work either, I turned to secular management books. And then to church consultants. And then to . . .

Does any of this sound familiar?

The myth of the silver bullet is alive and well—and it's not because of old reruns of *The Lone Ranger*, or teenage novels about werewolves. It's alive and well because we want the quick fix. We have been conditioned for the instant. It's our hidden addiction.

The myth of the silver bullet is alive and well because we all want the quick fix.

If our computers take longer than a minute to start, we think something's wrong. Do you remember when it would take so long for your computer to start up, that you'd have time to brew a cup of coffee or make yourself a sandwich before you could even start using it? If we want to read a book, we can download it instantly. If we want to listen to one, we can literally press play the moment after we purchase it. If we want toothpaste, laundry detergent, or a few bananas, we can order it on Prime Now and get it within two hours. And now, with the launch of Amazon Go, we don't even need to line up and pay the cashier at the grocery store! Sure, this is convenient, but the unfortunate side effect is that we've been conditioned like Pavlov's dog to salivate at the sound of a bell.[12] The availability of goods and resources—and our consumption of them—have conditioned us to *need* instant gratification. Regrettably, this has seeped into our spiritual lives and the way we lead our churches.

If you've been around ministry long enough, you'll know that there are no perfect models, no one right way of doing ministry or leading a church (I'm talking about church practice, not theology). There are no silver bullets—one-decision solutions that will solve all your woes and unleash your church into a new season of fruitfulness. The only way change happens—significant, long-lasting, macro-level change—is through a series of small decisions, steps, or micro-shifts, that are put into action and completed one at a time.

Isn't that why the late great preacher of the Metropolitan Tabernacle in London, Charles Spurgeon, said, "By perseverance the snail reached the ark"? The snail had no silver bullet. It got to the ark one small step at a time.

Consider . . .

Let me ask you a few questions. Are you happy with your existing vision, strategy, and values, or do you need to revisit them? Are you producing disciple-makers, disciples, or consumers? Are you worried that what you're currently doing isn't sustainable or scalable? Do you need to overhaul your church, but aren't sure what to do differently? Are you thinking about planting a church or campus but want to make sure that you grow by multiplication, instead of addition?

Throughout this book, I want to invite you to consider. Consider what God might do in and through you and your church, if you were to implement the small changes, or micro-shifts, that you read about in each chapter.

As you work through each chapter, be sure to leverage the audits, frameworks, and questions. These tools will help you "consider the path for your feet" so that you can stop talking about change and instead do something about it (Prov. 4:25–26). Each chapter is designed to cut through the noise and complexity of ministry to provide you with sensible wisdom to make your next micro-shift. After all, isn't that better than the one silver bullet that is larger than life, one-size-fits-all, and often too complex the more you learn about it? I think this is what Solomon was referring to when he contrasted sensible wisdom with "the stupidity of fools" (Prov. 14:8).

Five Micro-Shifts

In this book, we're going to consider five micro-shifts that will produce macro-change in your church. In chapter 1, we will start by looking at discipleship from a systems perspective. We will define the various ways churches approach discipleship from a fifty-thousand-foot level. We'll do this by looking at the two spectrums that influence your approach, and then by examining how they intersect.

Then, in chapter 2, we'll zoom into discipleship at the individual level. We'll go from looking at the systematic discipleship of the many to the personal discipleship of the one. We'll do this by unpacking the results of one of the largest research projects on discipleship to date, in order to determine the right metrics for maturity.

Technology has forever changed the way individuals learn. Moreover, adults learn differently from children. We simply can't teach the way we were taught. In chapter 3, we'll unpack these issues and explore what it looks like to move from being a sage on the stage to a guide on the side when it comes to discipleship and leadership development.

In the New Testament, we read more about the function of ministry, which is to be in community, than any particular form or model of ministry. As a result, in chapter 4, we'll survey four environments where discipleship and development occur. This will help us uncover and adopt a kingdom vision for community, rather than a whatever-works-for-the-successful-church-down-the-road model.

How do you define the church? Through the lens of God's mission or your mission? In chapter 5, we'll look at the marks of a church and compare what happens when the end goal for discipleship is maturity, and what happens when the end goal for discipleship is mission.

Whereas the first section of this book laid out the shifts, the second section will focus on the path to implementation. Your church is a system and it's interconnected. To think that you can introduce change quickly and easily, without it affecting the other areas of your church, is naïve at best.

This is why, in chapter 6, we'll examine expectations, the change process, and three steps for introducing change.

In chapters 7 and 8, we'll focus on your church's discipleship pathway and help you uncover and/or create the intentional route, steps, and paths for developing missionary disciples for kingdom impact. If your church does not have a discipleship pathway, these chapters will help you uncover what's underneath the skin of your church, so that you can build one that's right for your context. However, if your church already has a discipleship pathway, I want to challenge you to consider how the vision, strategy, and values of your church are getting you there. Are they integrated and working with one another? Or are they like the situation we read of in 1 Corinthians 12, where each body part is saying they don't need the others?

These last two chapters will offer you ideas to integrate the five micro-shifts into the way you disciple and lead your church. In other words, if you're planting a church, replanting, or revitalizing it, you'll learn how to build a discipleship pathway from scratch. If, however, these systems are already set up in your church, but you aren't quite sure if they are the right ones or if they're performing at full capacity, then you'll learn how to clarify and tweak them. In both instances, the goal is to unleash your ministry toward greater Kingdom impact.

By the way, it was the Texas story. Pecos County is real, but Hester Griggs and his sugary solution aren't.

Let's get started with the first micro-shift and discover why twelve disciples should always be preferred over twelve hundred consumers.

SECTION I

THE SHIFTS

CHAPTER 1

FROM DESTINATION TO DIRECTION

*"You can create a stronger movement with twelve
disciples than with 1,200 consumers."*
—Alan Hirsch

We had made it. We had finally made it. I no longer had to make up excuses, bend the truth, or gripe when I would share what we did during summer vacation with my friends. Long gone were the days I would complain that my summer was filled with Kumon math problems, Korean language school, violin practice, and hanging out on dairy crates at the back of my parents' grocery store. My family was going to Disneyland.

You heard me right—Disneyland! And I was going to make sure all my friends knew about it when I came back from summer vacation. Me and Mickey—it would be glorious.

I had a simple childhood. My parents immigrated from South Korea to Canada in the 1970s and had nothing. They literally started with nothing. So in order to support my three older sisters and me, my parents had to work. And I'm not talking about a forty-hour desk job with nice perks. I'm talking about working all day and night, without any help, benefits, sick days, or vacation. In fact, the only time we ever took a vacation was when my parents decided that they were done with their business. So they sold it and we went on vacation. I'm guessing they were burned out.

As a kid, I didn't care. It didn't bother me that my parents sold their only means of making an income. Or that they didn't have plans on what was next—at least to my knowledge. I was just happy that we were going to go on a real vacation to a faraway land!

After a week in the van, we finally arrived at my long-awaited paradise—Disneyland. Now I understand that it shouldn't take a whole week to drive to Disneyland from Vancouver, Canada, but when there are four children in the van and one parent doing the majority of the driving, things often take longer than they should. I was so excited we were finally at Disneyland, that right after entering the park, I bee-lined to Autopia—the ride with a real-working gas pedal and a steering wheel. Sure, we had been in a car for a week, but now I could be the driver and I could be in control. I mean, come on; as a five-year-old boy, what else could you expect? It was a dream come true.

After a full day of lining up and relining up for Autopia, we hit the sack. The next morning, my dad announced . . . that we were going back home. I couldn't believe it. After a week of driving, and only one day at Disneyland . . . that was it?

What injustice! How could he? This felt like torture. No amount of griping, begging, crying, or negotiating worked. We couldn't change my parents' minds. So we left paradise and began our trek home. To be honest, I guess I was so depressed and upset that I don't even remember the trip back.

The Journey Matters Too

As an adult, I wish I knew then what I know now about vacations. The journey is as much a part of the vacation as is the destination. Instead of viewing that vacation as an epic failure—since we were only at Disneyland for a day—what do you think would have happened if I had shifted my perspective and viewed the entire journey as an equal part of it?

Perhaps I would have remembered the fun that we had on the way backstopping in San Francisco and spending *way too much time* in a gift shop buying T-shirts and snow globes—don't ask me why we bought snow globes in San Francisco.

Or maybe I would have remembered the beauty of the Grand Canyon-esque valleys we saw during one of our rest stops. And how during that rest stop, I was dressed up as a great safari explorer intent on wielding my plastic sword and killing all the imaginary bad guys!

I may have even remembered the special time my parents let us sleep at a Motel 6 because "cabin fever" can actually apply to long road trips in a van too. As cool as our maroon Ford Sidewinder was—with captain seats in the second row, and a third row that reclined into a bed—six people in a van all day and night can get a bit taxing at times.

If I had only shifted my perspective, the ride home might have been as enjoyable as our time at Disney.

The journey is just as much a part of the adventure as the destination.

In hindsight, it's a good thing this is how I see it now—the journey, or the direction, really is as much a part of the adventure as is the destination. In fact, those three memories are as vivid, if not more real to me, than the numerous times I went on Autopia.

How ironic.

From Mourning to Intentional Celebration

When I pastored in Korea, I named our ministry Nine37 after Matthew 9:37: "The harvest is abundant, but the workers are few." The leadership team and I did this because we knew that we would only have our church members for a few years before they would leave us. After all, as globe-trotting expats, they were only ever going to be with us temporarily before moving onto their next big thing. So we would regularly give them a guilt trip and tell them that they had to stay with us, because the harvest was abundant in Korea and the workers were few.

Okay, not really. But we did have to intentionally shift our perspective in order to deal with this reality. So instead of trying to keep them from leaving, we decided to send them out instead. Instead of mourning, we decided to rejoice and celebrate.

As a result, every week during our pre-service Sunday morning prayer time, we would literally pray Matthew 9:35–38 over our church. Our leadership team would intentionally ask God to transform our church members into Kingdom-focused harvest workers. We prayed that wherever they went, they would be a greater blessing there as a result of their time in our ministry here. So when the time came for people to leave, instead of giving them the cold shoulder, we commissioned them. This could not have happened without shifting our perspective.

The Same Is True for Your Church

Think about your church. What do you long to see for them? What do you regularly pray over them? If God were to answer your deepest prayers for your church, what would happen? What would change?

Would your church be filled with a movement of disciple-making disciples that infiltrated all areas of your region (Matt. 28:18–20)?

Or maybe your worship service would be filled with "a vast multitude from every nation, tribe, people, and language" worshipping beside one another (Rev. 7:9)?

Perhaps your church would be meeting daily, living life together, meeting one another's needs, praising God, receiving favor from all people, and being used by God to save people on a daily basis (Acts 2:42–47)?

Whatever dream God has given you for your church, I want to be the first one to tell you that it's possible. After all, the fact that you're even reading this book and praying for your church means that you're on the right track.

But I also want to be the first one to tell you that achieving those dreams does not require a radical change; you don't have to blow everything up and start over. All it requires is a series of micro-shifts, taken one step a time. After all, let's be honest with ourselves—there's no silver bullet in life, so why would we assume that there's one in ministry?

But . . .

I love the following quote—often attributed to Harriet Tubman—about dreams: "Every great dream begins with a dreamer. Always remember, you have within you the strength, the patience, and the passion to reach for the stars to change the world." And this one by Walt Disney: "All our dreams can come true, if we have the courage to pursue them."[1]

The problem though, is that a dream is precisely that—a dream. Dreams are not reality. They are the hidden potential for the future that lies dormant within each and every one of us. Dreams are like the statue that's imprisoned in the walls of marble, awaiting the sculptor to set it free—as the iconic Italian artist Michelangelo once said. So while I like inspirational quotes as much as the next person, inspiration can only get us so far.

Dreams require courage and strength. They cannot be achieved on a whim, since they require a strategy and a plan. I mean, do you really think the Underground Railroad was built without a strategy or a plan? And what about the Disney Empire?

The Three Influences on Your Church

If you're like me, one of your dreams is maturity—to see the people in your church grow in their walk with Christ. While I also want my church to grow numerically, I actually care more about spiritual growth than numerical growth. Just imagine what a hundred sold-out followers of Christ can do compared to five hundred seat warmers? Or as Alan Hirsch once said to me, "You can create a stronger movement with twelve disciples than with 1,200 consumers."[2]

> Dreams are the hidden potential for the future that lies dormant within each and every one of us.

In order to help individuals mature and grow, which we'll address at depth in chapter 2, you first need to understand the orientation or posture that your church has toward growth. There are several factors that affect this, most significantly the church's leadership, culture, and history (see Figure 1.1).

So take a moment and work through the following two assessments to discover your church's posture to growth. Upon completing them, I'll introduce you to the Influences Matrix, which will help set your church on the right trajectory to both spiritual and numerical growth.

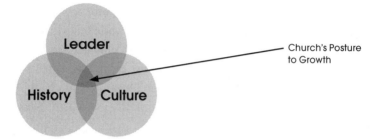

FIGURE 1.1: CHURCH'S POSTURE TO GROWTH

Self-Assessment: The Leader's Influence

1. Who do you look up to as a pastor and church leader? Who has shaped your view of church practice and practical theology? Is it Eugene Peterson? J. I. Packer? Tim Keller? It could be someone you know personally, or someone you've admired from a distance. The people you look up to hold the greatest power to shape you. In other words, the ones you follow are the ones you model.

Write down the names of the pastors, missionaries, theologians, leaders, and thinkers that have shaped you most:

_____

_____

_____

_____

_____

2. How have others shaped you? How have the individuals above shaped the way you approach church practice and practical theology? Is it the way you preach? Or the way you approach discipleship? Perhaps it's the way you cast vision, or your view of church planting, multisite, and multiplication?

Write down the ways that your church practice and practical theology have been shaped by the previous list of individuals:

_____

_____

_____

_____

_____

3. What type of leader are you? Let me paraphrase one of my favorite quotes from the Chinese general, military strategist, and author of *The Art of War,* Sun Tzu: "If you know your enemy, you'll win half of the battles. But if you know yourself, you'll win the other half."[3] Following up from the previous points, we too often model our ministries after the ones we follow—sometimes intentionally and other times unintentionally. As a result, their influence on us inevitably leaves a mark on the way we view and do ministry. This is not a bad thing per se, but it has the potential to turn into a bad habit if left unchecked.

So going back to Sun Tzu's wisdom on war—are you only winning half of your battles? Do you know what type of leader you are? Are you more task-oriented or people-oriented? Do you like solving problems or finding solutions? Do you like starting things, improving them, or maintaining them? Do you know your strengths? Are you managing your weaknesses? Do you like to do everything, or do you develop, delegate, or dump?

Take a few personality profiles and write your results here (I recommend StrengthsFinder,[4] Kolbe,[5] and any of the numerous versions of DISC, just to name a few):

_____

_____

_____

_____

_____

4. How do you view accountability? Is it your direct responsibility to grow those in your church as disciples? Or rather, is it your responsibility to create an environment in which they can grow? Do you have someone that holds you accountable as a leader? These questions are important because your view of accountability from a systems perspective directly influences the way your church measures growth, as we'll discover later in this chapter.

Write down your view of accountability here:

_____

_____

_____

_____

This self-assessment on your leadership is the first step to understanding your church's existing orientation and posture toward spiritual and numerical growth. However, that's only a third of it, since culture and history also have a deep impact on the way your church views growth. So take some time now to assess the other two influences that affect your church in this next combined assessment. If you are a ministry leader and not a part of the senior leadership of your church, then answer these questions for your ministry area. Otherwise, answer them for your church.

Completing this next assessment will pave the way to the heart of this chapter, where you will discover a new paradigm that will help you make a micro-shift that will lead to macro-change—setting your church on the trajectory to both spiritual and numerical growth.

Church Assessment: The Historical and Cultural Influences

1. Who are the celebrated pastors/leaders in your church and in your region? While your church may never hand you a pastor-of-the-year award, many in your church are trying to shape you into their image. Okay, maybe not into *their* image, but they are definitely trying to shape you into *an* image of some pastor they knew from yesteryear. This was the pastor who preached the best sermons, cared for them, and did ministry in just the right way. This is what I like to call *pastoral nostalgia*. The problem with nostalgia is that it's simply not accurate, since we tend to overemphasize the good characteristics and experiences, while underemphasizing the bad. This is why it's important to know who those nostalgic leaders are for your church because they are subtly influencing your church's posture to growth.

If you did not plant the church, ask people to describe their experience with the previous pastor(s) in your church. If there are a large group of individuals who came from another church in your region, ask them the same question. Carefully watch their body language while you're listening to them. What are they verbally and nonverbally saying? How do they view spiritual and numerical growth?

---

2. What kind of leaders do you have in your church? Assess the way that your staff, key ministry leaders, and volunteers lead. Do they function like surgeons, calling all the shots while others follow? Or are they more like lieutenants who receive their instructions from their commanders and faithfully lead those under them accordingly?

Perhaps they're more like union workers who always seem to refer back to the policy manual anytime a change is made. Are leaders the same across ministry areas? Or are they unique to each ministry area? The types of leaders you have in your church will affect your ability to implement the Influences Matrix.

Write down all the different types of leaders that you observe in your church:

_____

_____

_____

_____

3. What happens when the church is challenged or asked to do something? In a typical church, you'll have a portion that will respond with a resounding, "Yes!," others who will require a bit of convincing, some who will wait to see how the majority responds, and a few who will resist with their arms folded. When you look at your church, do you have more on the yes side or no side?

Alongside writing your observations here, can you identify the names of your greatest supporters and your most challenging resisters? How about the "swing voters"? This will help in chapter 6 of this book as you learn how to introduce change.

_____

_____

_____

_____

_____

4. What gets celebrated in your church? While this may seem similar to the first question in this assessment, this question actually focuses more on the types of activities, accomplishments, and stories that get celebrated than the individuals who are celebrated. This is not an idealistic question either. While your church may have its past accomplishments on banners, the names of significant donors engraved somewhere, and its vision on the wall, what you really need to identify are the things that get celebrated down the hall—since these are the very things that often shape culture.

Write down what your church truly celebrates, from the pulpit and down the hall:

Two Spectrums, One Matrix, and a Micro-Shift

Before you could buy an overpriced, ethically sourced, organic, fair trade coffee that was poured for you by a hipster barista at an indie coffee shop, there was Starbucks. Before you could mail order hand-selected, single origin, small batch, whole coffee beans within forty-eight hours of being roasted, there was Starbucks. Starbucks was doing both of those things way before anyone else.

While I know many coffee aficionados may scoff at the idea that Starbucks would serve a good cup of coffee, the fact is, Starbucks introduced the Italian art of coffee and espresso to North America and much of the world. They raised the bar and are still doing so today. Believe it or not, there was a time when coffee was weak, espresso was hard to find, blended and flavored iced coffee drinks were nonexistent, and lattes were only served at high-end restaurants.

Starbucks not only popularized the love of coffee, but they also shifted the way that we consume it. Howard Shultz, in his book *Onward: How Starbucks Fought for Its Life without Losing Its Soul,* writes, "We had evolved millions of people's relationships with coffee, from *what* they drank to *where* and *when* they drank it."[6]

I believe this shift was key to their success. If Starbucks had only focused on the *what,* without making an intentional shift to the *where* and *when,* they would not have experienced the widespread success that they have. After all, people do not just go to Starbucks for the coffee; they also go to relax, read, work, and have conversations.

This micro-shift from the *what* to the *where* and *when* has not only led to success for Starbucks—and the success of other retailers who have copied their strategy—but it has actually led to a macro-change in our culture. This micro-shift by Starbucks has essentially changed *where* and *when* many of us choose to live, work, and play.

What if you could make a similar micro-shift as a church leader that would result in a macro-change in your *church* culture? What if this micro-shift would set your church on a trajectory to both spiritual and numerical growth? Would you consider it?

In order to uncover this micro-shift, we first need to take a look at two spectrums.

The Destination/Direction Spectrum

When it comes to developing a process for discipleship, most churches fall somewhere along this first spectrum (see Figure 1.2):

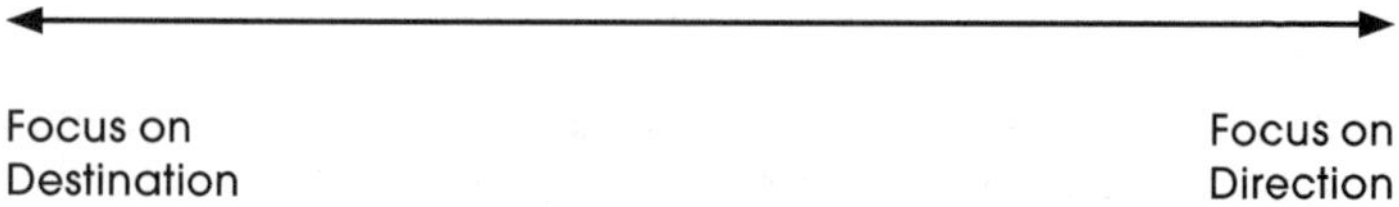

Focus on
Destination

Focus on
Direction

FIGURE 1.2: THE DESTINATION/DIRECTION SPECTRUM

A church that focuses on destination is one that measures the maturity of disciples based on how much they have achieved, what they know, their observable behaviors, and whether they have completed certain classes. The destination-focused church has clear metrics for success that are objective and outward in nature.

By contrast, a church that focuses on direction is one that sees maturity as an ongoing process without an endpoint this side of eternity. Maturity is first measured by the direction the disciple is moving—toward Christ or away from Christ—and then how far along they are in that journey. As a result, the direction-focused church has broader metrics for success that are both objective and subjective in nature.

Maturity is an ongoing process without an endpoint this side of eternity.

Let's compare and contrast the major differences between these two approaches using this table:

A Discipleship Process Focused on Destination	A Discipleship Process Focused on Direction
When you arrive, you are mature	You mature when you're moving in the right direction
There is an end destination	There is a clear direction
You must believe in Jesus before you can belong with the church	You can belong with the church before you believe in Jesus
Standardized	Personalized
Formulaic	Non-formulaic
Bounded-set	Centered-set

FIGURE 1.3: COMPARING AND CONTRASTING DESTINATION AND DIRECTION

Destination (Bounded-Set) vs. Direction (Centered-Set)

If you are familiar with missiologist Paul G. Hiebert, you may have noticed his inspiration on my two categories. In his landmark article,

"Conversion, Culture and Cognitive Categories," Hiebert described two different ways to understand what a Christian is based on set theory from mathematics: bounded sets and centered sets.[7]

Bounded sets are easy to understand, since most nouns in English are bounded sets. For example, if your neighbor has a four-legged furry animal that barks, pants, asks for belly rubs, and chases its tail, it's most definitely going to be some type of dog, and not a bird. Dogs and birds are different sets or categories. Though they might come in different shapes, sizes, smells, and varieties, one dog is not more of a dog than another. When you see the world this way, there is no way to mistake a dog for a bird, or a banana for a plum, since there are clear boundaries and a set distinction between them.

In contrast, centered sets are more of a foreign way to view the distinction between categories, since there aren't as many concrete examples in English as there are with bounded sets. Every centered set has a center point, and things are either moving toward it or away from it, much like a magnetic field and its particles. Something is considered to be in the set only when it's moving toward the center. This means that if something is near the center, but is moving away from it, it's not actually in the set. As a result, in centered sets, it's not about proximity to the center, but about direction.[8]

Although Hiebert was initially viewing the two sets through the lens of his question, "What then does it mean to be a Christian?" I believe they can also be applied to the way that a church views its discipleship process.

When you look at discipleship through a bounded-set lens, you tend to view maturity based on how long you've been a disciple. As a result, it's easy to view discipleship simply as being all about the classes you've completed, the number of times you've read the Bible, and other visible factors that can be measured.

While the destination and the activities that get you there definitely matter, so does the journey. When viewing discipleship through a centered-set lens, maturity becomes more about relation to the center, which is Jesus Christ, and the direction you're moving toward. "The focus is on the center and of pointing people to that center."[9] As a result, discipleship through a centered-set lens is best viewed as "a long obedience in the same direction"[10] as put by Eugene Peterson.

The centered-set concept describes a process of discipleship that is more focused on the direction you're moving toward than the destination that you end up in, as we compared in Figure 1.3. This is not to say that the destination is insignificant, since the direction ultimately points to that destination; rather, it's a shift in emphasis.

The notion of discipleship as direction is seen in Scripture passages like Acts 20:24, Romans 12:1–2, and Hebrews 12:1–2, just to name a few. In these verses, we discover that the process of discipleship is akin to running a race with endurance, while keeping our eyes on Jesus (Heb. 12:1–2) and ultimately finishing well (Acts 20:24). We also learn that discipleship as direction is about *continually* not being conformed to this world, which is how Romans 12:2 is worded in the Greek, rather than having a one-time experience.

If discipleship were more about the destination than the direction, Paul would have been fully mature the moment he encountered Christ and submitted his life to him. But as we see in 2 Corinthians 12:7–10, this was obviously not the case, as God used a thorn in the flesh to shape, mature, and transform Paul more and more into his image.

The Accountability Spectrum

As you might have already guessed from the title of this chapter and the previous point, the micro-shift that will set your church on a trajectory to both spiritual and numerical growth is precisely this: *from destination to direction*. While this micro-shift might make sense when it comes to defining what a Christian is, how it will precisely set your church on a trajectory to both spiritual and numerical growth might seem a bit confusing.

Enter: The accountability spectrum (see Figure 1.4).

Without this additional spectrum, the destination/direction spectrum is merely a philosophy of discipleship. Unless you overlay the accountability spectrum onto this micro-shift, all you have is a solid lesson in a discipleship class. The accountability spectrum is what takes this micro-shift from the individual level to the organizational/church-wide level, where we can begin seeing discipleship as a system from a fifty-thousand-foot level. When a micro-shift is made at this level, you can bet your horses that your church will embark on a new trajectory to both spiritual and numerical growth.

So what is the accountability spectrum? It's not a spectrum focusing on whether or not individuals have personal accountability in their lives, which is definitely an important attribute of a disciple, as we'll see in chapter 2. No, this spectrum is actually a way of measuring one of the most important cultural aspects of a church: accountability from a systems perspective.

In other words, when the leadership of your church asks the congregation to do something, do they do it? Is the "ask" seen as conjecture, suggestion, a strong recommendation, or a command? And after the "ask" has been made, how is the follow-up process? Is it vertical from church leadership to church member? Horizontal from church member to church member? Or inversed from church member to church leadership?

| Low | High |
| Accountability | Accountability |

FIGURE 1.4: THE ACCOUNTABILITY SPECTRUM

Using this table (see Figure 1.5), let's break down the spectrum a bit more to see the major differences.

Low Accountability	High Accountability
Scattered	Organized
Lop-sided ownership	Mutual ownership
Exempt	Responsible
Lazy	Proactive
Laissez faire/indifferent	Involved
Proverbs 6:9–11	1 Peter 5:2–3

FIGURE 1.5: COMPARING AND CONTRASTING LOW AND HIGH ACCOUNTABILITY

A church on the left side of the spectrum, with a low accountability culture, will either let everyone choose their own adventure when it comes to discipleship, or they might not even mention it. The church's leadership assumes that discipleship is either the responsibility of the individual, or the result of their preaching and programming. As a result, many models, programs, and ideas, *if* implemented, have a short shelf life at the church. In contrast, a church with a high accountability culture, on the right side of the spectrum, will be highly organized. The church's leadership will craft specific pathways and steps for newcomers to become a part of the church and for the mature to stay engaged. There is a high degree of mutual ownership where both the leadership of the church and the members are keeping one another accountable, so that promises are kept and expectations are met.

So what happens when you combine the destination/direction spectrum with the accountability spectrum? You get the heart of this chapter: the Influences Matrix.

The Influences Matrix

I am convinced that ignorance is the main reason churches in North America, and in many parts of the world, are not experiencing growth—spiritual and numerical. No, I am not talking about pastors having low IQ levels. I'm referring to the type of ignorance where you don't know why you do ministry the way that you do. More than anything, it's a lack of self-awareness.

Remember that Sun Tzu quote from before? "If you know your enemy, you'll win half of the battles. But if you know yourself, you'll win the other half." As pastors and church leaders, many of us are guilty of only focusing on half of the equation. We've been so focused, not on our "enemy" per se, but on other successful ministries and pastors, that we've failed to pay attention to our local context to discover why things aren't working the way we want them to. What if the solution to unlocking a new season of growth didn't start with a new model? What if it started with self-awareness as a church?

> What if the solution to unlocking a new season of growth didn't start with a new model? What if it started with self-awareness as a church?

The Influences Matrix is designed to help you start with self-awareness so that you can pinpoint the way your church approaches discipleship as a system from a fifty-thousand-foot level. This matrix, combined with the work that you did earlier completing those two assessments to discover your church's posture to growth, is going to help you discover where you are as a church (see Figure 1.6). This self-awareness is the very thing that will pivot your church onto the path to unlocking a new season of growth.

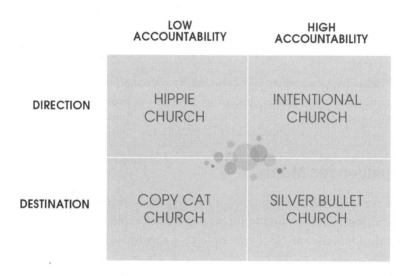

FIGURE 1.6: THE INFLUENCES MATRIX DEFINED

When you combine the destination/direction spectrum with the accountability spectrum, the result is a matrix with four quadrants. I call this the Influences Matrix because it illustrates the underlying systems that influence the way your church approaches discipleship.

For example, if your church is on the destination end of the spectrum, then you are typically trying to get everyone in your church to complete a formulaic set of discipleship classes because this is *the* defined way and best environment to grow people to maturity. If they finish the classes, then they're mature—they've arrived at the destination.

However, if your church is on the direction end of the spectrum, then you see discipleship as an ongoing process. So instead of focusing on a predefined set of classes to become mature, you create multiple non-formulaic learning experiences that help people take the next step in their walk with

Christ. In the same way, you understand that the classroom environment is only one of the many places that spiritual formation can take place.

On the Influences Matrix, if your church is on the low accountability end of the spectrum, you are typically scattered and indifferent. This is because you either let everyone choose their own path or because you aren't creating intentional on-ramps and off-ramps to help people get into discipleship classes or environments.

If your church is on the high accountability end of this spectrum, then your discipleship processes are typically organized and heavily involved. The particular nature of involvement and organization will look different depending on where your church is on the destination/direction spectrum.

Let's dig deeper into each of the quadrants so that you can pinpoint where your church is in this matrix (see Figure 1.7).

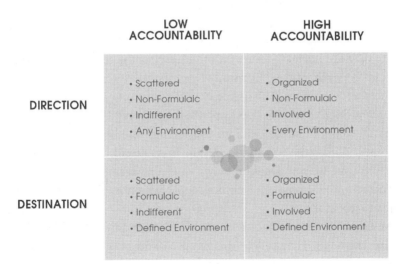

	LOW ACCOUNTABILITY	HIGH ACCOUNTABILITY
DIRECTION	• Scattered • Non-Formulaic • Indifferent • Any Environment	• Organized • Non-Formulaic • Involved • Every Environment
DESTINATION	• Scattered • Formulaic • Indifferent • Defined Environment	• Organized • Formulaic • Involved • Defined Environment

FIGURE 1.7: THE INFLUENCES MATRIX PERSONAS

In the Influences Matrix, there are four church personas: the Copy Cat Church, the Silver Bullet Church, the Hippie Church, and the Intentional Church.

1. The Copy Cat Church

With curriculum in hand, butcher paper marked up, and a new vision for what could be, Pastor Mark returned to his church invigorated. He had recently come back from an inspiring church leadership seminar where he learned the secrets to an effective discipleship ministry. He was told that if he implemented that church's straightforward 101, 201, 301, and 401 class model, people would be sure to attend, because it was obvious and straightforward, and disciples would be produced. They kept reiterating that it all comes down to the K.I.S.S. principle: "Keep It Simple Stupid."

His excitement soon turned to disappointment when he was met with opposition from his leadership. "What makes you think this model will work any better than the one we tried six months ago?"

● ● ●

This is the typical scenario for a Copy Cat church. They move from one model to the next, not just because they think each one is going to be the one that really works this time, but mainly because they're scattered, and only have short-term memory. This is the typical cycle: 1) Learn a new model for church growth or discipleship from a leading church at a conference or seminar. 2) Copy the model without considering whether it will work in their context. 3) Stop the previous model and immediately begin implementing this new one without regard to any change management. 4) If the new model doesn't produce enough fruit in a couple of months, then hit the reset button and repeat.

The Copy Cat Church is convinced that they are only one model away from breakthrough. They believe that maturity and growth are a result of pushing the right buttons and offering the right classes in the right order. As a result, they focus on creating a singular defined environment for everyone in their church to take a formulaic set of steps or classes in. In one model, they try to implement a 101–401 class approach that happens after the Sunday service, for four consecutive weeks. If that doesn't work as advertised, then they ask everyone to join a two-to-three-person discipleship group that happens on a weekly basis for Bible study and accountability. If the results don't deliver as promised, they then try to form small groups that meet in homes and discuss the topic of the sermon from that previous week.

In each and every one of those situations, the model doesn't work because there is no culture of accountability. To the church member, the leadership seems scattered and indifferent. Why join the new program when another is just around the corner? There is a deep lack of trust in the Copy Cat Church, so newcomers don't stick, members are reluctant to change, staff are frustrated, and there is a low participation rate in any new discipleship initiative. This inevitably kills any momentum that might have been generated from the pastor's enthusiasm.

2. The Silver Bullet Church

"Every one of our discipleship classes and environments have a distinct purpose and a clear next step. If we can mobilize our church to engage in this process from beginning to end, we will know for sure that they have been discipled. It's the only way to scale discipleship so that we can support the growth of our church," Pastor Dave shared with the Lead Pastor and the staff. He continued, "Every Sunday, we will have a discipleship class after each service: 101 on the first Sunday of the month, 201 on the second, 301 on the third, and 401 on the fourth. On months where we have five Sundays, we will designate that time to hold a ministry fair to help our congregation find opportunities to serve."

Dave, as the Pastor of Discipleship in his church, was a student of best practices. He stayed up-to-date on what the largest and most effective churches were doing in the area of discipleship. He went to multiple conferences a year, and when he couldn't travel to one, he carved out his schedule to tune into the live stream, so as not to miss anything. He even made trips to several of the most influential churches across the nation to meet with their Pastor of Discipleship and share notes.

In all his studying, he kept on coming back to the importance of being able to scale what they were doing to support the future growth of their church. As a result, he read books like Michael E. Gerber's *The E-Myth Revisited: Why Most Small Businesses Don't Work and What to Do About It* to learn about franchising, Robert Sutton and Huggy Rao's *Scaling Up Excellence: Getting to More Without Settling for Less* to learn principles about scaling, and Joseph Grenny's *Influencer: The New Science of Leading Change* to learn about motivation.

Based on what he was learning, Pastor Dave built a simple system for discipleship that was organized and formulaic. In each environment that progressed to the next, there was a sense of accountability to help move people along the path. The goal was to get everyone through the 101–401 classes so that they could end up in small groups, since that was the only scalable way to ensure everyone was cared for and being discipled.

After Pastor Dave finished explaining what the church's discipleship process was going to look like with the staff, he ended with this comment and then prayed, "This is our silver bullet, folks. I know this will work. Our people will finally be discipled. All we have to do is be on the same page and communicate this to our church with the sermon series that is going to start at the end of this month. Everyone will go through these classes and then get into small groups. I just know it."

• • •

Pastor Dave's plan is simple, linear, organized, and formulaic—it's a silver bullet. It's the classic *Field of Dreams* approach to discipleship, "If you build it, they will come." If you communicate the plan well enough, then you are sure to have high participation from your church in these 101-401 classes and then into small groups. The path is clearly set out and easy to follow. It's from one environment to the next. And it's scalable. Most importantly, though, this will ensure that everyone gets discipled.

Or will it?

At the heart of the Silver Bullet Church is the belief that simplicity wins the day. In contrast to the Copy Cat Church, the Silver Bullet Church is organized and its leadership is involved. Rather than blindly adopting and rashly implementing another church's model, the Silver Bullet Church makes sure to coordinate their ministries, implement a well-defined change management strategy, and contextualize language so that the model makes sense to their people. As a result, the Silver Bullet Church is able to move a large number of people through their discipleship process to their defined end.

While this model may seem slick and efficient—utilizing best practices from the business world to implement the model and move people through it—there are two glaring underlying issues. For one, at the heart of it is the belief that discipleship is programmatic, so people are discipled when they get to the end of a process. Secondly, it ignores the basic tenets of adult education and how adults best learn. Let's address both issues.

First of all, disciples are not widgets. They cannot be mass-produced on an assembly line. We see this in the Scriptures where it's evident that the only thing we can do is plant or water seeds in the lives of others. God is the only one who "gives the growth," as we read about in 1 Corinthians 3:5–9. To naively think that we are able to produce disciples when they complete a program—no matter how well thought out it may be—is simply unbiblical and foolish.

Disciples are not widgets. They cannot be mass-produced on an assembly line.

Disciples are not made when they get to a destination, which in the Silver Bullet Church is the end of their program. Disciples are formed *while moving* toward Christ. Discipleship is about direction, not destination.

Maturity and growth are not the result of pushing a button or offering the right set of classes in a sequenced order—a sniper approach. Nor is maturity the result of offering a plethora of discipleship classes or opportunities—a machine gun approach. Maturity is a result of equipping your church members with the right tools (or guns, to continue the illustration), at the right time, so that they can "run with endurance the race that lies before us, keeping our eyes on Jesus, the source and perfecter of our faith" (Heb. 12:1–2). More on this when I describe the last quadrant in the Influences Matrix—the Intentional Church.

Secondly, the Silver Bullet Church treats adults the same way they treat children. I'll share more on this in chapter 3, but here's the basic premise: we often teach the way we've been taught, so the way that we approach discipleship typically mimics the way that we were educated as children. As a result, the typical Silver Bullet Church attempts to move everyone through a set of sequenced classes, hoping that disciples will store and recall the content of those classes when needed. The problem, though, is that adults don't learn that way.

Unless you're an engineer or your occupation requires you to use these calculations on a regular basis, do you really remember what the Sine,

Cosine, and Tangent formulas are from trigonometry and calculus? To be honest, the only thing that I remember about those formulas is a silly rhyme that my eighth-grade math teacher taught me to remember five decimal points of Pi. It goes to the tune of a simple rhythmic cheer: "Sine, sine, cosine, sine, 3.14159."

Adults learn best when they see a need for the content and can apply the information to their lives immediately. This is why I only remember one of the lessons from my food science class in university. It was the class where I discovered that aspartame is only bad in high doses—to my satisfaction, this was my justification to drink Diet Coke, and now, Coke Zero.

Though a 101-401 approach is simple, easy to understand, and an effective way to move large numbers of people through a process, it is not educationally conducive to retention, application, and the transformation of disciples. I'm not against churches that use this model, nor am I saying that you need to throw out the baby with the bath water. All I'm saying is that this approach typically ignores the basic way that adults learn.

Furthermore, to the church member, a 101-401 approach looks and feels like school. So while it may be easy to grasp in that respect, there are hidden assumptions that accompany it. In college or university, when you finish your fourth-year classes, you have arrived, are an "expert," and are finished with your education. As a result, while you may never communicate this verbally to your church or even believe that it is true, the fact is, this is the assumption that a 101-401 approach carries for the typical church member. They think that they will have arrived when they finish the 401 class. In addition, you are going to be hard pressed to get those who already think they have arrived and are mature to even go through this sequence of classes.

Fear not! If you are a Silver Bullet Church, these shifts will not blow up your church or require you to radically change everything. You can even keep the core material from your 101-401 approach, with a small shift! More on that later though.

3. Hippie Church

"When Jesus says, you are the salt of the earth and the light of the world, he is not talking about you as an individual. He is using the plural form of you! He is saying, y'all are the salt of the earth, and y'all are the light of the world." In this sermon, Pastor Eric was giving an impassioned plea to his church to grow in maturity and into the "fullness of Christ" (Eph. 4:13 ESV). He continued, "Jesus taught his disciples, not in a classroom, but on a hill, in a boat, while doing ministry, and as they were walking to Emmaus. He taught them in the everyday with the everyday for the everyday. So go, be salt and light together in your everyday and in your community. As you do this, the Lord will mature you, he will shape you, and he will form you into his image."

Pastor Eric never had an average week. In addition to preparing his sermon, he always kept his calendar open to have coffee and meals with his congregation, so that he could constantly be spurring them toward love, good deeds, and maturity in Christ (Heb. 10:24). Since it was ultimately everyone's own responsibility to be growing as disciples in their own unique path and way, Pastor Eric saw his responsibility as being the chief cheerleader and motivator for his congregation.

● ● ●

No, I'm not describing American churches in the sixties, the organic church movement, communal living, or Woodstock. The Hippie Church describes churches that believe everyone is on a spiritual journey, where you belong before you believe, and can come as you are. They emphasize the ongoing journey of discipleship, more than the finish line.

As a result, Hippie Churches firmly believe that discipleship can happen and needs to happen anywhere and anytime. This is because they see discipleship as being deeply personal and not formulaic in any way, shape, or form.

There is nothing wrong with this directional view of discipleship! In fact, as you've seen throughout this chapter, this is the biblical view of maturity. The problems lie in the way that Hippie Churches implement this micro-shift and their underlying view of accountability. While their view of discipleship and the way people mature may be deeply biblical, they give way too much credit to the average church member. The church leadership assumes that as long as they teach the right things and have the right beliefs, people will just naturally grow and mature. After all, growth is God's responsibility, not theirs, right?

Hippie Churches have low-accountability cultures. They don't measure the growth or maturity of the individuals in their church, nor do they keep people accountable to regularly be in discipleship environments. They just teach the importance of it and leave the rest for their members to figure out—that is, if they have membership at all.

4. Intentional Church

Let's see what happens when Pastor Eric spends his week differently and changes his view of accountability. Instead of ending the sermon where he did in the Hippie Church story, let's change the ending and see how a high accountability culture works with a directional approach to discipleship. This will help us contrast the Intentional Church with our other churches.

• • •

"You need to be discipled in the everyday stuff of life! This is the biblical model for discipleship that goes all the way back to Deuteronomy 6:4–9. So that's why we as a church want to help you learn how to do this. This week, when you meet together with your group, ask one another this question: 'How have you shown the love of Christ to others this week?' If you're not in a group, then I want to invite you to a seminar that's going to happen two times this upcoming week. You can choose the one that works better for your schedule: right after the service today or on Wednesday evening at the church. In this seminar, we're going to take the next step and go deeper on the topic of today's sermon. We'll help you develop a plan to grow in your faith during the other six days of the week, so that together, we can be salt and light in our community. It will be fun and engaging, and I hope to see you there."

Instead of spending his time solely in sermon preparation and addressing the immediate pastoral needs of his congregation, Pastor Eric spent his previous week preparing all of his small group leaders for what was going to happen on Sunday.

He gave them cards to hand out during their small group time that asked this question: "How have you shown the love of Christ to others this week?" He asked his leaders to be praying for opportunities to have spiritual conversations that week. He even showed his small group leaders the material that he was going to be teaching from during the upcoming seminars.

He walked through the seminar material with his leaders for two reasons. First, he wanted to show them the importance of this material and how it was going to help the church, as a whole, live out their faith during the other six days of the week. And secondly, he wanted to give them the opportunity to consider inviting their entire group to one of the seminars.

• • •

The Intentional Church is exactly that—intentional. Instead of getting excited about a new idea, like discipleship in the everyday stuff of life—and then turning that into another program for people to add to their schedules—churches in this last quadrant look for ways to offer their congregation opportunities to take their next step spiritually and grow deeper, without taking them out of their regular rhythms of church life.

This method works because Intentional Churches have a high level of accountability. While discussing this topic with Dr. Robert Coleman, the author of *Master Plan of Evangelism* and *Master Plan of Discipleship,* he agreed with me on the importance of intersecting accountability with a directional mind-set for discipleship. "People need to be accountable for the progress they're making, or they'll get settled down and start drifting," he said during a phone call. "Accountability is what keeps you on course."[11]

For example, in this story, Pastor Eric finished his sermon with a call to go deeper toward Christ. This is about direction, not a destination. He didn't say that everyone had to attend the seminar, in addition to everything else they had going on that week—a typical machine-gun approach in the Silver Bullet Church. Nor did he say that this seminar was going to replace all other forms of discipleship in the church—a sniper approach in the Silver Bullet Church. Rather, he said, "If you're already in a small group, here are your next steps." And, "If you're not in a small group, here are your next steps." He understood that everyone was at a different place in their walk with Christ, so he challenged his church, not to get to a specific destination, but to simply take their next step toward Christ. This was an organized, yet non-formulaic, approach.

The beauty of this intentionality is that he was not giving his church mixed messages, since it was highly organized. To the newcomer or the individual who was not involved in a small group, they heard what their next step was. It wasn't to join a small group that had no end date, where everyone knows each other's dog's names. Instead, it was to attend a seminar that had a clear start and end time, on a topic that they were already prepped for, at either of two convenient times!

And for the individual that was already in community and growing deeper in Christ with her small group, her next step was clear—get together with her group! Since Pastor Eric prepped each small group leader with what was going to happen, each small group will have already made a decision about what they were going to do. They were either going to join one of the seminars that week together as a group, and then start asking one another that question in the following weeks, or, they were going to simply continue to meet together as a group, while letting anyone who wanted to attend the seminar do so individually.

Furthermore, in contrast to the Hippie Church, the Intentional Church is organized and very involved in creating environments where church members can take their next step toward Christ. Instead of leaving maturity totally up to the individual and hoping that sermons and programs will guide them in the right direction, as in the Hippie Church, the Intentional Church has guardrails and a moving sidewalk that their members can choose to use if they want.

Consider this metaphor. For the Intentional Church, the guardrails do not trap people in the church, any more than a moving sidewalk forces people to go in a direction. Instead, both are used as tools and guides to point people toward Christ, assuming that they want to move in that direction. If not, then people can get off the moving sidewalk as much as they can hop over the guardrail. The Intentional Church *intentionally* creates multiple environments to move people toward Christ, instead of assuming that people will move in that direction if given the opportunity to, like the Hippie Church.

Conclusion

I love what C. S. Lewis said in *Mere Christianity*:

The world does not consist of 100 percent Christians and 100 percent non-Christians. There are people (a great many of them) who are slowly ceasing to be Christians but who still call themselves by that name: some of them are clergymen. There are other people who are slowly becoming Christians though they do not yet call themselves so.[12]

Moving from destination to direction in your understanding of discipleship is not only biblical, it's absolutely critical for discipling individuals in today's post-Christian, pluralistic world, where Christianity is increasingly being pushed to the margins of society. In today's world where standardization is seen as suspect, and the church is seen as a broken institution, our world desperately needs faithful disciples who not only call themselves Christians, but who reflect Christ.

> Our world desperately needs faithful disciples who not only call themselves Christian, but who reflect Christ.

In this chapter, we looked at the way your church approaches discipleship as a system from a fifty-thousand-foot level. In chapter 2, we'll move to discipleship at the one-to-one level to discover what a disciple looks like, and how we can ensure that our churches are producing disciples who will create movements, rather than consumers who will, well, consume.

Reflection Questions

1. If you haven't done so already, fill out the two assessments in this chapter.

2. Where on the Influences Matrix would you place your church or ministry?

3. In your church or ministry, explain the Influences Matrix to one of your peers, someone you report to (or someone who disciples you), and someone you oversee (or someone you disciple). Ask them to pinpoint where they see your church or ministry. Then have a discussion on what it would take to move your church or ministry toward the Intentional Church quadrant.

CHAPTER 2

FROM OUTPUT TO INPUT

"Christianity without the living Christ is inevitably Christianity without discipleship, and Christianity without discipleship is always Christianity without Christ."
—Dietrich Bonhoeffer

God is more concerned with your faithfulness than your fame. Ministry to the few is as important as ministry to the many. While these two phrases might get you plenty of likes and shares on social media, they actually represent two of my deepest ministry scars.

"Can we please just play pool and hang out today?" said Joel.

I had crafted an epic eight-week sermon series on discipleship. I literally believed the heavens would open up, revival would break out, and my student ministry was going to triple in size. Montreal, Quebec, was never going to be the same! These students would almost instantaneously become like Christ. This sermon series was going to go down in the records of history and be canonized into thick, leather-bound books on the shelves of every seminarian—right alongside the sermons of Charles Haddon Spurgeon and the Matthew Henry commentary.

So instead of following my normal pattern of dismissing whatever Joel said—because he was the lovable clown that didn't know what the five-second-rule was—I actually agreed with him.

"Well, I was planning on starting our new sermon series today, but since—for some odd reason—you, Simon, Christina, and I are the only ones here today; sure, let's do it. Let's skip the sermon and just hang out!" And at that, I schooled everyone at a classic game of eight ball. (My dad owned a billiard hall while I was in high school, so I had *a bit of* experience when it came to pool.)

Typically, on a good Sunday, we had a few dozen students that showed up, so when Joel asked if we could hang out instead of learn, I thought to myself, *Why waste this epic sermon on one student? I would then have to catch everyone up the next week, since this was part one of eight in this series.* The logical thing to do was hold off on preaching this sermon until next Sunday. Also, this way, I could get one week ahead in sermon preparation. So not only did this benefit me, but it also made me look like the cool student pastor. It was clearly a win-win.

Until that afternoon.

Have you ever felt slightly off? It's like that moment, after entering the grocery store, when you suddenly feel like you forgot to lock your car doors. Or like that moment when you're joking around with your friends and you take it too far. Well, that's how I felt when I returned home that afternoon. Something wasn't right, and though I felt like I knew what it might be, I didn't want to admit it. I didn't want to walk back to the car and lock the doors. I didn't want to apologize to my friends for taking it too far. So I just tried to ignore that feeling.

No matter what I did to try to suppress that feeling, it just didn't go away. So I took a deep breath and decided to pray and ask the Lord why I felt the way I did. In that moment, I sensed the Lord saying, "That sermon that you worked so hard to prepare for was actually for today, not next week! It wasn't for the masses; it was for the few."

What at first seemed like a wise and common sense decision, ended up being the wrong one. And it was all because of my motives. I wanted to start the sermon series off with a bang and create momentum. I didn't want to have to play catch-up with the majority of the students in my ministry. I wanted the sermon to have as big of an impact as it could. So naturally, I didn't want to *waste* the sermon on a couple of people!

After repenting to God for being more concerned about my fame than being faithful with the message that he had entrusted me with for that Sunday, I ended up calling Simon, one of our leaders, to apologize. While it definitely felt awkward to apologize for not preaching and instead schooling him at a game of eight ball, during that call, as I listened to what he was going through, it clicked. That sermon was actually for him.

And that's when I discovered that ministry to the few is as important as ministry to the many. From that day forward, I promised myself that I would try to be faithful regardless of the size or *perceived* impact that any ministry opportunity had. Whether there was one person or ten thousand, I committed to choosing faithfulness and always bringing my A-game.

Instead of seeing every opportunity as a blessing from the Lord for Kingdom impact, I was judging effectiveness by attendance. My metrics were totally off. That experience, as minor as it may seem, was actually foundationally influential in shifting my perspective on success and effectiveness in ministry.

> Ministry to the few is as important as ministry to the many.

From the Many to the One

When it comes to developing a plan for discipleship and growth in your church, the one is as important as the many. In fact, the only way to see your entire church grow spiritually and numerically is to start by discipling one person at a time.

In the last chapter, we looked at discipleship as a system from a fifty-thousand-foot level through the Influences Matrix. This matrix, if you remember, is a simple tool that helps churches identify how they view discipleship from a big-picture perspective. Now, using that same matrix, we're going to switch out the spectrums, or axis labels, to uncover how the Copy Cat, Silver Bullet, Hippie, and Intentional Churches view discipleship at a one-to-one level. In this chapter, we'll move from looking at the systematic discipleship of the many to the personal discipleship of the one. We are going to see not only how ministry to the few is as important as ministry to the many, but where it actually all begins.

What Does a Disciple Do?

"Have you ever discipled anyone?" This was the question that I was asked before moving to Montreal to be one of the pastors at River's Edge

Community Church by another Joel—Joel Zantingh, from our denominational office.

"I think I have," I responded as confidently as I could. "I mean, yes, I definitely have."

That was probably not the best way to answer an interview question, but I was nervous. I was finishing up an internship as the sole pastor in a church plant in Ottawa, Ontario, and Christina and I were about to get married. Her internship was about to end as well, so getting this job to move to Montreal was a must—especially since we wanted to enjoy our wedding and honeymoon, and not wonder how we were going to pay next month's rent.

"Tell me about that experience. What happened, and how did you disciple them?" said Joel.

"Well, currently, I'm meeting weekly with a guy in my church named Matt," I responded. "We're reading the Scriptures together, I'm keeping him accountable on a few issues that he's struggling with, and we're praying for one another."

"That's good," Joel responded. "But, how do you know when you're done? I mean, how do you actually know when someone is mature as a disciple?"

"I guess, isn't it like that age-old question, 'How do you know if someone is the one?' Don't you just know when you know?" After thinking for a while, and taking another sip of my coffee, I continued, "Or, to be a bit more precise, perhaps it's when they live out the fruit of the Spirit?"

The Dilemma

What does a disciple look like? What do they do and what do they know? And how do you make disciples that make disciples that make disciples? These were the types of questions that I continued to wrestle with after moving to Montreal to join Lorenzo DellaForesta at River's Edge.

If someone were to have asked me to point out all the mature disciples in my church, I would've been able to point them out, and I'm sure you could have too. But if someone were to have asked me how he or she got there, I would've shrugged my shoulders and responded with the cop-out, "It's different for everybody," which is code for, "I have no idea."

The dilemma that many of us face today is that we don't have a sure-fire and reproducible way to make mature disciples in our churches. If we were honest with ourselves, we would probably admit that most of the mature ones in our churches were already mature before we met them! And for those that you could take some credit for, their maturity probably came about because you spent a lot of time with them during a crisis in their life. Not exactly something you would wish upon others.

Making disciples sometimes feels like a lot of grunt work with an unpredictable success rate.

Making disciples often feels like carrying heavy rocks from one place to another, only to find out the next week that many have rolled back to their starting point (see Figure 2.1). It's a lot of grunt work with an unpredictable success rate. Although you would never say this to your church, this demonstrates a conviction that only those who are strong enough (or mature enough) to lift heavy rocks are able to disciple.

FIGURE 2.1: A LACK OF METRICS

I hope you are balking at that unbiblical notion as much as I am! Of course, the mature can and ought to disciple others, but so can someone who has just encountered Christ for the first time. Just look at the conversation between the Gerasenes demoniac and Jesus in Mark 5:19–20 and how after Jesus freed him, he told him to "Go home to your own people, and report to them how much the Lord has done for you and how he has had mercy on you." At that, the man "went out and began to proclaim in the Decapolis how much Jesus had done for him, and they were all amazed."

This man, who was tormented by evil spirits, lived in the tombs because the community had ostracized him. We don't know how long this had been going on, why it started, or whether he had a faith background. What we do know though is that "Night and day among the tombs and on the mountains, he was always crying out and cutting himself with stones" (Mark 5:5).

But immediately after encountering Christ, this man went out and proclaimed the gospel to others! Did you hear that? He didn't go to seminary, take an inductive Bible study class, or sign a membership covenant. He didn't wait to become "mature." Rather, he responded in faithfulness, obeyed the Lord's command, and left the results up to the Lord . . . "and they were all amazed."

70:20:10 Discipleship

Discipling others while being discipled is actually one of the best ways to get discipled! We see this in the way that Jesus interacted with his disciples. After all, he did not wait for his death and resurrection to send the disciples out for ministry. He did this early on; in fact, shortly after the disciples saw the Gerasenes demoniac set free, Jesus sent them out in pairs for ministry (Mark 6:6–12).

Discipling others while being discipled is one of the best ways to get discipled.

We also see this in adult educational theory and leadership practice through the 70:20:10 principle (see Figure 2.2). This principle originated with Dr. Allen Tough in his book *The Adult's Learning Projects* and has since been elaborated and expanded by many others.[1] The principle states that 70 percent of our learning comes by doing. This is informal, on-the-job development that comes through trial and error, and growing in experience. Next, 20 percent of our learning is through receiving informal feedback from others, or through more formal coaching and mentoring relationships. This is primarily development through interacting with others. The last 10 percent of our learning is through conferences, seminars, and courses. This is structured formal education.[2]

70%	LEARNING BY DOING • On the job • Trial and error
20%	LEARNING BY INTERACTION • Feedback • Coaching and mentoring
10%	LEARNING BY LISTENING • Conferences, seminars and courses • Formal education

FIGURE 2.2: 70:20:10 PRINCIPLE

What's interesting is that most churches are unintentionally aware of the 70:20:10 principle and are living it out, but their application of it is backward. Seventy percent of their time is devoted to teaching, 20 percent to talking about it, and 10 percent to doing it.

What would happen to your church if you applied the 70:20:10 principle accurately? What if 70 percent of the time that you spent discipling others was helping them do the very things that made them a disciple? You would then talk about what they've done and provide them feedback 20 percent of the time, while only formally teaching them 10 percent of the time. Imagine the transformation that would happen in your church.

In order for us to disciple with the 70:20:10 principle in mind, we need to start with a basic question. What does someone need to do to grow as a disciple? In other words, what is the 70 percent that people can do that will move them toward maturity as a disciple? We started with this statement, and I believe it to be true: Discipling others while being discipled is actually one of the best ways to get discipled! However, discipling others is not the 70 percent—it's a part of it, but not the whole thing. So what else do disciples need to do to become mature and move toward Christ?

Before I present the results from one of the largest and most thorough research projects on discipleship to date, the first question we must answer is, "What is a disciple?"

What Is a Disciple?

As we introduced in the last chapter's micro-shift, a disciple is not someone who has completed all the discipleship classes set out by your church. Discipleship is not about arriving at some destination. Rather, discipleship, seen through a directional lens, is about setting our eyes on Christ and *continually* moving toward him. But while discipleship is more about direction than destination, there is a difference between someone who has just begun their journey toward Christ, and another who has been running this race of faith for decades. How can we tell the difference?

The Transformational Discipleship Assessment

In 2011, LifeWay Research embarked on their second in-depth study to examine the state of discipleship in the church today—the Transformational Discipleship Assessment (TDA). This survey was built on a longitudinal study that Brad Waggoner led on twenty-five hundred Protestants who attended church on a regular basis. The respondents were surveyed twice, once in May 2007 and again in May 2008, to determine their spiritual maturity and progress over time.[3] Waggoner's Spiritual Formation Inventory (SFI) laid the groundwork for the TDA and its three phases of research: 1) Expert Interviews; 2) A Survey of Protestant Pastors; 3) A Survey of Laity.

In the first phase of the TDA research, the LifeWay Research team interviewed twenty-eight global experts and thought leaders in the area of discipleship, like Dr. Robert Coleman, Alan Hirsch, and Henry Blackaby.[4] In the second phase, the team conducted a telephone survey with one thousand randomly selected Protestant pastors. While the first phase focused on uncovering expert opinion on the state of discipleship in North America and around the world, the second phase surveyed the state of discipleship in local churches.[5] "The survey revealed a great deal of paradoxes occurring between pastors' hope that people are maturing and the level of satisfaction they have that believers truly are maturing."[6] The last phase of this research project included a survey of over four thousand Protestant laity in North America, 30 percent of those respondents being Canadians.[7]

As a result, the research from these two projects present a solid framework that can help us determine what a disciple of Jesus looks like. Essentially, this research revealed that the following eight discipleship attributes—which are not anecdotal—consistently show up in the life of maturing disciples: Bible engagement, obeying God and denying self, serving God and others, sharing Christ, exercising faith, seeking God, building relationships, and being unashamed (transparency).[8]

Definitions of a Disciple

So what is a disciple? While you could definitely say a disciple is someone who displays those eight attributes in their life, that is more of a descriptive answer than a definite one.

If you look at the New Testament, the word *disciple* occurs 269 times, whereas the word *Christian* only occurs three times.[9] Although the term *Christian* has been watered down, and many see discipleship as an optional matter, it is clear that this is not what Jesus intended. After all, the early disciples were called Christians because they were learners, students, and apprentices of Christ. Thus, just as "being Canadian" is a part of the identity of a Canadian citizen, "being Christian" or "being a disciple" is an identity issue.

Dr. Robert Coleman describes a disciple as "a learner who's following Christ. You learn by following. And that means since we are finite and God alone is infinite, there's never a place in the journey where we stop learning."[10]

Pastor and martyr Dietrich Bonhoeffer defined a disciple as one who adheres to Christ.[11]

The philosopher and professor Dallas Willard defines a disciple as an individual who "desires above all else to be like him [Christ]."[12]

Henry Blackaby, author of *Experiencing God*, defines a disciple as "one being taught by many means intentionally, in a specific direction."[13]

Steve Murrell, author of *WikiChurch*, breaks down a disciple into three aspects: "It's following Jesus. It's fishing for people. And it's doing that in conjunction with others, in fellowship with others."[14]

Although all of the previous definitions of a disciple are nuanced differently, the common thread that holds them together is *movement toward Christ*. This is encouraging, because it lines up directly with our first micro-shift, from destination to direction.

While there may be agreement on what a disciple is, the problem is figuring out how to actually move people toward Christ and disciple them! The Joint Statement on Discipleship at the Eastbourne Consultation still proves to be right, even though it was released more than a decade ago. "As we face the new millennium, we acknowledge that the state of the Church is marked by growth without depth. Our zeal to go wider has not been matched by a commitment to go deeper."[15]

Discipleship is moving toward Christ.

To this dilemma we now turn.

From Output to Input Goals

There are four ways that people try to lose weight. The first is to simply just try to lose weight. No goals, no plan, and no vision—just a lot of hard work. This method of dieting reminds me of Figure 2.1, where you put in a lot of grunt work but find yourself with an unpredictable success rate.

The second way to is to have a clear output goal, like losing ten pounds before your beach trip at the end of the month. Output goals are the results that you want, or the future that you envision. So with your bathing suit hung up, a scale in your bathroom, and an image in your mind, you weigh yourself every day. Unfortunately, this method of dieting doesn't work either, because an output goal and a vision for what could be does not actually burn calories.

A third way to lose weight is to actually make the micro-shift from an output goal to an input goal. Input goals are the things that you can do today that will produce the results that you want tomorrow (output goals). In other words, input goals are the levers that you can pull to influence output goals. So focusing on input goals, like monitoring your calorie intake and exercising regularly, is another way to try to lose weight. Although you may get healthy by doing these two input goals, you won't necessarily lose weight, since you can easily just eat more calories than what you are burning through exercising.

The only sure-fire way to lose weight is to combine both input and output goals. So if you start with your output goal, which is to lose ten pounds before your beach trip at the end of the month, then you can reverse engineer your input goals. In other words, if your beach trip is a few weeks away, you would calculate what your daily-recommended calorie intake is based on your height, weight, and age. You would then eat fewer calories than your body needs, and exercise a few times a week to burn off a few hundred more calories. If you meet your input goals on a consistent basis, you'll get your output goal, which is to lose ten pounds and look good in a swimming suit.

Output and Input Goals in Discipleship

Churches tend to measure discipleship in the same four ways we approach dieting. There are those who try to disciple without any goal, plan, or vision. As a result, they put in a lot of grunt work without any predictable success. They carry heavy rocks from one place to another, only to find out the next week that many have rolled back to their starting point. There's definitely forward movement at times; it's just unpredictable. This describes churches without any goals or metrics, like we see in Figure 2.1.

The most common way that churches measure discipleship is through the use of output goals. Metrics like participation in a small group or Sunday school class, how often one attends weekend worship, how much one gives, whether or not one is serving, and if one is baptized are some of the most common output goals that churches measure. This is obviously much better than having no metrics at all, since you can measure these goals week over week, month over month, or year over year to see progress.

Unfortunately, output goals in and of themselves don't actually move people toward Christ! Output goals are the results of input goals. So if all you do is focus on output goals and let everyone choose their own input goals, you won't be able to reproduce any success that you might encounter! This is kind of like, as we see in Figure 2.3, being consumed with counting how many rocks have been moved to where you're standing, without having influenced or even knowing how they got there.

FIGURE 2.3: OUTPUT GOALS

Making the micro-shift from output to input goals is the first step to figuring out how to actually move people toward Christ and disciple them. Instead of just measuring the number of disciples that you have, you would influence them and then measure the things that produce disciples. You would focus on the things that you can do today that will produce the disciples that you want tomorrow. This shift from output to input goals would be like using a vertical pulley to lift those heavy rocks up from the ground and onto the bed of a truck as we see in Figure 2.4. Using this pulley is far easier than carrying the rock, but since you're just lifting the rock and then expecting others to move it from here to wherever they want to go, this is not an ideal solution either.

FIGURE 2.4: INPUT GOALS

In order to both lose weight and make disciples, you need to combine input and output goals. This is the best of both worlds, since you are pulling the levers (input goals) that directly influence the results you want (output goals)—and you have full visibility of both! This is like using a set of pulleys to lift a palette of rocks onto a train that is headed in a particular direction, as we see in Figure 2.5. You get to influence both the indicators and the results, the investments and the return, the input and the output.

FIGURE 2.5: INPUT AND OUTPUT GOALS

Output and Input Goals with the Influences Matrix

This is what Intentional Churches do. They not only have a clear picture as to what a disciple is (output goals), but they also create pathways (input goals) to help their church move toward maturity. In Figure 2.6, you'll see the Influences Matrix, but with the scales switched out to input and output goal spectrums.

Hippie Churches, on the other hand, have input goals, but lack output goals, like the input only example we walked through previously. They know the right behaviors (input goals) to do today, but have no idea whether or not these behaviors are actually producing disciples (output goals).

Silver Bullet Churches represent those who have clear output goals and metrics for maturity, but people are often at a loss as to what they need to do (input goals) in order to mature (output goals), since there are often too many options to choose from.

Lastly, Copy Cat Churches are like the first example. They have no input or output goals, so discipleship is haphazard at best. It's a free-for-all, and as my friend Todd Adkins likes to say, "It's the book of Judges where everyone is doing what's right in their own eyes" (Judges 21:25).

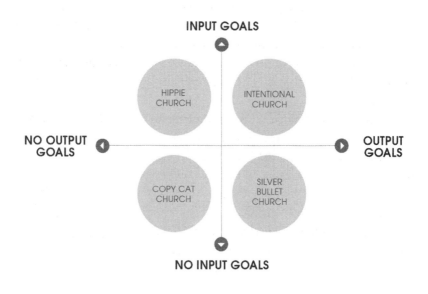

FIGURE 2.6: MODIFIED INFLUENCES MATRIX WITH INPUT AND OUTPUT SPECTRUMS

Input Goals + Output Goals = Mature Disciples

I love what Henry Blackaby said during the expert interviews phase of the TDA research:

> We automatically assume that if we teach a particular course, there's bound to be some radical change, but we never try to measure it. Don't ever teach or direct without having a means to measure the changes in people's lives as an outcome of what you're doing.[16]

No, he's not talking about an evaluation form. He's talking about something deeper. He's talking about the importance of being intentional in our discipleship processes and pathway. He's talking about the fact that input goals + output goals = mature disciples.

Let's get specific. If a disciple is someone who is moving toward Christ, then what does that disciple increasingly look like as they get closer to Christ? In other words, what are the output goals of a disciple?

Earlier I introduced to you the results of the largest study of its kind ever done on discipleship and what was discovered. In that research, the team discovered eight discipleship attributes in the lives of believers who were progressing in spiritual maturity, or moving toward Christ (see Figure 2.7). The more mature a believer was found to be, the higher they would score in each of these attributes. You can actually take this assessment yourself and do it with your small group, ministry area, or church at tda.lifeway.com.

I highly recommended using these attributes in the TDA as the output goals for the discipleship processes in your church, since they are rooted in Scripture, vetted by thought leaders, and backed by a massive amount of research. To not use them at least as the starting point for your church would seem like a missed opportunity to me. It's like I often say to the church planters and pastors that I help: "The first rule of ministry is this: Don't re-create the wheel."

The first rule of ministry is this: Don't re-create the wheel.

Discipleship Attributes (Output Goals)	Description
Bible Engagement	The Bible describes believers in Christ, those who follow him, as learners. The Bible contains many commands like "pursue truth," "seek wisdom," "renew the mind," "learn from one another," and "examine the Scriptures." It is impossible to fulfill God's invitation to follow him and serve him without committing to a lifestyle of learning, but "learning" in a biblical sense goes way beyond merely accepting facts. Learning incorporates the intellect and the will; it is both an attitude and a wide range of behavior and habits that lead to gaining knowledge, wisdom, and ultimately significant life change.
Obeying God and Denying Self	The Bible is filled with examples of and admonitions related to obedience and self-denial. To be a disciple is synonymous with following Jesus, and following Jesus is synonymous with self-denial in favor of obedience to God. This attribute will help you measure the degree to which you possess a "God-focus" versus a "self-focus."
Serving God and Others	The concept of service is vividly portrayed throughout the Bible. Jesus provided a great example for all Christians both through his spoken words and deeds. The apostle Paul states, "And our people must also learn to devote themselves to good works for cases of urgent need, so that they will not be unfruitful" (Titus 3:14 ESV).
Sharing Christ	A key mark of a growing disciple is an outward focus. For individuals, it means intentionally befriending and building relational bridges to non-Christians, and then inviting these friends and acquaintances to church with them.

Exercising Faith	A disciple is marked by a posture of weakness. Such weakness creates a great opportunity to exercise faith in a strong God. From Genesis to Revelation, the Christian experience is described using words like *believe, trust, rely upon,* and *act upon.* It's clear that above all, God desires active faith in his people, for without faith it is impossible to please God.
Seeking God	A disciple is one who seeks after and worships God. Jesus stated, "Yes, the Father wants such people to worship him. God is spirit, and those who worship him must worship in Spirit and in Truth" (John 4:23–24). A true disciple, a follower of Christ, is to engage in a lifestyle of worship, both privately and corporately.
Building Relationships	A disciple is one who is properly related to others, especially the community of faith. The Christian faith is neither a spectator sport (where self-professed Christians sit back and watch the local church in action), nor is it a solo sport (living in isolation from the body of Christ).
Unashamed (Transparency)	A disciple is not ashamed of the gospel of Jesus Christ. This quality is exhibited in their willingness to talk openly in church and community environments about his or her walk with God. We naturally praise and talk about what we love. Those unashamed of the work and presence of God don't wait for a predefined environment to talk about their beliefs in Jesus; rather, they embody the attitude of Peter and John who stated that they couldn't help talking about the ongoing work of God in their lives and world.

FIGURE 2.7: DESCRIPTIONS OF THE EIGHT DISCIPLESHIP ATTRIBUTES[17]

To be an Intentional Church, it's not enough to merely have these output goals and aimlessly try to work toward them. Instead, you need to make the micro-shift from wherever you are to an input/output combination, so that you can give individuals in your church a track to run on and tangible action steps that will actually move them toward Christ.

If you do a quick Google search of "what does a disciple look like," "what is a disciple," or "qualities of a disciple," you'll get a cumulative result of more than twenty million search results as of the writing of this book. There are many anecdotal lists out there on the qualities of a disciple. In fact, several books were also written toward that end! If you were to compare some of the qualities from those lists to this one in the TDA, you would definitely find overlap.

So while the list of these research-backed eight discipleship attributes is truly a significant finding, these results only just scratch the surface. When the LifeWay Research team dug deeper into this data (they conducted regression analysis, for you statistic geeks out there), they were able to discover what behaviors consistently led to these discipleship attributes. In other words, the gem of this research is that they discovered what input goals positively influenced and led to these output goals!

Faithfulness vs. Fruitfulness

Before I reveal what things we can do (input goals) that will influence the formation and maturity of the eight discipleship attributes in our lives (output goals), a quick note is necessary on the difference between faithfulness and fruitfulness. While it's easy for me to geek-out on this research, I need to remind myself that, while this research may find a high correlation between confessing my sins and sharing Christ, this is not a matter of causation. In other words, I cannot force myself or legalistically mature myself in Christ. I can be faithful, which will result in fruitfulness in God's timing and his providence, but I cannot make myself fruitful.

I can be faithful, but I cannot make myself fruitful.

This reminds me of Paul's first letter to the church in Corinth and all the infighting that was happening because of a lack of fruitfulness. There were some in the church who identified themselves as Paul's disciples, and others who sided with Apollos. Naturally, competition arose as to who was better, and which teacher would make them more mature and fruitful. To this, Paul responded aptly,

> For whenever someone says, "I belong to Paul," and another, "I belong to Apollos," are you not acting like mere humans? What then is Apollos? What is Paul? They are servants through whom you believed, and each has the role the Lord has given. I planted, Apollos watered, but God gave the growth. So then neither the one who plants nor the one who waters is anything, but only God who gives the growth. (1 Cor. 3:4–7)

Ultimately, there is nothing that you or I can do to cause ourselves to grow. God is the one who gives the growth! It's just like a vegetable garden. You can till the soil, put the right mix of fertilizer in, plant the seeds, and then water them. But you cannot truly force or cause the plants to grow. It's the same way with sleeping. You can't tell yourself to sleep and force it to happen. You can, however, create the conditions in which sleep will come.[18]

In the same way, no program, strategy, matrix, or pathway alone will cause your church members to grow. Growth is up to God and it's ultimately his responsibility. However, we cannot let that be a cop-out for doing nothing! We still have a role in the growth as outlined in the Scripture above.

As a result, what the micro-shifts outlined in this book will do—especially the one in this chapter—is help you create the right conditions in the soil of your church, so that you can unleash a movement of disciple makers who can plant and water effectively. After all, as I mentioned earlier, discipling others while being discipled is one of the best ways to get discipled.

Input Goals and their Output Goals

Through regression analysis in the TDA research, several input goals were found to correlate with a higher score in each of the output goals as we see in Figure 2.8. In other words, the research revealed that doing certain actions (input goals) would actually predict a higher score in each of the discipleship attributes (output goals).

For example, when individuals studied the Bible, which is different from just reading it, they scored higher on both the Serving God and Others attribute and the Sharing Christ attribute. In other words, the input goal of studying the Bible does more than just make you knowledgeable about Scripture and win Bible trivia games. Studying the Bible positively influences you to serve others and also evangelize! So the next time you want to inspire your congregation to share Christ with others, try offering an in-depth Bible study that will equip them with the know-how and skills to do so.

Furthermore, the input goal of making a decision to obey or follow God—knowing that this decision might be costly to you in some way—had an interesting effect on an individual's Bible Engagement output goal. The research revealed that this decision actually led individuals to a greater engagement with the Scriptures! Perhaps this is because courageous, faith-filled decisions often prompt us to search through the wisdom and truth in the Scriptures to know what our next steps should be. As a result, if you want to see your congregation stand up in the face of our culture and be "strong and courageous," as we read in Joshua 1:9, perhaps you should provide them with training and development to help them engage deeper with the Scriptures.

Input Goals (The following actions positively predict the score of the respective discipleship attribute)	Output Goals (Discipleship Attributes)
• Reading the Bible • Studying the Bible • Confessing your sins • Reading a book about increasing your own spiritual growth • Making a decision to obey or follow God knowing that this decision might be costly to you in some way	**Bible Engagement**

• Confessing your sins • Reading the Bible • Attending a worship service at your church • Praying for the spiritual status of people you know who are not professing Christians • Making a decision to obey or follow God knowing that this decision might be costly to you in some way	**Obeying God and Denying Self**
• Praying for the spiritual status of people you know who are not professing Christians • Getting involved in ministries or projects that serve people in the community • Discipling or mentoring a less spiritually mature person one-on-one • Praying for your church and/or church leaders • Setting aside time for private worship, praise, or thanksgiving to God	**Serving God and Others**
• Praying for the spiritual status of people you know who are not professing Christians • Sharing with someone how to become a Christian • Inviting an unchurched person to attend a church service or some other program at your church • Studying the Bible • Confessing your sins	**Sharing Christ**
• Confessing your sins • Praying for the spiritual status of people you know who are not professing Christians • Participating in a Bible study group or class that involved homework or personal study outside the group/class • Praying for fellow Christians you know • Setting aside time for private worship, praise, or thanksgiving to God	**Exercising Faith**

• Setting aside time for prayer of any kind • Setting aside time for private worship, praise, or thanksgiving to God • Confessing your sins • Praying for the spiritual status of people you know who are not professing Christians • Reading the Bible	**Seeking God**
• Attending small classes or groups for adults from church such as Sunday school, Bible study, and small groups • Praying in a group with other Christians • Having regular responsibilities at your church • Being involved in ministries or projects that serve people in the community • Studying the Bible	**Building Relationships**
• Reading the Bible • Praying for fellow Christians you know • Sharing with someone how to become a Christian • Being discipled or mentored one-on-one by a more spiritually mature Christian • Confessing your sins	**Unashamed (Transparency)**

FIGURE 2.8: REGRESSION ANALYSIS FOR THE TDA[19]

Confessing your sins was another fascinating input goal that positively influenced most of the output goals or discipleship attributes. It makes sense that confessing your sins would lead you to seek God, grow in your transparency with others, and better be able to obey God and deny self. However, what surprised me in the research is how confessing one's sins positively influenced an individual's ability to share Christ!

Let's think about that for a moment. What happens after you share Christ with someone and they believe? Are you the one confessing your sins, or is it the new believer? While it's typically the new believer that is the one doing the confessing, the research revealed that if disciples were regularly confessing their sins, they were more likely to share Christ with others.

As expected, praying for nonbelievers, sharing how to become a Christian, and inviting them to your church, were the typical input goals that led to a higher score in the output goal of sharing Christ. But how does confessing your sins relate? Perhaps it's confession that helps you get in the right posture to share your faith with others. Imagine the domino effect in maturity that would result if we continually led our congregation to confession on a regular basis. Now that would be an example of a micro-shift that leads to macro-change.

Patterns and Next Steps

As we come to the end of this chapter, the last thing I would want to do is to leave you with a whole ton of good information that you can't do anything with. In fact, that would go against every fiber of my being and the vision of this book. This book is about micro-shifts that lead to macro-change, not an overload of information that leads to paralysis.

So let's see what we've covered. First of all, you have several definitions of a disciple, but the common thread that holds them together is *movement toward Christ*. Next, we discovered that a mature disciple is an individual whose faithfulness (doing input goals) leads them to fruitfulness (evidence of output goals in their life). And herein lies the roadblock. While the list of the eight output goals is short and sweet, the list of forty input goals seems overwhelming! Add that to the fact that I didn't even list all of the input goals that led to those output goals, and it can definitely seem overwhelming to know where you should start.

With dieting, the input goals are easy: count your calories and exercise a few times a week. Doing these two things alone will inevitably lead to the output goal of either staying healthy or losing weight.

This is the classic 80/20 Principle or Pareto Law at work. This principle states that 20 percent of the things we do typically lead to 80 percent of the results. In Richard Koch's *The 80/20 Principle*, he asserts that it's the counterintuitive nature of this principle that makes it so valuable. He goes on to explain the principle:

We tend to expect that all causes will have roughly the same significance. . . . That each day or week or year we spend has the same significance. That all our friends have roughly equal value to us. That all inquiries or phone calls should be treated in the same way. That one university is as good as another. That all problems have a large number of causes, so that it is not worth isolating a key few causes. That all opportunities are of roughly equal value, so that we treat them all equally.

We tend to assume that 50 percent of causes or inputs will account for 50 percent of results or outputs. There seems to be a natural, almost democratic, expectation that causes and results are generally equally balanced. And, of course, sometimes they are. But the "50/50 fallacy" is one of the most inaccurate and harmful, as well as the most deeply rooted, of our mental maps. The 80/20 Principle asserts that when two sets of data, relating to causes and results, can be examined and analyzed the most likely result is that there will be a pattern of imbalance.[20]

This is further illustrated with the research that Joseph Grenny and his team did in their book, *Influencer: The New Science of Leading Change,*

Typically one or two vital behaviors, well executed, will yield a big difference. This is true because with almost any result you're trying to achieve, there are moments of *disproportionate influence.* . . . Even the most pervasive problems will yield to changes if you spot these crucial moments and then identify the specific, high-leverage actions that will lead to the results you want.[21]

Three Influential Input Goals

When it comes to maturity in Christ, are there a few input goals that will lead to the eight output goals? Can we find the 80/20 Principle at work here? Are there a few vital behaviors that will yield disproportionate influence toward maturity in Christ? I'm not talking about a few input goals per output goal; I'm asking if there are a few input goals, or vital behaviors, that will lead to a progressive increase of all eight output goals, resulting in an ever-increasing maturity in Christ.

While there's no silver bullet when it comes to maturity in Christ—especially based on our discussion above from 1 Corinthians 3 and the difference between faithfulness and fruitfulness—we do have the results of the TDA research! And believe it or not, there are a few input goals that consistently predicted a higher score across all eight discipleship attribute output goals. Here are three of them:

1. Reading the Bible
2. Attending a worship service at your church
3. Attending small classes or groups for adults from church, such as Sunday school, Bible study, small groups, Adult Bible Fellowships, etc.

Reading the Bible

When it comes to reading the Bible, hands down, this is *the* input goal that has a direct impact on the total score of all the output goals, or discipleship attributes, in the TDA. As you can see in Figure 2.9, when asked, "How often, if at all, do you personally read the Bible," individuals who read it every day had a significantly higher overall score in the TDA than those who rarely or never did.

Read the Bible	Average Total Score
Once a Month	63.90
A Few Times a Month	69.13
Once a Week	72.87
Every Day	82.60

FIGURE 2.9: ABOUT HOW OFTEN, IF AT ALL, DO YOU PERSONALLY READ THE BIBLE?

It's important to understand here that this question was not measuring whether or not an individual studied the Bible thoroughly or memorized Scripture. While those two were definitely important factors that predicted a higher score for the Bible Engagement output goal, this is not what we're talking about here. We're talking about the simple act of reading the Bible on a regular basis.

In other words, the more an individual did the input goal of reading their Bible, the higher they scored in all of the output goals. So the more you can help your church to read the Bible, the better they are going to be able to obey God and deny self, serve God and others, share Christ, exercise their faith, seek God, build relationships, and be unashamed about their faith.

This is astounding. While you might not need a research project to tell you that reading your Bible helps you mature broadly as a disciple, it is amazing that it helps you grow in all of these specific attributes. This impact makes reading the Bible a truly vital behavior, and, at its core, represents the importance of shifting to input goals.

Worship Services

In today's day and age, where you can watch church online and listen to the best preachers through podcasts, many in our congregations are questioning the importance of weekly church attendance. We see this because our membership rosters are typically twice, if not three times greater than our average weekly attendance.

Instead of viewing your membership roster as the total number of individuals you are reaching as a church, consider taking an average of your Christmas, Easter, and Mother's Day attendance numbers. This is because these are, according to a 2011 survey of Protestant pastors by LifeWay Research, the three highest attendance days in church life.[22] Now, don't misunderstand me. I'm not telling you to use the average of those three dates as the number you tout around conferences to boost your ego. I'm simply encouraging you to consider the total ministry reach that your church has.

There are three reasons why I recommend that pastors view this number as their total reach. First of all, on all three Sundays, the majority of your members will come. Secondly, on those same three Sundays, most of your semi-regular attendees will come. And lastly, those who still view your church as their church, but only come a few times a year, will typically come. It's often those three Sundays, when so many are present, that you'll have the greatest opportunity to develop momentum and help people understand the importance of attending on a regular basis.

As you can see in Figure 2.10, when asked, "In a typical month, about how many times (if any) do you attend a worship service?" individuals who attended four times or more had a significantly higher score than those who never did, or those who did on a semi-regular basis. In other words, the more an individual did the input goal of attending a worship service, the higher they scored in the rest of the output goals.

Attend a Worship Service	Average Total Score
0	61.81
1	68.29
2	66.61
3	67.74
4	73.47
5+	80.02

FIGURE 2.10: IN A TYPICAL MONTH, ABOUT HOW MANY TIMES (IF ANY) DO YOU ATTEND A WORSHIP SERVICE?

Do you view your worship service as a part of your discipleship process? Does your church see that too, or do they see it more as a ritual, and relegate discipleship to small group or classroom environments? Here's the bottom line: The research clearly shows that worship services matter and that the maturity level of a disciple is greatly influenced by the frequency that they attend worship services. So don't skim over this or minimize its discipleship implications for your church!

Small Classes or Groups

Typically, most people in your church think discipleship happens in the following TDA question: "In a typical month, about how many times (if any) do you attend small classes or groups for adults from church, such as Sunday school, Bible study, small groups, Adult Bible Fellowships, etc.?" While this is definitely an important part of a church's discipleship pathway, it is not the only place individuals are formed into the image of Christ, as we'll discover throughout this book.

If you take a look at the eight output goals, or discipleship attributes, you will probably assume that attending a small group or a class would help you grow in Bible engagement, since that's typically where you would study the Bible with others. And you'd be right! In the same way, you would probably assume that participating in a small group would help you build relationships and grow in transparency—and you'd be right there as well. As a result, your assumption would likely be that small groups or classes are one of the best environments for discipleship to happen and the most reproducible for growth. And once again, Sherlock, you would be right.

However, I'm sure you never would have imagined the actual total effect that it has on the maturity of a disciple, as we see in Figure 2.11. In the research, we discovered that the more often an individual attended a small community, the higher they scored in all of the output goals! So attending a small group positively influences your ability to obey God and deny self, serve God and others, share Christ, exercise faith, seek God, and be unashamed about your faith.

In fact, having led and managed systems of small groups and discipleship environments in a few churches, I know that small groups are as much of a discipleship environment as they are a tool to connect newcomers into community, care for members, develop leaders, and create a culture for multiplication. But to see how the frequency of attendance in this one input goal affects your total score in all the output goals is astounding. Frequently attending a small discipleship environment is not only the best place to get connected with a church, it's one of the best places to grow as a disciple into the image of Christ.

Attend a Small Community	Average Total Score
0	66.09
1	74.73
2	73.37
3	72.26
4	78.05
5+	82.29

FIGURE 2.11: IN A TYPICAL MONTH, ABOUT HOW MANY TIMES (IF ANY) DO YOU ATTEND A SMALL COMMUNITY?

Conclusion

Micro-shifts *do actually* lead to macro-changes. When Southwest Airlines shifted their metric for success from happy customers to happy employees, everything changed. Traditionally, many airlines and companies put customer satisfaction as their top priority. Unfortunately, since customer satisfaction is a typical output goal, it's difficult to know what input goals will actually produce it. So companies that have customer satisfaction as their *de facto* output goal are essentially letting their employees choose their own path or input goals to try to get there. The result is inconsistency in service and experience.

Southwest has always stood out in the airline industry, since they've been profitable for forty-three consecutive years, which is unheard of, especially during the recession when other airlines struggled. When asked what the secret was behind their success, Gary Kelly, the CEO of Southwest Airlines, said, "Easy: our People."[23] They believe that a strong culture with a unique "order of importance," where they put their employees first, then their customers, then their shareholders, is what has led to their success. "We believe that, if we treat our employees right, they will treat our customers right, and in turn that results in increased business and profits that make everyone happy."[24]

The simplicity of what Southwest has done is that they've made the micro-shift from output goals to an input/output combination. They've discovered that the input goal of happy employees is what results in the output goal of happy customers, which is why they are seeing increased business/profits and happy shareholders! No wonder Kelly, their CEO, believes that his employees are his company's "single greatest strength and most enduring long-term competitive advantage."[25]

The same thing will happen when your church makes the micro-shift, outlined in this chapter, and begins using the TDA input/output goals. You will begin to see macro-change toward maturity in your church, and maybe, prayerfully, you'll experience forty-three years of consecutive growth in maturity, and more.

I love this quote by the legendary UCLA basketball coach, John Wooden:

When you improve a little each day, eventually big things occur . . .
Not tomorrow, not the next day, but eventually a big gain is made.
Don't look for the big, quick improvement. Seek the small improvement one day at a time. That's the only way it happens—and when
it happens, it lasts.[26]

In section 2 of this book, we will integrate all of the micro-shifts
that we've uncovered into your church's discipleship pathway. While the
Influences Matrix, in chapter 1, is the foundational paradigm for any
church's discipleship pathway, the input/output goals of the TDA are what
will make discipleship tangible for your church. These goals are the railroad
tracks that will help your church move closer to Christ and allow you to
measure their progress at the same time.

Reflection Questions

1. Do you already have output goals for your church? What are they?
    How do they compare to the ones listed in this chapter?

2. Do you already have input goals for your church? What are they?
    How do they compare to the ones listed in this chapter?

3. What surprised you most about the research?

4. What is one input goal you can do this week to help your church
    move toward the output goal of maturity in Christ?

CHAPTER 3

FROM SAGE TO GUIDE

"Discipleship is not the path of least resistance,
since the devil never gives up."
—Dr. Robert Coleman

I was furious and out of breath, my head was spinning, and I had no money. I was running away from something, with absolutely nowhere to go. I just knew that I had to leave before I did something that I would've regretted.

I was very confused as a teenager. The fact that I loved to please others did not help much either, since it caused me to act in different ways depending on the situation. I basically put on whatever mask was required of me to get the best grades, to form the right impressions, and to fit into all the desirable groups—I did whatever I had to do to be accepted and get ahead.

To my parents, I was an honors student, a violin virtuoso, a hockey player, a black belt in Tae Kwon Do, and a future Harvard Medical School neurosurgeon who was going to complete his fellowship at John Hopkins. To my friends at school, I was a hip-hop break-dancer, a karaoke star, and an underage drinker who could get into bars. To the people at my parents' church, I was the first baby born in our church plant, a stellar Bible verse memorizer, a star actor in the Christmas musicals, and the violin player on the church's worship team. Like I said, I did whatever I had to do in order to be accepted and get ahead!

The only problem was when my worlds began to collide—and it was all because of a girl. I guess my mom was smarter than I put her out to be because she started to notice the inconsistencies in my stories. I don't know if she ever checked the "library" where I always told her I was going to go and study, when in fact I was hooking up with my girlfriend. Or if my violin teacher ever asked her why I was consistently late to my violin lessons, even though I left home with ample time to get there—another opportunity to be with my girlfriend. The fact is, when I got my report card and my grades were not where they were "supposed" to be, my mom took matters into her own hands. She began systematically shutting down all the opportunities that I had made to live out my alternate identities, and I just could not take it.

So I stormed out of the house and ran away, with nowhere to go. I just started running. I didn't have a wallet, a plan, or a phone; I just knew I had to get out. By the time I arrived at Park Royal—a shopping mall in my hometown—I was furious and out of breath, my head was spinning, and I had no money. I was running away from something, with absolutely nowhere to go.

It was Friday night, and I had no idea where I was going to sleep—the only thing I did know was where I was not going to sleep! I began asking random people in the mall for a quarter so that I could use the pay phone. Once I looked pitiful enough to warrant a quarter from a random stranger, I tried to figure out who I was going to call. It was not going to be my girlfriend because we were going through a rough spot. It certainly wasn't going to be my parents. I couldn't get in touch with my best friend. So the only other number that I had memorized was my pastor's. I know it's hard to believe, but there was a day—before cell phones—where you had to memorize people's numbers and use a pay phone to call someone. Remember those days?

Once I got in touch with my pastor and told him what was going on, he calmly convinced me to take the bus to church because I had nowhere else to go. He said he would feed and house me, so as a young sixteen-year-old, nothing could have sounded better.

When I think back to that time in life, I cannot help but laugh at my naiveté. The fact is, running away never solves anything; it just delays the inevitable. In addition, lying is foolish, because the truth will always be exposed in a matter of time.

After another stranger gave me money for bus fare, I took the ninety-minute bus ride to church and participated in the church's Friday night activities like nothing was wrong. After we were finished, I got into the car with my pastor. My expectation was that I was just going to crash on his couch, but I soon realized that, if his couch was the destination, we were driving in the wrong direction.

Over the next hour, while he was driving me home, he prayerfully listened as I began sharing, venting, confessing, and crying all at the same time. I do not remember quite what he said, nor do I remember what he said to my mom when we walked into my house together. What I do remember is that he was present, he listened, he gave me perspective, and he prayed for me.

We Teach the Way We've Been Taught and We Lead the Way We've Been Led

It's interesting that several years later, I found myself in the same situation again—only the roles were reversed. I was the student pastor—being present, listening, giving perspective, and praying for a student who was going through a difficult time with his family.

When was the last time you reflected on the way that you personally disciple others? In chapter 1 we took a look at how your church approaches discipleship from a fifty-thousand-foot level using the Influences Matrix. In chapter 2, we uncovered a way to make discipleship tangible to your church—using input and output goals—so that those in your church would understand what it looks like to move closer to Christ. In this chapter, we'll take a look at how and why you personally disciple others the way that you do, and the micro-shift that you can make that will lead to macro-change in this area.

So once again, when was the last time you reflected on the way that you personally disciple others? Are you more of a teacher or a shepherd? Do you like to take people through formal curriculum, or do you use their life situation as the starting point? Do you like to disciple one-on-one, in triads, in small groups, or in classrooms? When are people most apt to change? What role do the Holy Spirit, Scripture, and prayer play in the discipleship process?

Unless you have intentionally spent time studying the way people learn and different methods for discipleship, you probably disciple others the way you were discipled (or in the exact opposite manner). This is because our natural bias is to start with what we already know and have personally experienced.

If you are a parent, have you ever caught yourself saying or doing something to your children that your parents used to say or do to you? I catch myself doing this all the time. When my children are not listening, I just begin counting down from the number five. It's not like my parents told me this is what I should do, but it's what they did to me, and it worked. When I stop to think about it, I don't even feel like this is the best method for discipline; in fact, both my wife and I agree that it's not! But I often catch myself still doing it because of that natural bias.

Our natural bias is to teach the way that we have been taught and lead the way that we have been led, unless we make a conscious effort to change. In other words, until you reexamine the way you approach discipleship, you will naturally revert back to using the methods that others used to disciple you—much like I did when I found myself in reversed roles as a student pastor. This is not necessarily a bad thing, since you may have been discipled by some of the best deacons, elders, pastors, and small group leaders. But until you take a step back and realize why they did what they did, you will consistently hit a glass ceiling and have a hard time growing in the way you disciple others.

The point of this chapter is to help you reexamine the way that you personally approach discipleship. From one discipler to another, and from one church leader to another, I want to help you grow in the way you disciple, teach, and lead others toward Christlikeness, "until we all reach unity in the faith and in the knowledge of God's Son, growing into maturity with a stature measured by Christ's fullness" (Eph. 4:13).

This reminds me of Dr. Robert Coleman's definition of a disciple as "a learner who's following Christ. You learn by following. And that means, since we are finite and God alone is infinite, there's never a place in the journey where we stop learning."[1] After pressing Dr. Coleman on this definition recently, he elaborated on it by sharing that "learning is an active process because you never drift to become a disciple. Discipleship is not the path of least resistance, since the devil never gives up."[2] He continued,

"There's a continual sense that as we learn and grow more, we have to do what we've learned; otherwise, we wouldn't make as much progress."[3]

Adults Learn Differently than Children

"Grab a blank sheet of paper and in thirty seconds, sketch a portrait of the person sitting next to you. Ready? Go!" When training others, this is one of the key activities that I have learned to use in order to break the ice and help adults comprehend the way that they learn differently than children. After the thirty seconds pass, I ask the adults to reveal their masterpieces to one another. Inevitably, I will hear chuckles from a few; others will tilt their heads and scratch the back of their neck, while trying to respond with a comment. However, most will respond with an apology, while nervously showing their "masterpiece" to the one they drew.

Why is this the case? If you do the same activity with children, they will proudly show their masterpiece to everyone in the world. "I'm sorry," would be the last words you would hear from them after this activity! Whether my children are drawing stars, bubble words, and 3D cubes on the sticky notes in my office, stick figures of me with my pointy hair and them with their long hair hugging one another, or portraits of themselves with watercolors, their modus operandi is always confidence.

I love this quote by Pablo Picasso; in fact, Christina, my wife, framed it in our house: "Every child is an artist. The problem is how to remain an artist once we grow up." Picasso was onto something here. When you are a child, you're not afraid of what people might think or whether you'll be judged or graded, which is precisely why the thirty-second drawing activity plays out so differently among children and adults. Think back to when you were a child. If your teacher explained the difference between a noun and a verb, you probably did not respond by asking them to prove it. Most likely, your life experience was not brought into the learning equation much either. Instead, you just learned what the teachers taught. The teachers were in control, they were the experts, and they determined what needed to be taught.

> **Every child is an artist. The problem is how to remain an artist once we grow up.**
> **—Pablo Picasso**

Today, it's great that there are other pedagogical schools of thought that are trying to utilize more of a child-centered approach to learning, like Reggio Emilia. However, most adults today are the byproducts of a teacher-centered approach to learning. As a result, since we teach the way we've been taught, we pass along this teacher-centered approach to learning.

For example, when you were in kindergarten, you were expected to write between the lines, memorize Fry's First 100 sight words, recite your address and phone number, and repeat, repeat, and repeat until it was all ingrained in your brain. Why? Because the teacher said so. Sure, the teacher might have mentioned to your class the eventual benefits of knowing how to do all of this, but that's not the card that they led with. It basically went like this: "Students, take out your pencils and write your name. We are then going to do this, and then do that."

As an adult, how would you feel if that's the way someone treated you? If what you had to say didn't matter or necessarily affect what was going to be learned? If you were never given a sufficient reason for why you were learning a particular lesson? If the teacher disregarded your experience and just imposed his will and lesson on you? And if you were forced to learn things that seemed irrelevant or inapplicable to your life situation?

The fact is, adults learn differently than children. There is even a whole educational discipline devoted to this. It's called andragogy, which is the adult-oriented version of pedagogy.

Do you see the tension here? Since we often teach the way we've been taught and lead the way that we've been led, many of us are actually teaching, discipling, and developing adults using the methods that were used on us when we were children. No wonder there is such a lack of disciples in our churches! We are discipling adults the way that we were taught as children. We are shaping our small groups and classrooms for adults, in the same way we learned as children. We are training our volunteers and developing our leaders, in the same way we did twenty years ago. But times have changed! No wonder many of our current discipleship environments and processes are ineffective.

In order to move from pedagogy to andragogy, or a teacher-centered approach to a learner-centered approach, in the way that we disciple in our churches, we need to start by flipping the way we train our volunteers and leaders. This concept, which is rapidly gaining ground as the new standard among educators, is where this chapter's micro-shift is rooted.

Flipping the Classroom

A couple years after YouTube was birthed, high school chemistry teachers Jonathan Bergman and Aaron Sams found themselves experimenting with it to catch students up who had missed a class. They would record their lesson, complete with their voice and PowerPoint slides, convert it into a video file, and then post it on YouTube for their students. After a while of doing this, they discovered that many of their students, including those who had not missed any classes, were watching and rewatching the videos to review for their exams. Bergman and Sams, in their book, *Flip Your Classroom: Reach Every Student in Every Class Every Day*, explain the avalanche effect that then took place:

> We never could have expected the side effects of posting our lessons online: the emails began. Because our videos were posted online, students and teachers from all over the world began thanking us for them. Students just like ours who had struggled with chemistry found our videos and started using them to learn.[4]

After experimenting with this concept more, Sams had this insight: "The time when students really need me physically present is when they get stuck and need my individual help. They don't need me there in the room with them to yak at them and give them content; they can receive content on their own."[5] As a result, Bergman and Sams began asking one another, "What if we prerecorded *all* our lectures, students viewed the video as 'homework,' and then we used the entire class period to help students with the concepts they don't understand?"[6]

Though this was how the flipped classroom revolution was born, it certainly did not end there. In a financially challenged school near Detroit, where 75 percent of students receive a free or reduced-price lunch, the principal Greg Green decided to experiment with this approach to see if things would turn around. He describes the state of his school:

Every year, our failure rates have been through the roof. The students weren't paying attention, they weren't doing their homework, they were being disruptive, or they weren't coming to school at all. Sadly, these issues are not that uncommon, particularly in this economic climate, where the percentage of students who fall into the poverty category is increasing by the day.[7]

As a result, Clintondale High School tried the flipped classroom approach to see if things would turn around. And turn around they did! Over an eighteen-month period they saw their attendance increase, discipline decrease, and their failure rate drop significantly. In fact, when they first rolled out the flipped classroom to their ninth-grade students, their "student failure rate dropped by 33% in one year. . . . In English, the failure rate went from 52% to 19%; in math, 44% to 13%; in science, 41% to 19%; and in social studies, 28% to 9%."[8]

Talk about a micro-shift that led to macro-change!

Flipping the Classroom in Your Church

Imagine for a moment the implications of introducing this concept into the way that you train your volunteers, develop your leaders, and disciple your church. And no, I'm not suggesting that you digitize discipleship or depersonalize the spiritual formation process! If anything, flipping the classroom is a more personable, learner-centered approach to development than the traditional teacher-centered approach, as we see in Figure 3.1.

Digitizing discipleship and depersonalizing spiritual formation are *not* the goal.

When you leverage technology for the lecture component of the lesson, you free yourself up to spend more time with people. So instead of spending the majority of your time in a monologue, you get to spend it in dialogue. And instead of learning through a passive lecture, you get to learn through activities. In other words, flipping the classroom is high tech and high touch, rather than the low tech and low touch approach of the traditional classroom.

In the traditional classroom . . .	In the flipped classroom . . .
The teacher is the sage on the stage.	The teacher is the guide on the side.
The classroom time consists of the teacher lecturing, possibly answering questions, and then assigning homework.	The students watch the lecture at home via video, and then complete their homework in class. So, if a student doesn't understand something, she can ask her teacher.
The teacher needs to standardize the lesson, so she can't possibly engage both the lowest common denominator, and the overachiever.	Since the classroom time consists of homework, case studies, discussion, projects, and processing, every level of learner can be engaged.
Homework is completed at home. So, if the student doesn't understand something, he has to either ask a parent, tutor, or friend, or go back to class with his homework incomplete.	The teacher is able to customize learning to every student— spending more time with those who don't get it, and in turn, catalyzing the students who do get it.

FIGURE 3.1: THE TRADITIONAL VERSUS FLIPPED CLASSROOM

Let's take a look at two different ways that you can implement the flipped classroom model into your church.

Flip Your New Leader's Orientation Training

What happens when you recruit a new leader to serve in your children's ministry, as an usher, on your worship team, or as a group leader? There are two ways that orientation is typically done in churches. If your church is small, you would typically have one-on-one orientations based on necessity. If you are a bit larger, then you might still do one-on-one orientations occasionally mid-semester, but you would typically standardize your orientation times into a training event at the beginning of each semester.

In each orientation, you are essentially repeating the same thing. It goes like this: "Here's the vision of the church and this particular ministry. This is what it would look like to lead in this ministry. This is how you do it." And then you would answer any questions before you ask them to commit to serving for a period of time.

Well, what would new leader's orientation look like if you flipped it instead? Much like the traditional orientation, you would still have one-on-one orientations based on necessity, or you would have standardized orientation times at the beginning of each semester. This is really up to your bandwidth and church size.

However, the orientation wouldn't begin at the start of the event or the meeting; it would actually begin before you met with the leader. In other words, before the one-on-one meeting or the orientation event, you would ask the potential leader(s) to watch a video that would describe the vision of your church and your particular ministry, and also what it would look like to volunteer in this ministry.

Then, if you are meeting with the potential volunteer one-on-one, you would spend time getting to know him, discern whether or not he would be a good fit in your ministry area, and then answer any questions that he might have, before you ask him to commit. If you are meeting with a group of new recruits together, you would do the same thing as you would do one-on-one, but as a group.

What's beautiful about this flipped model is that you would better be able to discover whether potential leaders would be a good fit. This is because when you're together with them, you would have more time to ask them questions and get to know their story. After all, most of what you would have said anyway would have been covered through the video.

Once an individual commits to leading in your ministry, you would release them to serve, while concurrently assigning them a series of training videos that they could complete at their own pace. This is beneficial because you would be engaging them in ministry right away, while also helping them develop the skills that they need to serve effectively.

Are you beginning to see the advantages of flipping the classroom in your church? It's been revolutionary to me, and to all those that I have trained and consulted with.

Flip Your Training Events

Think about the last time you trained your volunteers and leaders. In a traditional training event, you would typically start with some sort of announcement or invitation asking for an RSVP. At the training event, you would have time for fellowship as people were arriving. You would possibly serve a meal, or at a minimum, serve Styrofoam cup church coffee, watered-down juice, and some cookies. You would then share the vision of why this training event was happening, go on to thank your volunteers and leaders for their commitment, and get into the lecture or lesson. Afterwards, you might have a brief time for some group discussion, but you'd always end with prayer. If you were keen, you might assign some sort of homework or application point to implement the concept that your leaders just learned in their ministry area. Sound familiar?

What would happen if you flipped this training event? Well, with the invite asking for an RSVP, you could link to a short video (fifteen minutes or less) that they could watch. This video would be the main concept that you wanted to train your volunteers and leaders in. For example, if you were training your small group leaders and wanted to teach them the art of asking good questions, that short video would explain the why, the what, and a few examples of the how. After the video, there would be some sort of brief assignment to complete to indicate basic understanding of the material, or how the concept would relate to their leadership and role. For example, you might ask them to write down a few follow-up questions that would help encourage discussion within a group setting.

At the flipped training event, there would still be many of the same elements as the traditional training event; however, the time allocation would be vastly different. Instead of spending the majority of the training event with a sage on the stage teaching the lesson, in the flipped classroom, you would spend the majority of the time in work groups.

When people arrived, you would still have time for fellowship, food, and bad coffee, but when it came time for the teaching portion and group discussion, you would flip the amount of time that you'd typically spend on both. So instead of a 30 to 45-minute talking head, you would spend 5 to 10 minutes casting vision, encouraging the volunteers and leaders, and reminding them of "the why" and "the what" from the video that they watched.

The majority of the time would then be spent in groups where the volunteers and leaders would be able to better focus on how to implement the concepts that they learned in the video. They would do this by working on case studies, revisiting concepts that might be difficult, and sharing best practices with one another via group brainstorming. Through this model, you would be able to better implement adult-education techniques—many of which we are going to explore later on in this chapter—and also cater to a variety of learning styles. If you're keen, when this training was finished, you could even assign ongoing training via a series of videos.

The Genius of the Flipped Classroom Approach

You can't disciple everyone in your church by yourself. This reminds me of Jethro's advice to Moses when he was spending morning until evening judging, guiding, and leading the Israelites by himself. "What you're doing is not good. . . . You will certainly wear out both yourself and these people who are with you, because the task is too heavy for you. You can't do it alone" (Exod. 18:17–18).

In order to develop disciples, rather than consumers, you need to train up leaders who understand that discipleship is more about direction than destination. These leaders need to understand what input and output goals are, and how they relate to one another. They need to be like those God-fearing and trustworthy leaders that Moses placed over the Israelites to help him lead and judge (Exod. 18:21, 25–26).

With these two micro-shifts in place, your leaders need to learn how to teach and disciple others using a learner-centered approach rather than a teacher-centered approach. In other words, they need to move from being a sage on the stage to being a guide on the side.

Leaders need to move from being a sage on the stage to being a guide on the side.

It's not just the higher level of engagement, retention in learning, and scalability of the flipped classroom approach that makes it an effective method to train your volunteers and leaders. The real genius is the fact that the flipped classroom approach subconsciously teaches and trains your leaders to view learning and discipleship from a guide-on-the-side point of view, rather than from a sage-on-the-stage point of view.

Once you've trained leaders using the flipped classroom approach, use the following four principles in your discipleship environments to help the rest of your church take their next step closer to Christ. These four principles are core to a guide-on-the-side approach to discipleship. They will help you integrate a learner-centered, adult-education oriented, guide-on-the-side approach to ministry into your discipleship curriculum, Sunday school classes, spiritual formation seminars, small groups, volunteer training opportunities, and leadership development environments.

So let's start with the first principle.

Principle #1: Lower Anxiety

Anxiety is real and must be addressed. The reason many adults apologize and are hesitant to show their "masterpiece," after the thirty-second drawing activity is because of anxiety. Anxiety is one of the major side effects of our educational testing and grading system. Do you remember how anxious tests made you feel? What about the anxiety of getting back the grade from a test that you did not study enough for? And what about the time your grades were not what you thought they should have been, or what you needed them to be, in order to get accepted into a particular college? School-induced anxiety was the worst, especially when you had to show that test, your report card, or a college rejection letter to your parents. I am not saying we do away with tests, calculus, and report cards— all I am doing is pointing out how those things tend to increase our adrenaline and anxiety levels.

Anxiety is real and must be addressed.

The key word here is *levels*. A little bit of anxiety, like a manageable due date, acts as a positive motivator to get our reports in, our presentations done, and our inboxes down to zero. Too much anxiety, like an overwhelming number of tasks all due in the next hour, causes many of us to panic, to be careless in the details, or ultimately, to shut down.

Everyone in your church deals with anxiety in a different way, so understanding and reducing the different levels of anxiety in your discipleship environments is the first key to facilitating adult learning.[9]

When you announce a discipleship class, a new small group, or ask someone if they would like to be discipled, what is the typical reaction at your church? If everyone cheers and signs up, then you can probably skip this point and go straight to number two. But for the rest of us, the reaction is often mixed. There are those in your church who always sign up for everything. They are the faithful few, the jolly Janes, the ones who always come up after service and say, "Thank you, pastor." These folks probably do not have an anxiety issue when it comes to learning.

There are others in your church who will attend based on the topic or their schedule—their anxiety level is somewhere in the middle. Then there are others who won't go to anything other than your worship service once a month—their church-related anxiety levels are on the higher end of the spectrum.

What will it take to help the latter become more engaged in your church and in these opportunities for discipleship? Well, it starts with reducing their anxiety by overcoming the barriers to entry. Let me explain.

There are three barriers that often prevent an individual from engaging in discipleship environments outside of the Sunday worship service. They are knowledge barriers, relational hurt barriers, and learning environment barriers.

Knowledge Barriers

The moment someone in your church hears about a discipleship opportunity and says, "I won't learn anything from that," you are facing the knowledge barrier. This barrier is the easiest one to overcome because it boils down to messaging and the way that you communicate.

According to a 2007 Yankelovich study quoted in the *New York Times*,[10] the average person living in a city saw up to five thousand ad messages a day. Imagine how much more that would be today. Whether you live in a big city of a few million, or a rural town of five hundred, the fact is, everyone in your church is being constantly advertised to.

So when you announce a discipleship opportunity to your church, guess who you are going up against. Let me give you a hint: it's not the other discipleship opportunities your church is offering. It's the millions of dollars that professional marketing firms spend on advertising their films, the seemingly unlimited hours of content on Netflix, the dozens of emails filling up inboxes, and all the extracurricular activities that parents are driving their children around to.

If the title or "elevator-speech" of your discipleship opportunity cannot compete against those five thousand other messages, how do you expect to help the nominally engaged in your church grow deeper in their relationship with Christ? Yes, I understand that in the grand scheme of things, your discipleship opportunities are *meaningful*, whereas many of the other activities are *shallow*. But unless you can peak the curiosity of the nominally engaged—or those who have high anxiety levels—and overcome the knowledge barrier, they will never fully experience how meaningful your discipleship opportunities can be.

When you announce a discipleship opportunity to your church, who do you think you're competing with?

Overcoming this barrier just requires a small change. The next time you are advertising a discipleship opportunity at your church, try titling the name of your seminar or class differently. Instead of being descriptive, try titling it with catchphrases. For example, in university, I had to take a history of religion course. My professor could have easily titled it, "The History of Religion in Canada," and I probably would not have even noticed the class. But instead, she titled it, "Missionaries, Medicine Men, and Methodists," and the class was packed.

Try titling your next discipleship opportunity by outlining the benefits of attending. For example, instead of titling your next men's breakfast the "April 10 Men's Breakfast," try calling it, "Bacon, Biscuits, and Bravery." I guarantee you that this title will cut through the noise and pique the curiosity of all the men in your church.

Another way you can overcome the knowledge barrier is to align your discipleship opportunities with the sermon series. If people are coming on Sunday, they typically aren't facing the knowledge barrier, because they have voted with their feet. So what if your small groups studied the sermons at a deeper level? Or what if you held an in-depth seminar for every sermon series that you preached? Or what if you handed out Scripture reading plans or articles that aligned with your sermons? Doing any of these options would definitely result in an uptick in participation, since you would be eliminating the knowledge barrier.

Relational Hurt Barriers

This second barrier is the hardest one to overcome, because it deals with an individual's past. Everyone has experienced betrayal, his or her trust being broken, and varying levels of conflict—both inside and outside the church. As a result, the extent to which an individual knows how to reconcile, forgive, and deal with their emotional baggage, determines their likelihood to join a discipleship opportunity where they will need to open up to others—like in a small group.

Similarly, the extent to which an individual builds relationships with others influences how mature a disciple they are. We see this in the TDA research that we examined in chapter 2. One of the output goals, or discipleship attributes, of a mature disciple is building relationships. This output goal is self-explanatory, as it measures the depth to which a disciple is connected to and properly related to others, especially fellow Christians.

As we explored the last chapter in Figure 2.7, there are several input goals that actually predict a higher score in the Building Relationships output goal. This is helpful to our discussion here because the higher someone scores in the Building Relationship output goal, the more likely they would be to overcome their relational hurt barriers. What are some examples?

First and foremost, developing healthy relationships is one of the best antidotes to healing broken ones. We see this in the research because when individuals are in small classes or groups that pray with one another (both are input goals), we see them scoring higher in the Building Relationships output goal. In other words, getting over that initial barrier and joining a discipleship group is one of the best ways to address your relational hurt barriers.

Furthermore, input goals like praying for your church and/or church leaders, having regular responsibilities at your church, and serving others in your community, all positively impacted the Building Relationships output goal. This shows us that the more you take the focus off yourself and your hurts, and instead focus on praying for and helping others, the more likely you will be to overcome your relational hurt barriers. This is all good and well, but statistics alone don't change people. According to authors Chip and Dan Heath, in their book *Switch: How to Change Things When Change Is Hard*, change happens when you appeal to an individual's rational side and emotional side, and then shape their path to make it easy to change. Since relational hurt barriers are so emotional in nature, you can't start by preaching statistics and appealing to the rational side. "Join a small group and pray with others! The research says that this will help you build relationships with others and overcome your hurts," is not the way you want to start addressing this barrier in your church.

Instead, you want to start by appealing to the emotional side and convincing it that people can be trustworthy. In order to do that, you will need to help those in your church who are struggling with this barrier create a new point of reference around community and transparency. You can do this by sharing before-and-after stories of life change from your small groups during the weekend service. And when you preach or teach, you can model transparency by sharing your imperfections, and how you are working through them with others in community. Both of these simple suggestions would appeal to the emotional side, which would then cause an individual to want to make a switch and join a small group environment where, according to our research, we know that deeper change would take place.

You can also overcome this barrier by making it easy for people to bring a friend or come with their spouse. This would be a way to "shape the path," in Chip and Dan Heath's words, making it easier for individuals to change. So, for example, if you charge for materials for a small group or some other kind of event, have a buy-one-get-one-free offer where every registration comes with a free registration. If childcare is the issue, provide a stipend to small groups to help them offset costs for those who need it. Or provide onsite children's programming at your church during seminars and classes. After all, is it not worth it to find the extra volunteers and increase your budget lines if the end result is life transformation and more people experiencing Christ?

Learning Environment Barriers

This last barrier is brief and relates to your experience in school. If you struggled through school, then any learning opportunity as an adult will inevitably conjure up old memories and feel threatening. To overcome this barrier, have a good description that outlines the content that is going to be covered and the manner in which it will be covered.

You probably will not want to do this during a Sunday morning announcement, since a long explanation like that will introduce the knowledge barrier into the equation. As a result, have a printed flyer that people can pick up after the service, or create a place on your website where people can learn more and register. You can also have a welcome booth or an information table where people can ask any questions they might have to a well-informed volunteer. The point is, information and explanation are the keys to overcoming this barrier.

Principle #2: Start with Experience, Not Theory

Lowering anxiety levels by addressing the barriers to entry are an effective way to get more people into discipleship environments. But once you get them there, you need to keep them engaged and ensure that you are giving them an opportunity to grow; otherwise, they won't return. In order to do this, you need to start with experience, not theory.

One of the key pillars of andragogy (adult education theory) is that adults are not blank slates. In other words, when adults enter into a new learning environment, they are not starting from zero; they're bringing their past knowledge, experience, and assumptions on the topic, as well as their stress, workload, and emotional baggage from the past few weeks into the learning experience.[11]

Adults are not blank slates.

Because adults aren't blank slates, if you start with theory or an abstract concept in your next discipleship opportunity, many of your adult learners may not engage for several reasons: 1) If they already understand the concept, they will tune out. 2) Some individuals may have recently argued with a loved one, or had to deal with conflict at work, and will be emotionally unprepared to connect with theories or abstract concepts. 3) Some might not even understand the complexities of the theory that you are trying to present because they need something more basic.

So instead of starting with theory, you need to start with experience. Start with your own story on the subject matter, or ask others to share their stories in smaller groups of two to three people. For example, the next time you are leading a newcomers class, do not start with the vision of your church. Instead, start by sharing a recent experience you had when you were the newbie in a room, or what it felt like when you first came to the church. You could then ask those who are attending to share with each other, in groups of two to three, how they heard about the church, why they are at the newcomers class, and what they hope to get out of it.

Or, when you are in a discipleship group, start by sharing personal stories about the subject at hand. Do this before even reading through the passage, discussing what it means, and how it would apply to your life.

By starting with experience, you can help everyone focus on the task at hand, regardless of how busy their week might have been. You can also prime the pump for learning by drawing out their past experiences related to the topic at hand. By doing this, you would essentially be lowering their anxiety and helping them become aware of what they already know internally. This is beneficial because it'll help them get into the right posture to learn the new concept that you want to introduce.

A Ball of Yarn and the Journey of Learning

Another way to understand what's happening inside of a learner is by thinking about a ball of yarn. I know it sounds silly, but bear with me. While I may not know how to knit, I am the proud owner of a hand-knit scarf that my wife, Christina, knitted for me while we were dating. Okay, well, to be completely honest, she hand-knitted half of it and asked her grandmother to finish the rest. But that's the beauty of this analogy! Let me explain.

Let's say you are leading a study on the spiritual disciplines. Everyone who is a part of it has probably heard a message on Scripture reading or prayer before and will have some level of experience in practicing those spiritual disciplines. Some may have even read books on the topic. In other words, everyone in your study has some level of experience and knowledge on the topic.

Let's imagine that a ball of yarn represents all of that past experience and knowledge. The first time you opened up the Bible, you got your first piece of yarn and your spiritual disciplines ball of yarn began. The first time you prayed, you tied the next piece of yarn onto that first piece. When you heard a message on fasting, you added another piece, and so on, and so on.

Now you're an adult, and that spiritual disciplines ball of yarn is pretty big—it's also complicated, messy, and probably all tangled. After all, just as you might have had seasons of your life where you were regularly adding pieces of yarn onto it, I'm sure there were other moments where that wasn't the case. When you walked away from God, had that summer of regret, or were consumed with the opposite sex for the first time, perhaps you threw your ball of yarn in the corner of your room, into a backpack, or somewhere else where it could get easily tangled. As a result, it probably doesn't look anything like those picturesque balls of yarn that you can buy at your local craft store. (How do they even make those anyway?)

The Effect of Neglecting Experience

Here's the thing. The next time you teach, if you start with theory, you're basically saying you don't care what everyone's ball of yarn looks like. There are a couple of issues with this approach. First of all, because adults aren't blank slates, if you fail to draw from their past experiences, and if you fail to take the time to help them become aware of what they know about the subject at hand, all you'll be doing is giving them knowledge. Until people figure out—if they ever do—how this learning applies to their lives, they'll have a difficult time retaining what you're teaching. And this is precisely because of the second issue with this approach—adults don't learn best when they're just storing up information for later on.

Think back to a recent work orientation. What do you remember most? The paperwork you had to fill out so that you could get paid, or the policy about year-end budgeting requirements? While you definitely needed to know both, most likely, during orientation, you focused on the paperwork to get paid, and when it came time for year-end budgeting, you asked a coworker what to do, or you revisited the orientation manual. The fact is, adults are most engaged when they see the relevance of the lesson to their life, and when they can immediately apply it.

So coming back to our yarn analogy, what happens if you start with theory and neglect experience and relevance? You would essentially be handing a new piece of yarn to everyone you're discipling and expecting them to find the end piece and tie it on themselves. This would work in a perfect world, but what if they didn't even know where their ball of yarn was? Or what if they hadn't looked at their yarn in a while? In other words, what if they didn't know what they knew about the subject at hand? What if they weren't consciously aware of all the ways they were shaped by others and their past?

Or better yet, what if their ball of yarn was tangled because they had learned so many different approaches and perspectives on the subject—in this case, spiritual disciplines? One pastor said it was all about a list of things to do—good works as outlined in Ephesians 2:10. And then another said it was all about grace as outlined in Ephesians 2:8-9. And then another said Ephesians 2:10 always comes after Ephesians 2:8-9, so it's a combination of both grace and works. In addition, a pastor might have told them the SOAP (Scripture, Observation, Application, Prayer) way to read the Scriptures, but then in reading a book on the spiritual disciplines, they discovered *Lectio Divina*. Or maybe, after years of praying for a loved one, and not seeing any fruit, they're doubting whether prayer works at all.

Have you ever tried to untangle a necklace or a ball of yarn? Nothing frustrates me more than acts of futility—and that's what I feel like that is. It's complicated and it always takes way longer that I expect, so I often give up. This is basically the situation you're placing all your learners in when you start with theory. You're giving them a tangled necklace or ball of yarn, and saying to them, "Have at it! Call me when you're done!"

Starting with Experience Respects the Learner

What would happen if you started with experience instead? Well, you would be admitting that everyone has a perspective on the matter—a mix of both conscious and unconscious beliefs that affect their practice of spiritual disciplines. You would, in fact, be recognizing that everyone has a ball of yarn. As a result, when sharing your own experience with those you're discipling, you would be showing everyone what your ball of yarn looks like—in all of its messiness and glory. This, in turn, gives courage to those you're teaching or discipling to take out their ball of yarn and show it to a few others when you ask them to share their experience. While each learner shares his or her own experience, they have the opportunity to remember the different experiences that created their ball of yarn, and find their end piece. This is what it means to help the learner verbalize what they already know internally.

Once you have helped those you are discipling pick up their ball and find their end piece, they have a decision to make: Are they going to accept that piece of yarn and integrate the new learning into their life? If so, you have positioned them in the optimal place to integrate and apply it into their lives. If not, then this is still okay, since you will have helped them focus their knowledge and belief on the topic.

Just like Christina's grandmother took over for her and finished knitting my scarf—Christina, myself, or anyone else for that matter, could easily pick that scarf back up and make it longer. That's the beauty of learning and the importance of starting with experience. Every time you teach or disciple another, you build upon what they already know and their life experiences. So start with experience, not theory.

Principle #3: Move beyond Your Lectern

One of the easiest and safest things to do as a teacher is to prepare your lesson, teach it as a monologue, and then go home. This way, you are in complete control and there are no variables to deal with. I remember one of my university professors was like this—he did not like questions. So when anyone was brave enough to ask him one, he would always react annoyed and respond with big words and complex theories. If you did not agree with what he said, or act like you understood, he would look at you like you were the stupidest person in the class. If it were not for tenure, he would have been fired. (No, I'm not bitter.) Unfortunately, since many of us teach the way we have been taught, this detrimental model of teaching continues to proliferate today—even in the church.

Instead of being a sage on the stage, what would it look like if you were a guide on the side? This principle is core to this entire chapter's micro-shift. Being a guide on the side is not just about letting people ask questions or interrupt your teaching; it is a wholesale change in the way that you look at the learning process. Aside from my horrific university professor example, in most classes, the teacher will often teach their lesson, *nicely* answer any questions, and then assign homework. In the same way, during a class on serving and spiritual gifts, you will probably teach the class, answer questions, and then talk about next steps. In the sage-on-the-stage model of teaching, the teacher is the expert, the teacher has the knowledge, and the teacher is passing his or her information onto the learner.

Seeing Yourself as a Facilitator

If you want to move from being a sage on the stage to a guide on the side, you need to start seeing yourself less as the master teacher, and more as the master facilitator. Instead of teaching a concept, what if you helped learners discover it themselves? Instead of sharing your own examples, what if you had students share their examples with one another? Instead of being the only lecturer, what if you had your students take turns teaching the concepts they needed to know?

Being a guide on the side is about moving beyond your lectern and crafting a learning experience for everyone in the class. This means that your preparation time will be spent less on what you are going to say, and more on creating learning activities for your students to move from discovery to application.

> **Being a guide on the side is about moving beyond your lectern and crafting a learning experience for everyone in the class.**

A Classroom Example

Let me give you an example. Let's say you were teaching a class on serving and spiritual gifts. Instead of lecturing out of 1 Corinthians 12, Ephesians 4, and Romans 12, what if you divided your class into groups of five to six people and gave each of them one of those passages. Each group would then be responsible to study that passage and craft a lesson on the spiritual gifts, which they would then teach the rest of the class. After each group presented, you would have the other groups ask questions, as if the presenting group were the teacher. When all the groups finished presenting, you would go up to the front and facilitate a conversation for the class to share the learned insights that were consistent across all the presentations.

Once that was done, and only then, you would add your thoughts on whatever was missed.

Do you see the difference? If information transfer were the only goal, it would be quicker and more efficient if you, as the teacher, prepared the lesson and lectured it. However, if retention and transformation were the goal, the latter method would be far superior. After all, haven't you ever noticed that you learn and retain something the most when you yourself are the teacher? If that is the case, then why not allow the student to become the teacher, and the teacher to become the guide?

A Small Group Example

During one small group, I wanted to teach on disciplining children. I spent quite a bit of time preparing because I wanted my group to grow in their ability to parent and discover different ways to discipline. However, instead of writing out a lecture, I crafted a learning experience.

I found two articles on the Internet that each explained a different way to discipline. So I printed them out and handed those articles to the group. The men got one, and the women got the other. Then I split them up. I asked each group to read through the article, discuss it, and come back to teach the rest of the group the concept that was outlined in the article. Except I told them that they could not lecture—they had to role-play the particular style of disciplining in a skit. Then, to shake things up, I invited the children to participate and said that they were the judges and got to determine which group won, and who would get the best award for acting.

> **Allow the student to become the teacher, and the teacher to become the guide.**

I guarantee you that was one of the most memorable lessons and learning experiences that my group had, since they were active learners processing the material and teaching it themselves, rather than passive listeners sitting idly by while the lecturer dumped information.

Being a guide on the side is not a time saver, since you still need to understand and grasp the concept that you are trying to teach in order to create learning experiences. In fact, oftentimes, it is more difficult to be a guide than a sage because it feels so good to be the authority, the teacher, and the lecturer. But if this is what will lead to transformation and greater engagement, since those you're discipling are active learners instead of passive listeners, isn't it worth it?

Principle #4: Apply the Learning Today

So far, we have explored ways to implement the micro-shift of moving from sage to guide before the actual discipleship opportunity begins and also while it is happening. Before leading a discipleship experience, you will want to address anxiety so that a larger number of individuals will participate. Next, you will want to keep them engaged, which is why you would start with experience, rather than theory. As a result, during the learning opportunity, you will want to craft experiences rather than lectures for optimal transformation.

But what happens at the end? Do you finish with the learning experience, pray, and dismiss? Or is there a better way to apply the learning?

Incorporate Time for Practice

The first thing you will want to do is carve out time during the lesson to apply the learning. For example, if you are teaching a lesson on journaling, provide time during the class for the students to journal. Or if you are introducing a new method of studying Scripture to your small group, give your group members time to independently study a short passage during your group time. If you are teaching on forgiveness, then have people role-play with one another and practice forgiving and receiving forgiveness, or have them write out letters to the ones they need to forgive, and/or ask forgiveness from.

By carving out time during the lesson to apply the learning, you give learners the opportunity to practice what they have learned, which is usually when most questions arise. This gives you the opportunity to provide feedback and troubleshoot in a safe environment, rather than leaving them to do that at home or by themselves. Does this remind you of the flipped classroom approach?

Use Horizontal Peer-to-Peer Accountability

Secondly, homework is great because it provides a sense of accountability. The only downside is that it is vertical accountability, so unless you are providing a grade, a certificate, or some sort of incentive that will motivate people to complete their homework, you'll never get the majority of your learners to complete it.

Instead, what would it look like if you introduced horizontal peer-to-peer accountability? At the end of the discipleship opportunity, what if you asked people in your group to follow up with each other by sending one another a quick text message sometime in the following week, or connecting with one another on Facebook or other social media platforms? This form of accountability is less direct, but it is often just what is needed to nudge each other to revisit what has been learned and work toward application.

Conclusion

Consider the way that we now communicate with one another via writing, compared to when we were children. We have moved from long-form letters, to postcards, to emails, to text messages, to 140 characters on Twitter, and now to emojis. What's next?

In the same way, the average shot length of a movie scene has decreased significantly from 12 seconds in 1930 to 2.5 seconds today.[12] This was most apparent to me when watching *Star Wars: The Force Awakens* (2015). I couldn't believe how quickly the shots transitioned and the movie progressed, especially when comparing it to the original trilogy of Star Wars films. If you don't believe me, go ahead and watch the original trilogy and time the scenes—especially when they're talking! It moves so slow.

With the increasing proliferation of smartphones and being constantly connected, a recent study from Microsoft proves that we now have a shorter attention span than goldfish. They discovered that our attention span has decreased from 12 seconds to 8 seconds since the mobile revolution began in the year 2000. If only we could hold our attention for another second or two, we could still claim to have the upper hand on the nine-second attention span of goldfish![13]

Oh, how times have changed! And the rate of change is only going to increase. Just look up "Did You Know" by Karl Fisch, Scott McLeod, and Jeff Brenman on YouTube from several years ago, and you'll be floored by the way things have changed. Anyone remember MySpace?

We cannot continue teaching the way that we were taught. We cannot assume that those we are discipling and leading today will participate in our discipleship opportunities just because we offer it to them. Nor can we expect them to stay engaged and experience transformation with mere lectures anymore. We need to change the way that we disciple others, and the way that we train our disciplers, volunteers, and leaders. So will you make the micro-shift from being a sage on the stage to being a guide on the side?

Reflection Questions

1. How will the concepts in this chapter affect the way that you train your volunteers and leaders?

2. What is one thing that you can do differently the next time you teach a discipleship class or seminar?

3. How can you equip your group leaders to be more like a guide on the side than a sage on the stage?

CHAPTER 4

FROM FORM TO FUNCTION

*"The only possible hermeneutic of the gospel
is a congregation which believes it."*
—Lesslie Newbigin

"Why don't you come to *our* community group?"

I couldn't believe my ears. These were words that I never thought I would hear coming out of Angela and Chris's mouths.[1] Jeff and Kari on the other hand? Of course, they started the group with my wife, Christina, and I. But why in the world would Angela and Chris invite others to our group? They hadn't been for months. And why would they use the personal pronoun "our," anyway? Did they really feel like this was *their* group, despite their inconsistent attendance and apparent lack of care for community?

You know those people who regularly come late and leave early for your worship gathering? They're nice, pleasant, and even fun to talk to when they show up, but they always seem to have other plans when you try to get together with them. Or how about those people who tend to become engaged every few months because of a crisis, only to grow distant again once things settle down?

Both of these descriptions fit Angela and Chris to a tee. So you can guess my surprise when I heard them refer to our group with the personal pronoun, and when they invited others to come as well! These are behaviors I would have expected from regular attenders and those who were wholly bought in to the vision of our group, but certainly not from those who hardly came or returned my calls.

This messed me up.

What if I had been looking for success in all the wrong places? What if I had the wrong perspective when it came to community and group life? What if success was more about their perception of the group than my metrics like frequency of attendance? In fact, what if success in community and group life was ultimately about cultivating a sense of belonging? Then, wouldn't engagement increase accordingly? If someone felt like they belonged and it was their group, even if their attendance was hit and miss, wouldn't they ultimately turn to the group in a time of need?

Yes. Yes. Yes.

I've seen this happen time and time again. With Angela and Chris, I saw them engage back into our group when they found out they were pregnant. I saw this happen for them again when they were going through a rough patch in their marriage.

I've seen this happen with people like Jason and Melissa as well. Although they were relatively consistent in their attendance, they typically wouldn't open up about their lives. Nor would they make an effort to connect with others outside of Wednesday night and Sunday morning. That was, at least, until Melissa's mother passed away. It was a slow process. Initially, they would miss group meetings here and there because of doctor appointments and hospital visits. And when her mother passed away, they had to arrange for the funeral and host family from out of town. Their absence from the group was definitely excusable and understood. But as the months went by, their engagement continued to drop. So instead of missing an occasional group meeting, weeks would go by before we saw them again. And even then, it was hit and miss.

It wasn't until a year later that Melissa finally opened up to our group and shared how she was going through depression. This was honestly the first time we had ever heard her open up about anything personal. During prayer time, it would always be about others. In fact, both her and Jason always seemed to have things together and be the perfect little family with their two daughters, son, and quaint, white, picket fence.

So when Melissa shared some intimate details about the depths of depression that she was fighting, it took a second for our group to know what to do. Sure, Christina and I had sensed something had been off, but we didn't know that it was this serious. So we gathered around her as a group and prayed.

There was something about that night and the subsequent weeks that changed the way Melissa and Jason engaged with our group. Instead of being distant, they were connected. Rather than attending sparsely, they were consistently present. Instead of just keeping to themselves, they began hanging out with others from our group outside of the regularly scheduled meetings.

It wasn't that our group did anything different. It wasn't the study, nor was it really the fact that we prayed for them, since we always prayed for each other. What changed was their perception and perspective of the group. They felt like they finally belonged.

The Tension of Playing Matchmaker

I was never much of a matchmaker. Shows like *The Bachelor* or *The Bachelorette* feel awkward, contrived, and frankly cause me anxiety. In fact, I can still feel the cold sweat from the time my friends set me up on a blind date.

So you're probably not surprised by the fact that I hate playing matchmaker at church. And no, I'm not talking about the singles ministry. I'm talking about placing people into existing groups or classes.

You know how it goes. We appeal to our congregation to get into a group because *life is better in community.* Or we say things like, "Groups are the way to go deeper and find community at our church." So when we get that email, connection card, or have a conversation with someone who wants to find a group, we look through our list of groups and classes and suggest a few that might work best for them.

For some, that's the beginning of the end. Either they don't follow up, or we let them slip through the cracks. For others, they will get in touch with a group leader or meet with them for coffee, but then never show up at the group. In other instances, they might attend a group meeting, but never return. And then you have a small percentage of individuals who will visit a few groups until they find the one that fits for them. This is partially why

I've yet to meet a church that has a *consistently* high rate of success in *placing* newcomers into *existing* groups or classes.

When I was serving as a small groups pastor, I wasn't that concerned with newcomers who were mature in their faith. We had our systems and groups set up in a way that would help individuals like them get quickly plugged in and find the right fit. Instead, my attention was toward those who did not show any initiative to get into community. I was trying to help people like Melissa and Jason, or Angela and Chris, who were either disillusioned with community because of a bad experience in the past, kept to themselves, or simply did not sense the need for community. Group fairs, short-term groups, new groups starting every month, group connects, and even online groups—I tried everything and anything to get them in, but the results always seemed to be lackluster and less than expected.

There had to be a different way.

A Kingdom Vision for Community

Imagine how you would feel if you belonged to a community where love was a verb and was characterized by action, rather than shallow words that didn't do or mean anything? Where blessing each other wasn't a second thought, but a normal part of our daily schedules? Where apathy and indifference weren't the normal attitude, but we passionately praised God, were all grounded in the Word, were filled with the Holy Spirit, and were empowered with his strength? Imagine if serving one another was our normal posture, and proclaiming the gospel was our priority?

Can you see this? Can you imagine this sort of community? Can you taste it? This is what the early church was like in Acts 2:42–47, and what was the result? Three thousand people were baptized on a single day, and that was just the beginning.

Just imagine what it would feel like to belong to this kind of community, where no one had any need? Where everyone came with the posture to give, instead of the agenda to take?

For a moment, let's think about the impact that this would have. It's 2:00 p.m. and one of your colleagues needs caffeine to get through the rest of the day. So you decide to walk with him to the local café. How would you feel if, when you arrived, your coworker reached into *your* pocket, took five dollars from *your* wallet, and bought himself coffee without even asking you? If you're from the South you'd probably say something like, "Oh bless your heart," while thinking to yourself, *I can't believe this just happened . . . the nerve.*

Let's replay the situation. As you're walking into the café, you decide to bless your colleague and buy him coffee. How would you feel then? The end result is the same in both situations for your colleague—his need is met and he gets free coffee. But there's one stark difference. Instead of feeling cheated, you would feel generous. Instead of feeling empty, you would leave filled.

This is the difference between giving and taking, and it's the same way in our churches. If everyone came with the posture to give, rather than the agenda to take, everyone would leave filled, while also getting their needs met. We would be a community where the "one anothers" in Scripture would take on flesh. Where we would be serving one another through love (Gal. 5:13), carrying one another's burdens (Gal. 6:2), forgiving one another (Eph. 4:32), submitting to one another in the fear of Christ (Eph. 5:21), spurring one another on toward love and good deeds (Heb. 10:24), loving one another (1 John 3:11), confessing our sins to one another, and praying for one another (James 5:16).

> **What if everyone came with the posture to give, rather than the agenda to take?**

This is what I want. This is what gets me excited. This is the type of church that Jesus describes in the Sermon on the Mount as the salt of the earth and a city on a hill that cannot be hidden (Matt. 5:13–14). When we do this, and we function as the type of church that God intended us to be, then those who are far from God will see our "good deeds and glorify God on the day he visits us" (1 Pet. 2:12 NIV).

A Sign, Instrument, and Foretaste

Lesslie Newbigin (1909–1998) is one of my favorite missiologists, and I attribute much of the way that I think about mission and the church to him. In short, after serving as a missionary to India for thirty-five years, he returned to England in the 1970s at age sixty-six, only to realize that England had completely changed. Once a Christian nation, it was now post-Christian, and he realized that the West needed the gospel just as much as the East. So rather than retire and play golf, he felt convicted to devote the rest of his life to equipping the church in England to be missionaries, not just overseas, but right where they were.

The church is to be a sign, instrument, and foretaste of the kingdom of God.

There is this one phrase that he says about the church that has consumed the way that I view discipleship and community life. He says that the church is to be a sign, instrument, and foretaste of the kingdom of God.[2]

In order to unpack that phrase, we need to first define the kingdom of God and its relationship to the church. George Eldon Ladd does this well in his book, *A Theology of the New Testament,*

> The Kingdom is primarily the dynamic reign or kingly rule of God, and derivatively, the sphere in which the rule is experienced. In biblical idiom, the Kingdom is not identified with its subjects. They are the people of God's rule who enter it, live under it, and are governed by it. The church is the community of the Kingdom but never the Kingdom itself. Jesus' disciples belong to the Kingdom as the Kingdom belongs to them; but they are not the Kingdom. The Kingdom is the rule of God; the church is a society of women and men.[3]

So while the church is not the Kingdom, it is certainly a sign, instrument, and foretaste to it. Let me explain.

The Church as a Sign of the Kingdom

Though I grew up in Vancouver, and would regularly spend my summers at the beach, the sand was certainly nothing to brag about. It was coarse, rocky, and sometimes covered with seaweed and driftwood. I would sometimes hear from my friends that there were these faraway lands where the sand was white and so fine that it felt like cornstarch underneath your feet. However, until I actually saw it with my eyes, felt it with my hands, and walked over it with my feet, these white-sanded beaches were as real to me as the Loch Ness monster.

After moving to Nashville, I quickly discovered that these mythical white-sanded beaches were only a day's drive away down on the beaches of Destin, Florida, lining the Gulf of Mexico. So the first chance I got, I decided to take my family down on a vacation. While driving down, it wasn't until we passed through Birmingham and Montgomery, Alabama, and then crossed over the state line to Florida, that we finally saw the sign: Destin, Florida, sixty miles! I'm sure you could've anticipated the excitement that my wife, Christina, and I both felt after eight hours of driving with three young children. That sign gave us hope that the end was near. And the closer we got to Destin, the more excited we would get when we would see more signs: Forty miles. Thirty miles. Ten miles. Welcome to heaven on Earth.

This is how a healthy church should function—it should be a sign that points everyone to the kingdom of God. After all, the purpose of a sign is not to point to itself. We weren't excited to see the sign because it was pretty and green and said Destin; we were excited because of what the sign was pointing us to. In the same way, churches are not called to ultimately point people to themselves. They are called to be signs that point people to the kingdom of God.

> **Churches are not called to ultimately point people to themselves.**

The Church as a Foretaste of the Kingdom

I love meat. I especially love steak. But what I love the most is free steak. Being a pastor, I would sometimes be blessed by church members with gift cards to local restaurants. Boy, did I ever love those gifts of appreciation! Especially when the gift card was to a steakhouse.

I remember this one time that my wife and I had a $100 gift card to spend on dinner. Growing up in an immigrant household, I couldn't even fathom how someone could spend that much on a single meal, but nevertheless, I was on a mission. I wanted to have a memorable date with my wife, celebrate our anniversary, and eat meat.

So I ate a light breakfast, half a sandwich for lunch, skipped that Snickers bar in the afternoon, and finally got home from work ready to take my wife to a feast. When we arrived at the restaurant and got out of the car, my stomach was roaring and ready for battle. While being escorted to our table, I was planning my course of action. We were going to start with grilled jumbo shrimp and calamari for an appetizer. A New York strip with Portobello mushrooms, French green beans, string fries, and a loaded baked potato for my main course. And then crème brûlée for dessert. It would be magnificent.

Here's the thing though. By the time our appetizers came, I felt like I had already eaten. The anticipation throughout the day and the aromas from the restaurant had already given me a foretaste of the food—even before I took my first bite.

This is exactly what the church is called to be. A healthy church that is making disciples of all nations is supposed to be a foretaste of the kingdom of God. It's supposed to give people a taste of what is to come.

The Church as an Instrument of the Kingdom

When I read Revelation 21:4, "He will wipe away every tear from their eyes. Death will be no more; grief, crying, and pain will be no more, because the previous things have passed away," I cry out with the author of Revelation, "Amen! Come, Lord Jesus!" (Rev. 22:20). This is a picture of what life will be like when the kingdom of God is fully present after Jesus returns.

The reason we read stories of healing and restoration during the life of Jesus, and after his death and resurrection, is because when he came to Earth, he ushered in the kingdom of God. "For you see, the kingdom of God is in your midst" (Luke 17:21). This is why Jesus told John the Baptist's disciples, that "the blind receive their sight, the lame walk, those with leprosy are cleansed, the deaf hear, the dead are raised, and the poor are told the good news" (Matt. 11:5). These are signs of the Kingdom that demonstrated its arrival. However, the reason signs like these don't always happen is because the kingdom of God is not fully here.

Though Satan has been ultimately defeated through the death and resurrection of Christ Jesus, the war is not over yet. John Piper puts it well: "Sin must be fought, Satan must be resisted, sickness must be prayed over and groaned under (Romans 8:23), and death must be endured until the second coming of the King and the consummation of the kingdom."[4]

Until Jesus returns, we will experience both glimpses of the Kingdom and absences of it. As the church, we are called to be God's instruments of healing, hope, transformation, and restoration to this broken world. In those instances when we pray for healing, and see it actually happen—either physically or emotionally—let us praise God, for that's a glimpse of his Kingdom! And in those instances when we pray for healing and it doesn't happen the way we were hoping, we need to recognize that this is an absence of the Kingdom, since it's not fully here. In those situations, let us also praise God because there is a day that is coming when his Kingdom will be fully present, and all sickness and death will be gone. Furthermore, we see glimpses of God's Kingdom today when people respond to the proclaimed Word of God, and are born again in Christ and set free to walk in relationship with God. In these instances, all those who prayed for that individual to find Christ are instruments of the Kingdom. The one who preached or shared the gospel was also used as an instrument of the Kingdom. The community group that this individual is a part of, to help him or her grow in Christ, is an instrument of the Kingdom. And so on, and so on.

Wrapping Things Together: The Church as a Hermeneutic of the Gospel

I remember walking through my college cafeteria with the Four Spiritual Laws in hand looking for people who might be interested in having a spiritual conversation with me. Sometimes I'd open up the conversation with, "If you were to die tonight, do you know where you would go?" Or I'd ask, "On a scale of 1–10, how interested are you in spiritual conversations?" I was often rejected. Other times, I was met with skepticism. And on the odd occasion, I was actually able to share the gospel and see that individual discover a new life in Christ.

While evangelism strategies that rely solely on the verbal proclamation of the gospel still have their place, they are definitely waning in influence. The solution is not necessarily to swing the pendulum the other way and just live out the gospel and love people to conversion, either. Tim Keller frames it well,

> If the gospel were primarily about what we must do to be saved, it could be communicated as well by actions (to be imitated) as by words. But if the gospel is primarily about what God has done to save us, and how we can receive it through faith, it can *only* be expressed through words. Faith cannot come without hearing.[5]

Since the gospel is more about what God has done than what we can do, it needs to be proclaimed through words. But since crusades, street preaching, and spontaneous evangelism are waning in their effectiveness and influence in many parts of the West, we need to figure out different ways to invite non-Christians into the types of environments where they can hear the gospel proclaimed to them.

This is why we need a both/and approach to sharing the gospel! There needs to be something different about the way Christians live that forces non-Christians to ask questions. If a non-Christian looks at your life and sees the same fruit, or lack thereof, as theirs, they will see your faith as mere empty religious behavior. Isn't that why Peter urges us to live as "foreigners and exiles" and "to abstain from sinful desires, which wage war against your soul" (1 Pet. 2:11 NIV)? We need to live as *outsiders* and be distinctly different from society. We need to "live such good lives among the pagans that, though they accuse you of doing wrong, they may see your good deeds and glorify God on the day he visits us" (1 Pet. 2:12 NIV)!

It's important to understand that this is not a solo effort. Though Western culture is staunchly individualistic, the Scriptures aren't. In 1 Peter 2:12, Peter isn't talking to an individual; he is talking to the church corporate. We know this because he uses the plural form of "you." It's like Peter is saying, "Now y'all live such good lives . . ." It's the same way with the Sermon on the Mount. Jesus is saying, "Y'all are the salt of the earth, and y'all are the light of the world" (Matt. 5:13–14). I guess living in the South is rubbing off on me . . .

Though Western culture is staunchly individualistic, the Scriptures aren't.

Seriously though, this plural use of the word *you* has massive implications for the way we need to live out our faith. Since these passages are written to a community, rather than an individual, you cannot actually live these out alone! God has intended for the gospel to be lived out and proclaimed together in community. Isn't that why we have the *body* of Christ, rather than the *individual* of Christ? "For the body does not consist of one member but of many" (1 Cor. 12:14 ESV).

I'm convinced that the early church saw the results they did because they both preached the gospel in word and lived it out *together* in deed. The early church understood that when they functioned as God intended them to, they would be a living demonstration of the gospel. Lesslie Newbigin put it well: "The only possible hermeneutic of the gospel is a congregation which believes it."[6] In other words, a congregation that believes in the gospel and lives out its implications *together* as a community is the way the gospel comes to life. A healthy church is how the gospel takes on flesh today! A healthy church is how this lost world will actually "taste and see that the LORD is good" (Ps. 34:8). And it's precisely through experiencing the gospel lived out through healthy churches that this lost world will want to hear the gospel.

So practically, what will it look like if your church functions as a hermeneutic of the gospel and lives out its identity as a sign, instrument, and foretaste of the kingdom of God? Well, the next time you see your neighbor while doing yardwork or picking up your mail, instead of having the same old conversation, you might share how the gospel took on flesh and came to life in your church community. Let me share a few stories.

When one of my community group members got into a car accident, her husband posted on our Facebook group and asked for help. Immediately, a few of our members responded. While he went to go help his wife, others picked up their children from daycare and took care of them. The rest of the group prayed.

Another time, when the mother of one of our group members passed away, a few of us would take turns watching their children whenever they had to tend to details, in addition to the entire group providing meals for them.

Whenever group members or neighbors had to move, a bunch of us from church would always go over to help.

By regularly sharing stories from your church community to your non-Christian neighbors, you are helping them see the gospel lived out tangibly. Not only will this give you opportunities to have spiritual conversations with them, it will also provide you with opportunities to invite them into your community so that they can personally see, feel, and experience the gospel lived out. So invite them to wherever your community gathers, such as one of your group meetings, a block party, a service opportunity, or to your church service. When they enter, they will not only hear about the power of the gospel that is working in and through your lives, but they will experience the gospel through the love that you show to one another. After all, "evangelism is best done out of the context of a gospel community whose corporate life demonstrates the reality of the word that gave her life."[7]

Church communities that are a sign, instrument, and foretaste of the kingdom of God put flesh on the gospel and make it tangible for our world today.

From Form to Function

In the late nineteenth century, steel-framed skyscrapers emerged on the American scene of densely populated cities like Chicago, St. Louis, and New York. During this time, American modernist architect Louis H. Sullivan, the father of Chicago's skyscrapers, wrote a landmark paper on the way skyscrapers should be designed.[8]

In his paper, "The Tall Office Building Artistically Considered," he coined the phrase, "form ever follows function."[9] He believed that the form of a building should always be developed based on its function or intended purpose. Little did he know this phrase would not only influence modern architecture, but would be applied to products, design, and systems throughout the twentieth century, and even to this day. In fact, at the time of this writing, a Google search on "form follows function" results in 3.7 million webpages.

Does this phrase still stand true today in architecture, design, systems, products, and beyond? Up until the creation of digital products, yes it did. Think about a rotary phone. The phone in and of itself had one purpose—to call someone else—but so did its components. The handset had one purpose—to listen and speak. And there was one hole for each respective number. The rotary phone's form followed its function.

Compare that to today's smart phone where its form definitely does not follow its function. For example, is the block shape of a smart phone the best form for a car racing game? To read a book on? To take notes with? Or how about to monitor your heart rate or count your steps? If form followed function, it would surely take an odd-looking device to do all those things!

Think about your church for a moment. Does form follow function?

Did Jesus Talk about Function or Form?

In the previous section, what came to mind when you read "community," "group," or the two words placed together? What form of group meeting did you imagine? Was it a discipleship group at a café? A small group of twelve people in a home? A Sunday school class of fifteen in a classroom? A missional community of thirty? A seminar or class of fifty? Or was it a large group of women or men sitting at round tables in the fellowship hall of your church?

Whatever form of group came to mind, we need to understand that Jesus talked about function more than form. Let me explain. Did Jesus ever tell his disciples to meet weekly in small groups? Or did he say that a discipleship group of two to three people is the best environment for discipleship? Did he suggest Wednesday nights as church programming evenings? Or Sunday morning as the Sunday school hour? Did Jesus even prescribe an ideal size for a community group of believers?

In *Planting Missional Churches: Your Guide to Starting Churches that Multiply*, Ed Stetzer and I shared "that God used the megachurch to reach Korea and the house church to reach China. The lesson here is to hold models loosely and the gospel firmly."[10] Though we were talking specifically about models of church planting, I believe this equally applies to different models, or forms, of community.

Function > Form

If you were to survey the landscape of churches in North America, and even around the world, it would seem to appear that the mandate for both small groups and Sunday school came directly from Scripture. Although these two forms of community, and other related ones, have dominated the landscape of churches for decades, they are not the only ones that exist. Nor are they a mutually exclusive biblical command! In fact, in the New Testament, we read more about the function, which is to be in community, than any form or model in specific.

In other words, when you look through all of the "one anothers" in Scripture, you read more about the function of being in community and what that should look like, than any specific form or model. For example, in Romans 12:10, "Love one another deeply as brothers and sisters" is function. If this were really about the form of community, it would read like this,

"Show family affection to another with brotherly love *when you are together in your small group meeting.*"

Or, take a look at Ephesians 5:21: "submitting to one another in the fear of Christ." This is function, because it can happen in any form regardless of culture, preferences, or context.

Furthermore, consider the most quoted verse by discipleship pastors and preachers: "And let us consider how to stir up one another to love and good works, not neglecting to meet together, as is the habit of some, but encouraging one another, and all the more as you see the Day drawing near" (Heb. 10:24–25 ESV). How often has that verse been used to justify a particular form of community? "This is why Sunday worship is important!" Or, "This is why our church is a church of small groups!" The fact is, the author of Hebrews was talking more about function than form.

Hold Your Forms Loosely and Your Functions Firmly

Now, I'm not saying that you need to get rid of all your forms and go straight to function. After all, many of our forms of community in today's church came out of the function to be in community. What I'm saying is, hold your forms loosely and your functions firmly. Revisit the "one anothers" in Scripture. Revisit Acts 2:42–47. Develop a Kingdom vision for community as outlined in the previous section. And make this micro-shift from form to function, *so that*, you can develop the right forms of community that work for your context today.

> Shifting from form to function allows you to develop the right forms of community that work for your context today.

When we make the micro-shift from form to function, we are freed up from feeling like we have to base our ministries on the most popular forms or models of influential churches. This also frees us up from being bound by those forms because Scripture, which is the function, always trumps any and every form, or church model, out there.

In order to develop the right forms of community that will allow your church to be a sign, instrument, and foretaste of the kingdom of God in your local neighborhood and city, we need to take a look at Edward T. Hall's research on proxemics.

Four Spaces for Community

Have you ever noticed that you relate differently with others depending on the environment or space you're in? For example, think about a time you went to a sporting event. When your team scored, weren't you the best of friends with the strangers sitting next to you? But if you were to meet those same people at the grocery store, or in another space, would you be able to recognize them? Probably not; yet, during the sporting event, you probably felt an inspirational sense of community and belonging.

Or think about the last time you went to a standing reception. The feeling of belonging or community was different than the sporting event, but it was still there, wasn't it? In this space, community feels less inspirational and more like an extended family gathering. After all, in this space, you can have side conversations with friends, as well as group conversations with strangers. It's kind of like those large awkward holiday family dinners where you get to come with the family you live with, eat with the cousins you haven't talked to in months, and say hi to the uncles and aunts that you see once a year.

Next, consider a time you had dinner with a few friends and their significant others. You were all sitting around a large table, sharing memories, stories, and updating one another with what's been going on. The feeling of community and belonging you felt was probably more exclusive and private than in the previous two examples.

Now think about the last time you had a one-on-one coffee with your best friend, spouse, or significant other. Nothing was held back and everything was up for grabs. You might have even shared your thoughts behind your thoughts. This space is the closest and the most intimate sense of community.

Proxemics and the Study of Space

The reason community feels and looks different in each of these environments is outlined in Edward T. Hall's theory called "proxemics." He discovered this in the 1960s when he was examining the relationship between space and culture. In his research, he discovered that humans, just like birds and other mammals, have an intuitive sense of territory and personal space that will trigger their flight-or-fight response if someone or something gets too close.

For example, consider how the distance between you and another affects the volume of your voice. Just read through the above examples again and you'll see what I'm talking about. I will shout and scream at a sporting event, project my voice when trying to speak to a group of friends over the white noise at a party, wait for my turn and speak in a conversational tone over the dinner table, and whisper when together with my wife before we turn the lights off to sleep. What's fascinating is that no one told me that this is what I had to do. I didn't read it in a book or hear it in a class. It's just intuitive.

In his research on proxemics, Hall discovered that there are four distinct spaces or environments in which humans relate differently to one another. He labeled them *public, social, personal,* and *intimate* spaces.[11] In each space, he determined that there is a measured distance that would often influence behavior. For the public space, it is 12 or more feet; for the social space, it's 4–12 feet; for the personal space, it's 1–4 feet; and for the intimate space, it's 0–18 inches.[12]

> **There are four distinct spaces or environments in which humans relate differently to one another.**

Space and Belonging

Joseph Myers, in his book *The Search to Belong,* advances Hall's work by relating it to how individuals belong and find community with one another. While explaining Hall's research on proxemics to a college classroom, Myers made this critical connection: "These four spaces communicate how we belong to one another."[13]

I love how Erwin McManus illustrates the primal craving that we all have for community in *Soul Cravings,* "We are born to belong, we are created for connection, and whether we admit it to ourselves or not, we spend our whole lives trying to fit in, get in, and stay in. It almost doesn't even matter what 'in' is; we just want to belong somewhere."[14]

This is true for everyone in your church, neighborhood, community, city, and region. We all long to belong. We all crave to be a part of a community where we can learn how to live beyond ourselves. Where we are best positioned to make our greatest contribution. Where we are loved just the way we are. And where we can come as we are and know, without a shadow of a doubt, that we are accepted.

Although Hall and Myers concluded that there were four spaces for community, neither of them said that one of the spaces were superior to the others:

> A healthy strategy for those working to build community entails allowing people to grow significant relationships in all four spaces—*all four*. It means permitting people to belong in the space they want or need to belong. Insisting that real, authentic, true community happens only when people get "close" is a synthetic view of reality that may actually be harmful.[15]

From Form to Function to Four Forms

Earlier, we made the micro-shift from form to function, in order to discover what a Kingdom vision for community looks like. This set us free from basing the way we disciple on *what works* in other churches, and allowed us instead to get back to Jesus' commands and what the Scriptures say. But we cannot stay there. If we are going to disciple others, the biblical function or command of being in community has to manifest itself in some type of form(s) or model(s) of community. After all, we cannot live in the ethereal world of concepts. We need to put our boots on the ground.

So take a look at your church. If people naturally connect to one another in these four spaces, are you providing them with opportunities to be discipled in each of them? Can your church grow into and live out their identity as disciples of Jesus—being a sign, instrument, and foretaste of the kingdom of God—in each of the four spaces? Or do you emphasize one or a couple of the spaces more than the others? Are you missing any? Take a look at how the four spaces manifest themselves in a church context (see Figure 4.1).

Space	Description
Public Space	A church worship service or a sporting event is what the public space looks like. You belong, you are part of a community, and you somewhat get to know those around you, but there is not much of an opportunity to really get to know others because it's so large. This environment is typically when 75+ people come together.
Social Space	This is a large group, or party-like environment where you are safe to decide whom you would like to grow a deeper relationship with. It's big enough that newcomers won't feel like they're the center of attention, yet it's small enough that no one will fall through the cracks. It's big enough that everyone will find someone to connect with, but it's small enough that meaningful conversation can take place without people being uncomfortable. You belong, you are part of a community, and it's a safe place to take that next step. This environment is typically when 20–50 people come together.
Personal Space	This is the typical small group environment where you are intentionally connecting with others to go deeper, sharing life together, praying with one another, and allowing yourself to be known. Private information is shared, but this isn't the place where you are completely vulnerable and baring your whole soul. This environment is typically when 8–12 people come together.

Intimate Space	This is an environment that you let only a few people into. It could be a spouse, a best friend, or an accountability group. This is an environment where nothing is held back, and there is a lot of intentionality in sharpening one another, being accountable to one another, and being intentional in community. This environment typically consists of two or three people.

FIGURE 4.1: THE FOUR SPACES DEFINED IN A CHURCH CONTEXT

The Neglected Social Space

If you survey the landscape of churches in the West, unless you belong to a small house church, nearly all will have a public space, which is their weekly worship gathering. Most will have some form of a personal space for small groups or Sunday school. Fewer will advocate for an intimate space, like accountability groups. And only a very small percentage will take advantage of the social space.

This is problematic because it's in the social space that you most naturally find those that you connect with. The social space is that unique sized gathering of approximately twenty to fifty people that is big enough that you're not the center of attention when you're new, but also small enough that you're bound to find someone that you connect with. It's that fascinating environment where both extroverts and introverts can coexist and feel a deep sense of belonging. The extroverts, on the one hand, have plenty of people to talk to and can naturally move from one conversation to the next easily. The introverts, on the other hand, can find a corner of the room and engage in a deeper conversation with two to three others throughout the night.

There are plenty of books that explain best practices for discipleship in one or more of these spaces. For example, *Discipleship that Fits* by my friends Bobby Harrington and Alex Absalom provides a good, comprehensive overview of discipleship in these four spaces. Check out *The Church as Movement* by my friends JR Woodward and Dan White Jr. for a missional treatment on this subject. And don't forget *The Master Plan of Evangelism* by my mentor Dr. Robert Coleman.

It's my conviction that unless we have the social space in the life and rhythm of our churches, we will never be able to live out what it means to be a sign, instrument, and foretaste of the kingdom of God. Now don't misunderstand me! I am not saying that the social space is *the* form of community and that it's some sort of silver bullet! I'm just saying that it's the neglected form of community in many of our churches, and, when utilized in partnership with the other forms or spaces of community, will result in greater Kingdom impact and greater opportunity for discipleship in your church. The remainder of this chapter is devoted to explaining the social space in our churches.

The Mid-Size Community

When I was pastoring at Beulah Alliance Church in Edmonton, Alberta, Canada, my mission was twofold: I wanted to increase the number of people engaging in community, and I wanted to help the church be a sign, instrument, and foretaste of the kingdom of God. So I began to do some research.

I discovered that over the last ten years, the population of Edmonton had boomed by 24 percent. When looking at our average weekend attendance over the same ten years, I was excited to see that our church had grown by 31 percent! Hopeful about these trends, I decided to take a deeper look and see what had happened in community life and the engagement of groups over the same ten years. The result? Zero growth. That number was approximately one thousand people ten years prior; ten years later, it was still one thousand. Apparently, something was wrong, and we needed to figure out what.

This led me on a journey to discover and learn from Edward T. Hall, Joseph Myers, and the plethora of churches in England that had been utilizing the social space to engage people both in community and on mission in their neighborhoods. Many of the churches in England that I contacted had discovered a way to connect post-Christians into community and see them discover Christ. Since Canada and the U.S. were rapidly moving toward a post-Christian context like Europe, I wondered if this might be the key to breaking through that 0 percent growth trend at my church.

Spectrums of Churches Utilizing the Social Space

My first call was to the Alpha church, otherwise known as Holy Trinity Brompton (HTB) in England. When Keith Taylor, Darren Herbold, and a few others from Beulah came back from a leadership conference at HTB, they told me I had to get in touch with them, since HTB had been utilizing the social space for ministry since 1982. Until a couple years ago, they called them pastorates. Their pastorates met on a biweekly basis during the midweek. During a typical group meeting, they would eat, worship, hear a lesson, discuss it, and then pray and minister to one another.

St. Andrews Chorleywood in England was the next model that I encountered through Mark Stibbe and Andrew Williams's book, *Breakout.* They called their social space groups Mission-Shaped Communities (MSCs). Due to a building refurbishment and inability to find a space that would fit their entire congregation, the leadership of the church decided to transition their MSCs from being mid-week groups to meeting on three out of the four Sundays a month. As a result, church members met in school halls, community centers, coffee shops, and other venues. On the fourth Sunday, they would all come together for inspiration and be re-envisioned.

When Mike Breen took over St. Thomas Crookes in Sheffield, England, in 1994, he introduced the social space group concept that he had been experimenting with since 1988. They called them Clusters, and their story is outlined in Bob Hopkins and Mike Breen's book, *Clusters.* Their Clusters focus more on the fact that they're a community of Christians on mission, rather than a regularly occurring gathering. This is their distinction from HTB's pastorates: "It's the cluster mission focus above anything else that sets them apart, holds them together, gives them identity and motivates them."[16]

As I continued my discovery process by calling, emailing, and comparing websites of churches utilizing the social space in England, I noticed how most of them fit somewhere within this spectrum in Figure 4.2.

Social Space Group
as Church

Social Space Group
as Program

FIGURE 4.2: SOCIAL SPACE SPECTRUM

The difficult thing about naming and placing churches on this spectrum is the fact that models often change when leadership changes. To be frank, this is why I even hesitated to name the churches that I researched above, since all three of them have changed their models because of leadership change! Now, before you skip the rest of this chapter and dismiss the social space as a viable and necessary environment for ministry, let me explain.

Although HTB, St. Andrews Chorleywood, and St. Thomas Crookes are all utilizing a different model today than when I first researched them, the fact is, they were pioneers in our generation who leveraged the social space in the church. As a result, when you look throughout Europe and North America today, you'll actually find hundreds of churches continuing to use the social space to move people into community and engage them on mission. For example, take Soma[17] and the V3 Movement.[18] Both of these church planting networks actively teach how to create groups using the social space in their training. As a result, they have helped plant churches that are integrating the social space environment into the life of their church. Consider other American churches doing this like The Austin Stone,[19] as well as churches in England, like The Crowded House,[20] Guildford Baptist,[21] ChristChurch,[22] and Network Church.[23] The important thing to take away from this section is just how wide and flexible the spectrum is to implement the social space environment in your church.

Case Study: Beulah Alliance Church

While I was conducting this research on the landscape of churches using the social space, my wife, Christina, and I decided to pilot the concept and see what would happen. After all, at this point, not only did I hate the *matchmaking process* to get people into the *right* group, but we were seeing over one thousand new people visit our church every year, with a minimal growth rate year-over-year. Our backdoor was wide open, and people weren't sticking. We desperately needed to get people into community because once a newcomer engaged in a second environment (any sort of group, event, or experi-

Is your backdoor wide open? Are people sticking?

ence outside of the Sunday service), their likelihood to stick and become a part of the church vastly increased.

After meeting bi-weekly for a few months, we soon found ourselves with a regular gathering of about twenty adults, with over fifty on our roster. In addition, since we were a young families group, we always seemed to have at least twenty additional children running around every time we met. We decided to call these social space gatherings Mid-Size Communities (MSCs) because I didn't like the acronym for mid-size groups. It reminded me too much of bad Chinese food.

What fascinated me about this experiment was that the majority of individuals coming to our MSC (over 95 percent) weren't previously in any form of group life! In fact, one couple blatantly told me why they didn't want to join a small group when I first tried to invite them to our MSC. After explaining the difference between our MSC and traditional small groups, they quickly apologized and asked when the next meeting was going to be.

Not only did we have unengaged church attendees become deeply engaged with our church as a result of the MSC, we also saw non-Christians experience and taste the gospel because of the way our MSC loved one another, loved them, and lived out the gospel. Our community was, as Lesslie Newbigin said, a hermeneutic of the gospel.

I remember one time our MSC gathered together to pack shoeboxes for children overseas. I had encouraged our group, as I usually do, to invite non-Christians to this gathering. Do you remember Angela and Chris from the beginning of this chapter? Well, when they arrived with a Muslim on their arm, I was surprised on many levels. Not only did they hardly ever attend, but I wasn't even sure of where they stood in their relationship with God, let alone the Muslim. After eating together as a community, we packed the shoeboxes, and I asked if anyone would volunteer to pray for all the children who were going to receive the shoeboxes—that they would experience the love of God as a result of this small act. Guess who volunteered to pray? The Muslim.

After this awkward moment, and as people were beginning to leave, I engaged the Muslim gentleman in a conversation. What fascinated me was that this guy grew up as a Christian, but decided to convert to Islam. My prayer that night, and since, for non-Christians like him, has been that my interaction with them would always result in seeds of the gospel landing on good soil, so that it would later bear fruit in Christ (1 Cor. 3).

This reminds me of another one of our mid-size communities that actually had more non-Christians than Christians! In this particular MSC, there was one couple, David and Metz, who discovered what it meant to follow Christ. When I asked them about their experience, they said that it was "through sharing and assisting the MSC and small group gatherings, that we became more aware of God's fingerprint in our lives. We understood our sins, our shortcomings, and the power of God's grace. Through this, we gave our lives to Christ." Praise God for the leaders of this MSC, Eduardo and Kenya, and the work of God through them! This group really understood what it meant to be a hermeneutic of the gospel.

So in my pilot group and the others that we started, not only did we see the unengaged get plugged in and find community, but we also saw them get discipled. What I loved about our MSCs was the fact that all of these individuals who never would have joined a class or traditional small group in the first place actually ended up in a small group as a result of our MSC!

Since our MSCs met every other week, we created opportunities in the off weeks for smaller groups to form and meet. Sure, there was a level of discipleship that would happen during the MSC gathering, but the point of that social space was to get to know one another and create a larger environment for missional engagement. Discipleship and life change is often a result of transparency, and it's hard to be open about your life when you're with twenty to fifty people. As a result, we not only had a men's and women's group that met in the off weeks, but we also had smaller groups of two-to-three people and four-to-six meeting together to disciple one another!

This was true for Monica as well. For eight years, she attended our church with her husband Del without getting plugged into community. Deep down they wondered whether anybody would notice if they didn't show up. This realization prompted them to be more intentional at connecting with others. Small groups scared them and they didn't feel like they had the bandwidth to participate in one. But since MSCs were larger and seemed a bit less threatening, they decided to join one. After participating in one, not only did they rarely miss the gatherings, but they also started a discipleship group with others they met through the MSC!

I have story after story like these that not only demonstrate the unengaged getting engaged in biblical community, but also the lost coming to know Christ, leaders being developed, lives being restored, care and prayer happening both in and outside of the groups, and both introverts and extroverts finding community. It's the "one anothers" being lived out and the church functioning as a sign, instrument, and foretaste of the kingdom of God!

By the time I left Beulah to head up the church planting, multisite, and multiplication initiative for LifeWay by starting NewChurches.com, in just three years, we had started more than seventeen MSCs with more than seven hundred individuals engaged in them. This was on top of the hundreds and hundreds in other forms of group life! Today the number is even higher, as MSCs continue to multiply.

MSC Frequently Asked Questions

As I've continued to speak, train, consult, and help churches figure out their unique approach to leveraging the social space environment, I've compiled a list of some of the most frequently asked questions I encounter. Here are my answers regarding mid-size communities and how we designed them at Beulah.

What Are Mid-Size Communities?

- Mid-Size Communities are groups of twenty to fifty people who journey together to celebrate, grow, and be a blessing to those they live, work, and play with.
- A community that is formed around a common affinity, geography, or societal need—and this gathering point becomes the mission focus of the group. They are a community on mission with one another.
- A community where you belong before you believe. It's not just a scheduled meeting, either. Typically, there is a large group gathering every other week, with smaller groups for study and get-togethers in the off weeks.
- Not a large small group, nor a small weekend gathering.
- An open, inclusive, and safe environment where friendships are formed and you can discover who you could potentially grow a "deeper" relationship with.

Where Do You Meet?

- Homes that have at least fifteen hundred square feet of space are the ideal environment. You don't need seating for everyone attending, since the MSC has a standing-room-only feel. Think standing reception, not small group.
- Community halls and parks work as well, depending on the time of year and where you live, but discussion is a bit more difficult to have in these locations.
- Your church building is not the ideal place to host MSCs, since it's not reproducible or scalable.

What Does a Typical MSC Gathering Look Like?

- Think of a standing reception. People are eating and chatting with one another. Some people are gathered in groups of five or six and others are talking in groups of two or three. These gatherings are large enough that you won't be the center of attention when you're new, but small enough that you'll find someone you can connect with.
- They typically last anywhere from ninety minutes to three hours.
- There are three different types of gatherings: discussion, social, or mission focus:
  - A discussion night starts with food. There is then a five- or ten-minute big idea teaching time, that is followed up with individuals forming into ad hoc small groups to discuss, process, pray, and apply the ideas.
  - A social night might have large or smaller group games, like Pictionary, but it will definitely have food. Its purpose is to build relationships and allow conversation to happen naturally.
  - A mission focus night can range anywhere from determining the group's mission focus, having a discussion on it, praying over it, or going out and doing it. For example, one of the MSCs in my church would regularly reach out

to the international students at the university. So for one of their MSC gatherings, they chartered a bus, invited the international students out to our Good Friday services, and then had dinner together afterwards.

Who Leads a Mid-Size Community?

- MSCs are led by a leadership team of three-to-six people.
- The MSC leadership team is a co-discipling environment. The team members are praying for one another, supporting one another, discipling one another, and pointing one another toward Christ.
- Every team member has the following: a missional mind-set, a solid foundation, leadership capacity (able to lead up to fifty people), and previous and/or concurrent participation in an MSC.

How Are Leaders Trained?

- In a three-dimensional way: initial, ongoing, and practical.
- Initial: All MSC Leaders and Lead Team Members are invited to our exclusive MSC Leadership Training Course. This course has a total of four sessions and a retreat. You can download my workbook for this course at danielim.com.
  - Session 1: Missional Ecclesiology
  - Session 2: Leading Yourself
  - Session 3: Leading a Team
  - Session 4: Leading a Movement
  - Retreat: The Heart of a Leader, Counseling and Ethics, and Teachers as Leaders
- Ongoing: There are four components to this.

  1. The Live Forum: We offer periodic live forums where all MSC Leaders and Lead Team Members will come

together to be inspired and tackle relevant issues for better leadership.

2. Online Forum and Resources: This is an online hub where MSC Leaders and Lead Team Members can share lessons and resources, collaborate on ideas, solve challenges, and dream together.

3. Leadership Coaching: Our pastoral staff team offers leadership coaching for all of our MSC Leaders.

4. Facilitation Training: As you launch smaller groups within your MSC, we offer small group facilitation training in an online format to better empower your team and the individuals desiring to launch a smaller group.

- Practical: The training is both high tech and high touch. It's high tech because we offer online training. It's high touch because our coaching is pastoral and adult-education oriented.

What about Small Groups?

- Small groups are a personal space for people to connect and support one another in more vulnerable and intimate ways. They are a great environment for study, spiritual growth, accountability, and depth in relationship. As a result, small groups need to form organically and naturally, since relational chemistry is of the utmost importance for a great small group. That is why smaller groups are able to form organically and naturally through MSCs—they can meet in the off weeks.

- If people come to the church asking to join a small group, we intentionally share that the only way to join a small group is through an MSC. In fact, we would even tell them that this is why we had a vibrant small group ministry.

What Didn't Work Well with Small Groups That Will Work Well with Mid-Size Communities?

- Assimilation:
  - Newcomers will not feel obligated to keep coming, nor are they the center of attention.
  - It's easy to step into an MSC environment, since the environment is conducive to this.
  - It's a great place to meet a lot of new people.
- Multiplication:
  - In small groups, multiplication is an incredibly hard and painful thing since the group is small and the relationships are tight. In MSCs, multiplication doesn't feel like radical surgery, since there are so many more people.
  - In MSCs there is less ambiguity as to who goes where, because multiplication happens based on mission. In other words, when my MSC multiplied, we sent out young couples without children to reach and minister to other young couples without children. The same happened with our Spruce Grove MSC. The new MSC multiplied to reach a particular neighborhood of Spruce Grove, so only those who lived around that neighborhood left.
- Discipleship:
  - The MSC lead team is an incredible environment for discipleship. In-depth discipleship happens here where it's a co-discipling environment.
  - All MSC leaders receive initial training and ongoing coaching/support from the pastoral staff.
  - Through an MSC, a disciple grows in knowledge (discussion nights and off-week small groups) as well as puts his/her faith to action, since every MSC has a mission focus.
  - Through an MSC, individuals discover that discipleship is an all of life thing, rather than just being a weekend thing.

Conclusion

Mid-size communities are not a silver bullet. Social spaces aren't either. In fact, if you try to implement this concept on top of what you're currently doing, it will probably fail! The point of this chapter was not to move you from whatever *form* of community you are using in your church, to the biblical *function* of community, and then to the *form* that worked for me. Instead, the goal was to help you step back from your models of community and discipleship, and be re-envisioned with a Kingdom mind-set.

In this chapter, I wanted to help you understand that there are several different forms or spaces for community. Since we are all familiar with examples of the public, personal, and intimate spaces for community in our churches, I wanted to introduce you to the way that churches are leveraging the social space, so that you can better engage people in community and get them on mission.

While the social space will help close your backdoor and better integrate newcomers, it won't do so magically. The social space won't automatically get everyone excited about mission, discipleship, or multiplication, either. Nor will it make everyone an evangelist and raise the level of baptisms and conversions for your church.

The social space is not a silver bullet. However, if you introduce the social space as a part of a larger strategy for discipleship, you just might see those things happen. Social space groups need to fit into the larger whole, and we'll see how this can work for your church in section 2. But before we get there, let's now move to our last micro-shift that leads to macro-change: from maturity to missionary.

Reflection Questions

1. What will it look like if your church functions as a hermeneutic of the gospel and lives out its identity as a sign, instrument, and foretaste of the kingdom of God?

2. What are the forms of community that you have in your church? What's missing?

3. What would it take to pilot a mid-size community in your church? Who would be on your leadership team? What would success look like two years down the road?

CHAPTER 5

FROM MATURITY TO MISSIONARY

*"As local congregations are built up to reach out in
mission to the world, they will become in fact what they
already are by faith: God's missionary people."*

—Charles Van Engen

"Everyone line up and get in position! The judges will be watching your every move. After your pattern is complete, we will score you, and then award medals."

Believe it or not, I'm a black belt in Tae Kwon Do. While it may not seem like it looking at my picture, it's true. I also have quite the collection of medals, trophies, and broken boards to prove it! And boy do I have stories. There was this one time I took on ten guys at once . . .

Okay, before I get too carried away, let me give you some perspective. That story about me taking on ten guys? Let's just say I may have exaggerated the numbers *a bit*. The fact is, I'm not a cut and chiseled master of martial arts. My black belt has a bit of dust on it—a few decades' worth, since it's packed up in a box somewhere in my parents' house.

I often think about those hours I used to spend sparring and practicing patterns. My favorite thing about Tae Kwon Do was being able to fight others and beat them—especially this one guy who would always annoy me at school. Since I wasn't allowed to fight at school, Tae Kwon Do was perfect. Not only would we get to fight one another, but my sixth-degree black belt instructor would teach us how to do so strategically!

Patterns were always a means to an end. My instructor would first make us practice them, before we could spar one another. In addition, the only way that he would teach us new moves is if we first memorized our patterns, performed them in front of him, and then passed the exam for our next belt. Like I said, patterns were always a means to an end.

Whenever I entered a Tae Kwon Do competition and performed my pattern before a set of judges, I never managed to rank or win a medal. Sparring, on the other hand, was a different story. I don't think I ever managed to not win a medal.

It wasn't until a few years ago that it finally clicked. I don't know what it was that specifically made the light go off in my head, but I finally got it. The patterns weren't just a way to test our memorization skills or perform an Asian version of line dancing. They were actually training us how to fight. The patterns weren't just rote *dance* moves. They were a pre-determined set of moves against an imaginary enemy. We were conditioning our bodies and minds to know what to do if, and when, we actually got into a fight.

If I had realized this back then, I would have taken the patterns more seriously. I would have imagined that I was blocking and fighting the bullies at school. I would have even integrated the moves that I learned in the patterns into my sparring. Perhaps, if I had made this micro-shift, I would have won silver or gold, instead of always finishing with bronze.

James Was Probably against Pet Peeves Too

Let me tell you my pet peeve. It's when people talk about their pet peeves. Honestly, it just annoys me when people talk about the things that annoy them. Instead of focusing on what annoys you and airing that out with the whole world, let's be constructive with our words! I'm pretty sure James felt the same way about pet peeves when he wrote, "Everyone should be quick to listen, slow to speak, and slow to anger, for human anger does not accomplish God's righteousness" (James 1:19–20).

What's fascinating about pet peeves, other than the fact that there are entire websites dedicated to them,[1] a National Pet Peeve week,[2] and over five-hundred thousand search results on Google, is that our ministries are often shaped by them. Let me share a few with you.

Have you ever been to a church whose pet peeve is bad worship or a lack of excellence on stage? These are the ones that time their service down to the second, pay their band members, have just the right amount of smoke coming out of their smoke machine, and use reverb on their vocals. I might be exaggerating just a bit, but I've seen churches like this, and for them, what happens on the stage drives everything. Decibel levels are the topic of staff meetings. Budget is never an issue for the worship and arts team, even though other departments might need to make cuts. After all, who needs Goldfish crackers for children when there are programmable moving head LED spotlights that need to be bought?

Or what about those churches whose pet peeve is a lack of involvement with global missions? The pastor might have been a former missionary or read multiple books by some. He is always using illustrations from the mission field and the persecuted church in his sermons. A significant portion of the church's budget goes toward global missions—at a detriment to local missions. And it seems like the only way to get discipled or feel like you belong is to go on a short-term missions trip with the church.

Or how about churches whose pet peeve is a lack of knowledge and love for the Scriptures? They pride themselves in being called a Bible-believing church. Everyone carries around their reference or study Bible that's edged with gold. In fact, pulling up the Bible app on your phone during a Sunday message or Bible study would probably be frowned upon! If you want to get discipled, there are one-to-one discipleship mentors ready to go. In addition, there are always Bible study classes going on that are studying the Bible book-by-book. And you know that Sunday school attendance is *healthy* because everyone often carries around their study guide along with their Bible to the worship service.

Do you recognize any of these examples? What are the pet peeves that drive ministry philosophy and strategy at your church? Is it an aversion to an attractional model of church? Or maybe it's skepticism toward missional models? Or perhaps it's a preaching style or particular church programming? Whatever it might be, the fact is, your pet peeves—or the pet peeves of the loudest voices in your church—often influence the purpose of your church and the way you lead.

Zooming Out

As we come to the end of this section in the book, let's take a look at what we've covered and how it relates to what we are going to cover in this chapter.

In chapter 1, we looked at how your church approaches discipleship from a fifty-thousand-foot level. This chapter was all about helping you discern how you view discipleship as a system and what it would take to make the micro-shift from destination to direction.

In chapter 2, we zoomed in to discipleship at the individual level. We went from looking at the systematic discipleship of the many to the personal discipleship of the one. As a result, we looked at the definition of a disciple and how churches can know whether they are developing mature ones. Instead of just setting some obscure metric of *maturity*, we outlined the output goals of a disciple and the input goals that led to them.

In chapter 3, we made the micro-shift from sage to guide by introducing the unique way that adults need to be discipled. Since we often teach the way that we've been taught and lead the way that we've been led, this is an important micro-shift to make, so that we can best engage and develop disciples in our churches.

In chapter 4, we explored the four different environments in which discipleship and development occur. We made the micro-shift from form to function in order to uncover and adopt a Kingdom vision for community, rather than a whatever-works-for-the-successful-church-down-the-road model of ministry.

Each of these four chapters could stand on their own. That's the beauty of this process—there really is no silver bullet. Each chapter presents an individual micro-shift that can lead to macro-change for your church. But if you're not careful, your church can become so consumed with implementing each of those micro-shifts, that you fail to realize the broader purpose that they are all moving your church toward.

And that's the purpose of this chapter. It's to help you understand the collective macro-change that these micro-shifts are moving your church toward. These micro-shifts, when put together, are intended to help you develop *missionary disciples* rather than merely *mature disciples*. Now don't get me wrong. I'm not advocating against maturity—just take a look through chapter 2! What I am advocating against is maturity as an end in and of itself.

In my experience pastoring, leading, and consulting with churches, I've discovered that when you focus on developing *mature disciples*, you do not necessarily find yourself with an army of missionaries. However, when you focus on developing *missionary disciples*, you will always get *mature disciples*.

When you focus on developing missionary disciples, you will always get mature disciples.

I'm not talking about training up overseas missionaries here. Nor am I advocating that you ask everyone to quit their job and become full-time local pastors. I'm using the word *mission-ary* as a noun referring to people who see their primary vocation as being sent on God's mission, rather than their own. I'm specifically talking about helping ordinary people understand that all of their life is about mission. This starts by helping them understand that their first and foremost vocation is to go and make disciples of all nations, *while* getting a paycheck from their employer.

In other words, every plumber, poet, and police officer in your church has the same vocation—to go and make disciples. This is our missionary mandate as the church! We are all sent and on mission with God *wherever* we are and in *whatever* we do for a living (John 20:21). And this precisely is our primary vocation.

When a church focuses on developing disciples with a missionary mind-set, they are not just pushing their pet peeve, like we saw in the other examples above. Instead, they are starting from a biblical foundation of the nature and purpose of the church, rather than a cheat sheet of the latest models and strategies.

The Church

What is the church and what's the best way to understand it? Should we start with the fact that the church is both visible and invisible at the same time?[3] Or is this too elusive of a concept? If the invisible church is the entire church composed of all true believers, how does this relate to and differ from the visible church—the human institution that people belong to? Is it possible to be a part of one and not the other?

Gandhi is often quoted to have said, "I like your Christ; I do not like your Christians. Your Christians are so unlike your Christ." There are many in our culture today—both non-Christian and Christian—who would agree with him. This is especially true in light of the prominent televangelist scandals decades ago and the growing number of megachurch pastors leaving the ministry for one reason or another. Not to mention hypocritical Christians who say one thing with their mouth and do another thing with their behavior!

This reminds me of that Brennan Manning quote popularized by the mid-nineties DC Talk song, "What If I Stumble?" "The greatest single cause of atheism in the world today is Christians who acknowledge Jesus with their lips, walk out the door, and deny Him by their lifestyle. That is what an unbelieving world simply finds unbelievable."

While the church is definitely both visible and invisible, this ontological approach to understanding it is too philosophical for the regular church member. It's too elusive and ethereal, since it's not tangible or practical enough. It's an approach that focuses on nature and being, instead of purpose and progress.

> **What if we defined and understood the church through the lens of *its* mission, rather than the lens of *our* mission?**

So instead of taking an ontological approach to understanding the church, what if we began with the end in mind? (This is called a teleological approach.) What if we defined the church by its purpose of existence, rather than an explanation of its existence? What if we defined and understood the church through the lens of *its* mission, rather than the lens of *our* mission?

If we do this, churches who once competed against one another would actually collaborate and do Kingdom ministry together because reaching and discipling the lost is far greater than any petty difference. This would also prevent churches from falling into the trap of being a loving community for their own sake, or being mistaken as a rotary club. For churches like these, their rallying cry would be, "In essentials, unity; in non-essentials, liberty; in all things, charity," as the late German theologian Rupertus Meldenius once advocated.[4]

No, this is not an excuse to ignore the nature of the church. It is however a plea for churches to define their being and existence *through* the lens of their God-given mission. Although the Yale professor William G. Rusch states "the more the Church understands its own nature, the more it gets hold of its own vocation,"[5] I actually believe the opposite is just as true. The more the church understands its own mission or vocation, the more it will grab hold of its own nature. In other words, the more a church sees its own mission as developing everyday missionaries to fulfill the Great Commission, the more it will understand its nature and live out its calling as the body of Christ.

The Missionary Nature of the Church

"When the Church . . . ceases to be missionary, it contradicts its own nature. Yet the Church is not to be defined by what it is, but by that End to which it moves."[6] Lesslie Newbigin seems to agree; or rather, I guess it's more appropriate to say that I agree with Newbigin.

Professor and prolific author in missiology, Charles Van Engen, agrees as well: "As local congregations are built up to reach out in mission to the world, they will become in fact what they already are by faith: *God's missionary people.*"[7]

The church finds its missionary nature in the sending nature of God. For just as the Father sent the Son into this world, and just as the Son sent the Holy Spirit into this world, so now the Father, Son, and Spirit are sending the church into this world (1 John 4:9; John 20:21–22; Acts 1:8).

It's easy for a church to look at a verse like John 20:21, get excited, and just run with it: "As the Father has sent me, I also send you." We are sent! That means we need to go and make disciples of all nations, doesn't it (Matt. 28:19–20)? We need to go to the lost because "How, then, can they call on him they have not believed in? And how can they believe without hearing about him? And how can they hear without a preacher?" (Rom. 10:14). It's our God-given responsibility, isn't it? So we cast vision, develop a strategy, equip our church, and march forward, right?

While that is completely true, it's really only half of the story. There's a verse that comes after John 20:21 that we often skip over, even though it's the very next verse! "After saying this, he breathed on them and said, 'Receive the Holy Spirit.'"

Conviction by itself is never enough—it always falls short. This is because the mission is hard. Jesus himself said that the enemy was going to sow weeds among the wheat, and that these weeds were going to grow together with the wheat until the harvest (Matt. 13:24–30). And in the same way, Jesus also said that not every seed that is sown will fall on good soil. Some will fall along the path, on rocky ground, and among thorns, and will not bear fruit (Matt. 13:3–9). This is why Jesus warned his disciples, "If anyone wants to follow after me, let him deny himself, take up his cross, and follow me" (Matt. 16:24)!

Conviction by itself is never enough— it always falls short.

Without the empowerment of the Holy Spirit, Jesus would not have taken that march to Jerusalem to ultimately be nailed to a cross. Without the Holy Spirit, three thousand people would not have found new life at Pentecost (Acts 2:41). Without the Holy Spirit, Saul would not have become the most powerful missionary in the early church (Acts 9). And without the Holy Spirit, the gospel would be powerless and the church would be dead. Without the Holy Spirit, there is no sending of the church. Our witness is powerless without John 20:22! This is because "mission is not just something that the church does; it is something that is done by the Spirit, who is himself the witness, who changes both the world and the church, who always goes before the church in its missionary journey."[8]

So when your church leaves their pet peeves at the foot of the cross and embraces their missionary identity, they are actually embracing their true nature. They are taking off their masks and seeing themselves in the mirror for the first time. This is ultimately not about changing your vision; it's about embracing God's original vision for you and me. "For the mission is not ours but God's."[9]

Marks of the Church

When it comes to the marks of the church, there are countless versions, paradigms, and lists throughout church history. John Stott believed that "love, suffering, holiness, sound doctrine, genuineness, evangelism and humility" were the marks of an ideal church.[10] The Augsburg Confession

(1530) defined the church as "the congregation of saints, in which the Gospel is rightly taught and the Sacraments are rightly administered."[11] In contrast, although John Calvin believed in the same two marks, he worded it differently as "the Word of God purely preached and heard, and the sacraments administered according to Christ's institution."[12]

Rick Warren famously advocates for five purposes or marks: worship, ministry, evangelism, fellowship, and discipleship.[13] Interestingly, Mark Shaw takes a look through church history and explains the different marks of the church via church leaders that embodied them: A vision for truth (Luther), spirituality (Calvin), unity (Burroughs), assurance (Perkins), worship (Baxter), renewal (Edwards), growth (Wesley), the lost (Carey), justice (Wilberforce), and fellowship (Bonhoeffer).[14]

Millard Erickson views the marks of the church through the lens of the church's function: evangelism of the lost, edification of believers, worshipping the Lord, and social concern for both believers and non-Christians. At the heart of all these functions is the gospel; it's the "one factor that gives basic shape to everything the church does."[15]

The Baptist Faith and Message (2000) views the marks of the church as a "local congregation of baptized believers, associated by covenant in the faith and fellowship of the gospel; observing the two ordinances of Christ, governed by His laws, exercising the gifts, rights, and privileges invested in them by His Word, and seeking to extend the gospel to the ends of the earth."[16]

There's even a book titled *9 Marks of a Healthy Church* by Mark Dever. He divides his marks into two categories: the preaching of the Word and leading disciples. The first five all fall under the preaching of the Word: expositional preaching, biblical theology, gospel, conversion, and evangelism. The next four fall under the other category, leading disciples: membership, discipline, discipleship and growth, and leadership.[17]

Missional Marks of the Church

If we go all the way back to the year AD 325 to the Council of Nicea, we encounter one of the first times the church had to clearly define itself in the face of heresy—the Arian controversy. The result of this council was the development of the Nicene Creed—the "most universally accepted Christian creed"—since it is accepted by both Western and Eastern churches, in contrast to the Apostles' Creed, which is only accepted by Western churches.[18] In the revised version of the Nicene Creed, which took place at the Council of Constantinople in AD 381, four words were added that outlined the marks of the church: "one, holy, catholic, and apostolic."[19]

In *God's Missionary People*, Charles Van Engen suggests a fascinating twist on these four marks from the Nicene Creed.

> Maybe it is time we begin to see the four words of Nicea not as adjectives which modify a thing we know as the Church, but as adverbs which describe the missionary action of the Church's essential life in the world. This would make the four be more than static "attributes," more than testing "marks," and even more than dynamic "gifts and tasks." It would see the four as planetary orbits of the Church's missionary life in the world.[20]

By rewording these four marks from adjectives into adverbs, we discover a view of the church that has the end in mind. We can call these the missional marks of the church. Let's walk through each of them (see Figure 5.1).

Nicene Creed's Marks (adjectives)	Van Engen's Missional Marks (adverbs)
One	Unifying
Holy	Sanctifying
Catholic	Reconciling
Apostolic	Proclaiming

FIGURE 5.1: THE NICENE MISSIONAL MARKS OF THE CHURCH[21]

1. ONE/UNIFYING

Churches can take one of two postures when it comes to the first Nicene mark of the church. They can either draw out clear boundaries and police them, in order to define who is a part of the one true Church and who isn't, or they can actively join Christ in the work of unifying, since he said,

"May they all be one, as you, Father, are in me and I am in you. May they also be in us, so that the world may believe you sent me" (John 17:21). As we see in this verse, churches that take on the task of unifying realize that unity is connected to mission. They also understand that while all churches may not agree on everything, the one thing that they can agree on is the Great Commission.

Consequently, this first missional mark is all about being a church that actively partners with others in Kingdom ministry around God's mission and plan for this world.

2. HOLY/SANCTIFYING

Churches can set themselves apart and detach from the world in their quest for holiness, or they can refuse to be like the priest and Levite in the parable of the Good Samaritan, and instead be a sanctifying force like the Samaritan—not just in their own members' lives, but in the lives of those outside their church (Luke 10:25–37). After all, Jesus did not just stay on the mountaintop after the transfiguration; he came down and immediately ministered to a man who was possessed by a demon (Mark 9:1–29). As Jesus cast the demon out of this man, he helped start this man on his journey of sanctification. In this second missional mark, the church is called to be a sanctifying force by showing and demonstrating the effects of forgiveness and healing in Christ to this world.

3. CATHOLIC/RECONCILING

The third mark is not a jab at the Protestant church. Rather, it's the generic use of the word *catholic*, which means "including many different things."[22] The missional adverb form to this adjective is *reconciling*. As a result, in the midst of the brokenness, hatred, racism, and wars in our world, the church cannot be exclusive if others decide to join. Instead, the church has to actively be about the ministry of reconciliation because we were first reconciled to God and then given this ministry (2 Cor. 5:17–20). It's the church's task to be "peacemakers" (Matt. 5:9), not peacekeepers. Jesus told us specifically to turn the other cheek, to give them our coats, and to go the second mile (Matt. 5:38–42). This is not passive catholicity; it's active reconciliation.

4. Apostolic/Proclaiming

Lastly, while it's definitely true that the church is built on the backs of the teaching and preaching of the biblical apostles, the fact is, the Word of God is still living and active today. Thus, we do not teach a dead historical document; rather, we proclaim the Word of God that "is living and effective and sharper than any double-edged sword, penetrating as far as the separation of soul and spirit, joints and marrow" (Heb. 4:12). The church is called to follow the lead of the biblical apostles—though not claiming the title for ourselves—in continuing to preach, teach, disciple, witness, mobilize, and send for the sake of the gospel and the salvation of others.

When we alter the Nicene marks of the church from adjectives to adverbs, we make the micro-shift from maturity to missionary. Instead of maturing our churches to be one, holy, catholic, and apostolic, we are sending them out as everyday local and global missionaries to be a unifying, sanctifying, reconciling, and proclaiming force in this world that desperately needs to hear the good news of Christ. Thus, mission becomes central to the identity of the church, rather than a peripheral task that it checks off. "The essential nature of the local congregation is, in and of itself, mission, or else the congregation is not really the Church."[23]

> Mission is central to the identity of the church, rather than a peripheral task that it checks off.

Marks of a Missional Church

When mission is central to the identity of a church, it is safe to call the church missional. The word *missional*, as Ed Stetzer and I wrote in *Planting Missional Churches*, "means adopting the *posture of a missionary*, joining Jesus on mission, learning and adapting to the culture around you while remaining biblically sound . . . *missional* means living and acting like a missionary without ever leaving your city."[24] I love how Christopher Wright breaks down the word, "missional is to the word *mission* what covenantal is to *covenant*, or fictional to *fiction*."[25]

When Ed Stetzer and I were writing the second edition of *Planting Missional Churches*, we wrestled with whether or not to change the title. Since the word *missional* has been around for a while, we were questioning whether it was still relevant to ministry today. While no one quite knows who coined the term or when it happened, we see that Francis Dubose, in his 1983 book *God Who Sends,* used the word in the sense that we use it today.[26]

In 1998, after a three-year research project to recover the church's missional call in North America, Darrell Guder and his team published the landmark book, *Missional Church.* Since then, some have used the word *missional* to refer to a specific style of ministry, in contrast to *attractional* models or other pet peeve models of ministry. For Ed and me, we decided to keep *missional* in the title of our book to reclaim its original meaning as ministry centered on God's mission, focused on the Kingdom, and part of the culture that we're seeking to reach, rather than a pet peeve style of ministry. Thus, being missional is really more of a posture than a style of ministry. Here is how we defined it: "Planting missional churches stems from the fact that the church's identity is wrapped up in God's identity. Since God is a missional God, his church should be as well. This is essentially our foundational understanding for writing this book."[27]

> **Missional means living and acting like a missionary without ever leaving your city.**

Regardless of where you live, whether it be in the rolling hills of Georgia, the Rocky Mountains in Alberta, French-speaking Quebec, Sin City, the Windy City, or the City of Angels, ministry today has to be missionary oriented (or missional) rather than maturity driven. How much more so in a post-Christian context!

Over a seven-year period, the Barna Group conducted research with more than seventy-six thousand adults around what makes a city post-Christian, and they measured for the following fifteen factors (see Figure 5.2).

1. Do not believe in God
2. Identify as atheist or agnostic
3. Disagree that faith is important in their lives
4. Have not prayed to God (in the last week)
5. Have never made a commitment to Jesus
6. Disagree the Bible is accurate

7. Have not donated money to a church (in the last year)
8. Have not attended a Christian church (in the last 6 months)
9. Agree that Jesus committed sins
10. Do not feel a responsibility to "share their faith"
11. Have not read the Bible (in the last week)
12. Have not volunteered at church (in the last week)
13. Have not attended Sunday school (in the last week)
14. Have not attended a religious small group (in the last week)
15. Have not read the Bible in the past week and disagree strongly or somewhat that the Bible is accurate
16. Not Born Again

FIGURE 5.2: BARNA'S POST-CHRISTIAN METRICS[28]

A city qualified as post-Christian if they met nine or more of those factors. If they met thirteen or more, they were considered "highly" post-Christian. In both 2013, 2015, and 2017, American cities like New York, San Francisco, Albany, Boston, and Portland appeared on the top-fifteen list.[29] If Barna had done this research in Canada, I'm sure cities like Montreal, Vancouver, and Toronto would have made the list as well.

If you live in an area that is not quite post-Christian, but seems to be on its way, it would be helpful to learn from those who have thriving missional ministries in a post-Christian context, like Tim Keller in New York. Because the church in our culture is increasingly being pushed to the margins, it's only a matter of time until the area where you live and minister becomes post-Christian too.

It's only a matter of time until the area where you live and minister becomes post-Christian.

In *Center Church*, Keller presents a missional view of the marks of the church that are actually helpful in any context—post-Christian or not (see Figure 5.3). However, in light of the fact that he is ministering in a post-Christian context, his are especially important to take note of.

1. The church must confront society's idols
2. The church must contextualize skillfully and communicate in the vernacular
3. The church must equip people in mission in every area of their lives
4. The church must be a counterculture for the common good
5. The church must itself be contextualized and should expect nonbelievers, inquirers, and seekers to be involved in most aspects of the church's life and ministry
6. The church must practice unity

FIGURE 5.3: TIM KELLER'S SIX MARKS OF A MISSIONAL CHURCH[30]

From Maturity to Missionary

Taking Keller's marks of a missional church as our starting point, let's explore what it would look like to shift our churches from a maturity mindset to a missionary one.

1. THE CHURCH MUST CONFRONT SOCIETY'S IDOLS.

What idols does your church face in the neighborhood, town, or city where you live? What are the sins that consistently come up in counseling? What are the strongholds that you address through your preaching? Is it materialism? Consumerism? Individualism? Some other "-ism"?

To develop missionary disciples, you need to train your church to do as Paul did in Athens at the Areopagus—to reason with the locals both in places of worship and in the marketplace (Acts 17:17). Paul noticed the altar "To an Unknown God" (Acts 17:23) and used it as a starting point for confronting the society's idols and sharing the gospel; you need to know the *local* altars and be equipped to share the gospel in your neighborhood today.

2. THE CHURCH MUST CONTEXTUALIZE SKILLFULLY AND COMMUNICATE IN THE VERNACULAR.

When I was pastoring in post-Christian Montreal, there was such a lack of awareness about basic Christian concepts like God, sin, and redemption among teens and young adults, that I couldn't assume anything. So the way that I would share the gospel had to be different than if I were doing it in the buckle of the Bible Belt.

Are you training your church to be "ready at any time to give a defense to anyone who asks you for a reason for the hope that is in you" (1 Pet. 3:15)? Are you teaching them how to do this "with gentleness and respect" (1 Pet. 3:16), while sharing the *whole* story of God, rather than assuming a common knowledge base of God, sin, and redemption?

3. THE CHURCH MUST EQUIP PEOPLE IN MISSION IN EVERY AREA OF THEIR LIVES.

At one point in time, we had to help our churches understand the Reformation doctrine of "the priesthood of all believers." I believe that today we need to make an even further shift: from priest to missionary. It's one thing to help our church members understand that they *are* the church and that it's the role of the pastor to equip the saints to do the work of ministry, rather than do it for them (Eph. 4:11–12). So in this sense, every member is a minister or every member is a priest. In this way, the concept of doing ministry is often seen as an internal matter of caring for the flock, and helping them mature. But we must move beyond priesthood and call people to see themselves as missionaries—the "sent out" ones.

> **To develop missionary disciples, you need to help your church see their primary vocation as being missionaries.**

To develop missionary disciples, you need to help your church see their primary vocation as being missionaries—wherever they live, work, and play—and their secondary vocation as being whatever they do to make a paycheck. This will require them "to be a verbal witness to the gospel," "to love their neighbors and do justice within their neighborhoods and city," and "to integrate their faith with their work in order to engage culture through their vocations."[31]

4. THE CHURCH MUST BE A COUNTERCULTURE FOR THE COMMON GOOD.

The late Archbishop of Canterbury, William Temple, lives on today through his often quoted saying, "The church is the only institution that exists primarily for the benefit of those who are not its members." Rather than seeing your church as a social club for its own good, what would it look like if your church embraced its missionary identity? What if you called your church to be "salt of the earth," and the "light of the world," since "a city situated on a hill cannot be hidden." After all, "no one lights a lamp and puts it under a basket, but rather on a lampstand, and it gives light for all who are in the house. In the same way, let your light shine before others, so that they may see your good works and give glory to your Father in heaven" (Matt. 5:13–16).

When we live out our missionary identity as a church and function together as the salt of the earth and the light of the world, something happens. We begin to realize that our true citizenship is not on earth, since we are actually "strangers and exiles" here (1 Pet. 2:11). When we live against the grain of culture and begin loving our enemies and praying for those who persecute us (Matt. 5:44), instead of plotting revenge, the church becomes "a counterculture for the common good." When we show the world that people from "every nation, tribe, people, and language" (Rev. 7:9) can actually worship together, live in community, and serve one another here on earth and not just in heaven, the church becomes "a counterculture for the common good." In this way, a healthy congregation is truly a "hermeneutic of the gospel."[32] A countercultural church brings the gospel to life and gives this world the opportunity to "taste and see that the LORD is good" (Ps. 34:8). Ultimately, a countercultural church opens up doors not only for the gospel to be shown, but also to be proclaimed.

5. THE CHURCH MUST ITSELF BE CONTEXTUALIZED AND SHOULD EXPECT NONBELIEVERS, INQUIRERS, AND SEEKERS TO BE INVOLVED IN MOST ASPECTS OF THE CHURCH'S LIFE AND MINISTRY.

A missional church has a direction mind-set, rather than a destination one, as we discussed in chapter 1. Instead of asking people to believe before they belong, a missional church invites everyone to belong before they believe. The door is open until you close it for the missional church, rather than being closed until you open it. As a result, for the missional church, both discipleship and evangelism can happen anywhere and at anytime, rather than being bound or restricted to a department or a program.

6. THE CHURCH MUST PRACTICE UNITY.

What I love about my role as the Director of Church Multiplication for NewChurches.com at LifeWay Christian Resources, is that it's my daily responsibility and privilege to serve church plants and multisite churches in their mission to multiply and make disciples. As a result, twice a year, I have the privilege to convene the Church Planting Leadership Fellowship (CPLF) with Ed Stetzer and Scott McConnell.[33] In this exclusive network of leaders who oversee church planting for their denomination or network, we discovered that more than 75 percent of the church planting in North America is represented by our members! While Baptists and Presbyterians or Lutherans and Pentecostals may never plant together, they can definitely train together and learn from one another. This is precisely the attitude that the missional church must embrace! As Meldenius said, "In essentials, unity; in non-essentials, liberty; in all things, charity." So instead of contrasting ourselves from one another, the missional church will seek to avoid unnecessary divisions.

The Maturity/Missionary Cycle

Charles Spurgeon once said, "Every Christian here is either a missionary or an impostor. Recollect that. You either try to spread abroad the kingdom of Christ, or else you do not love him at all. It cannot be that there is a high appreciation of Jesus and a totally silent tongue about him."[34] He goes on to say in this sermon, "that man who says, 'I believe in Jesus,' but does not think enough of Jesus ever to tell another about him, by mouth, or pen, or tract, is an impostor."[35]

When we live out our core identity as missionaries, the Lord matures us. However, if we focus on behaviors directly tied to the maturation of our souls, we may never go beyond ourselves. The interesting thing about both goals—to mature and to live as a missionary—is that they're cyclical. What matters is your starting point.

When we live out our core identity as missionaries, the Lord matures us.

If you start with the goal of maturity, then in the quest for Christlikeness, and having been influenced by our educational system, you may inadvertently focus on head knowledge alone. If so, as you grow in your knowledge of theology, doctrine, and apologetics, you may also neglect going out and telling others about Christ! "I'm not ready," "I don't know any non-Christians," or "my role is to equip others to do the work of ministry" are typically the excuses for Christians that are solely focused on maturity. If this is the case, then while you may be growing in head knowledge, true maturity is not happening. This is because maturity that does not result in living as a missionary is false Christianity. Remember that powerful Spurgeon quote? If you're not telling others about Christ, the question is, do you really love him?

If you start, however, with the goal of living as a missionary, you will surely mature, because the only way you can actually live on mission in a sustainable manner, is to mature! Ministry that does not flow out of a sense of rootedness and a deep understanding of your identity in Christ will always flame out.

Just consider the lives of Moses, David, Jesus, and Paul. All of them had desert experiences before the Lord released them into ministry. And even after being released for ministry, many of them experienced the desert again! For Moses, it was when he first fled to Midian (Exod. 2:14–15), and again during the forty years in the desert (Deut. 8:2). For David, it was after he was anointed by Samuel (1 Sam. 16:13), and again when he was chased out of his kingdom by his son Absalom (2 Sam. 15:14). For Jesus, it was when he was tempted by Satan in the desert after his baptism (Matt. 4:1–11), and again when he was nailed to the cross (Matt. 27:35–50). For Paul, it was during the three years after his conversion before he went to Jerusalem to get to know Peter (Gal. 1:15–18), and again during his house arrest in Rome, while awaiting his trial (Acts 28:30–31).

We don't fall into the desert when we are locked up in our study. The Lord matures us through seasons in the desert that occur while we are living as missionaries for his Kingdom. God uses these desert experiences to "humble you and test you to know what [is] in your heart, whether or not you [will] keep his commands" (Deut. 8:2). He did this in each of the above examples and more! The Lord used the desert to ready David for his kingship and Jesus for his ministry. He uses these desert experiences to refine our character and deepen our

The Lord uses desert experiences to refine our character and deepen our prayer lives.

prayer lives. After all, how many of the Psalms were written out of David's desert experience?

Normalizing Mission

In the 2015 State of Church Planting research LifeWay Research conducted with NewChurches.com, and in partnership with seventeen denominations and networks, we discovered a great deal about church planting and multiplication.[36] In the eBook that I wrote with Ed Stetzer, *Multiplication Today, Movements Tomorrow: Practices, Barriers, and an Ecosystem*, we focused on the 22 percent of churches—that started in 2012 or earlier—that started at least one daughter church within their first five years of existence (see Figure 5.4).[37] As we were studying what made these churches multiply, and others not, we discovered six common practices.

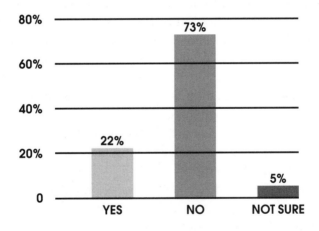

AMONG THOSE STARTED IN 2012 OR EARLIER, 22% STARTED AT LEAST ONE DAUGHTER CHURCH WITHIN 5 YEARS OF EXISTENCE.

FIGURE 5.4: PERCENTAGE OF CHURCHES THAT MULTIPLIED IN THEIR FIRST FIVE YEARS

Churches that multiplied in their first five years of existence not only had a deep love for the lost, but they were intentional about evangelism. For these churches, strategy was not as important as the fact that evangelism was happening. It's like that quote often attributed to D. L. Moody, "I like the way I do evangelism better than the way you don't do evangelism."

So whether a church used mailers, hosted a sports league, put on fun social events, used special children's activities, or offered Bible studies as forms of outreach, churches that were intentional about evangelism typically saw a higher number of new commitments made for Christ and more unchurched individuals attend their gatherings! In other words, when a church normalized mission, they were more likely to reach the lost, impact their city, and multiply.

> **When a church normalizes mission, they are more likely to reach the lost, impact their city, and multiply.**

Eric Geiger and Kevin Peck, in their book *Designed to Lead*, present a clear framework for leadership development that I believe lends itself well to normalizing mission. They describe their framework (see Figure 5.5) in this way: "Churches that consistently produce leaders have a strong *conviction* to develop leaders, a healthy *culture* for leadership development, and helpful *constructs* to systematically and intentionally build leaders."[38]

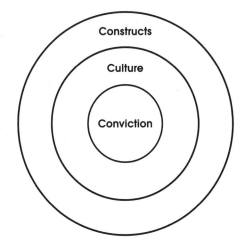

FIGURE 5.5: DESIGNED TO LEAD FRAMEWORK

Let's take this same framework and apply it to our discussion on the micro-shift from maturity to missionary.

Conviction

At the center of the *Designed to Lead* framework is conviction, because "without conviction to develop others, leadership development will not occur."[39] In the same way, without the conviction to go and make disciples of all nations, your church will struggle to reach the lost and participate in lasting Kingdom ministry. Unless you, your team, and your church understand the conviction that we are all sent and on mission with God *wherever* we are and in *whatever* we do for a living (John 20:21), developing missionary disciples will be nothing but a pipe dream.

In order to teach this conviction to your church, you need to first destroy the dichotomy between "church" and "mission." For many, the "church" is where worship, spiritual development, and pastoral care happen, whereas, "mission" is where the gospel is proclaimed, in order to make converts who are passed onto the "church."

When I was pastoring in Korea, I remember having a conversation with a young man in our congregation. He felt called to the ministry, so he wanted to get my advice and ask me some questions. When I joyfully met him for coffee, my first question was, "Why do you feel called to pastor?" His facial expression and response was so vivid, that it has stuck with me to this day.

"Pastor? No way. That's too easy. I don't want to do that. I want to be a missionary. That's better."

I guarantee you there are people sitting in your church service every weekend who feel the exact same dichotomy between church and mission. They are in the church to be spiritually cared for, fed, and kept safe; *others* are responsible for the mission. Isn't that why they *tip* when the offering plate goes by? Oh, I mean, *tithe*.

This is precisely why the micro-shift in this chapter matters! In order to destroy this dichotomy and lay the foundation for this John 20:21 conviction, you need to help your church understand that "mission is not primarily an activity of the church, but an attribute of God . . . [since] God is a missionary God."[40] Thus, when your church grasps that "the church is the church only when it exists for others,"[41] as Dietrich Bonhoeffer wrote from prison, the foundation for this dichotomy will begin to crack.

Culture

You will know that the seed of conviction has taken root and begun to germinate, when it becomes a part of your church's culture. "Culture is the shared beliefs and values that drive the behavior of a group or people."[42] As a result, you will know that this John 20:21 conviction has begun to take root in your church when the dichotomy between church and mission begins to break down.

For example, when you see your church members intentionally eating meals and hanging out with both non-Christians and Christians on a regular basis, outside of the Sunday worship gathering, conviction has begun to make its way into culture. After all, this demonstrates that your church comprehends that mission is something they do, not something they contract professionals to do.

> **Mission is something you do, not something you contract professionals to do.**

Constructs

Without constructs, which is a fancy word for systems, processes, and programs, culture and conviction can easily change on a whim, much like we saw happen in the Copy Cat and Hippie Churches in chapter 1. This is why "wise leaders implement constructs to help unlock the full potential of a church that seeks to be a center for developing leaders" and missionaries![43] Constructs also help solidify and normalize conviction and culture, since they are the programs that get implemented, the language that is used, and the way your particular conviction and culture are executed and become tangible.

One of the best ways to normalize mission is through the formation of a personal construct that anyone in your church can live out. Here are a handful of the popular ones (see Figure 5.6).

BLESS from Community Christian Church[44]	BELLS from Michael Frost	Rhythms from Soma Communities[45]	BLESS from The Edge Network[46]	Up, In, Out from Mike Breen
Begin with Prayer	Bless	Story-formed	Bless	Up
Listen	Eat	Listen	Listen	In
Eat	Listen	Celebrate	Eat	Out
Serve	Learn	Bless	Speak	
Story	Sent	Eat	Sabbath	
		Re-create		

FIGURE 5.6: MISSIONAL CONSTRUCTS

Conviction, Culture, Constructs Applied

When I was pastoring at Beulah Alliance Church in Edmonton, Alberta, my *secret agenda* was to make it missional. For many at the church, the dichotomy between church and mission was alive and well. Anything that was remotely related to missional engagement was a highly programmed, one-and-done service opportunity, like a clothing giveaway, a small group serving at a soup kitchen, short-term mission trips, or a disaster relief love offering.

While one-and-done service opportunities like these are a practical and scalable way (or construct) to give the masses a taste of serving, they simply cannot be the end. Instead, they need to be seen as the means to help individuals discover their true primary vocation, which is that John 20:21 conviction.

As a result, in addition to introducing mid-size communities as a way to help the church live as a sign, instrument, and foretaste of the kingdom of God, as I outlined in chapter 4, I also introduced the BLESS construct from Community Christian Church in Chicagoland (see Figure 5.7).

Since we had a high accountability culture, we made sure that this construct was not just going to be a flash in the pan. So I led our church on a quest to integrate this across every department and into every crack and crevice of the church. Being on the teaching team, I helped plan a four-week series to inspire, inform, and equip our church with this new construct. This sermon series was intended to help everyone discover that they were sent and on mission with God *wherever* they went and in *whatever* they did for a living (John 20:21).

Next, we made it a priority to communicate the BLESS construct on a regular basis. So when we shared stories of life change on the weekend or when the staff submitted stories to whoever was preaching, we made sure that each story illustrated at least one of the five letters in the BLESS construct.

We also designed a tract-sized pocket guide to help our church understand the conviction that was behind this construct. The pocket guide begins with many of the concepts that I wrote about in this chapter using everyday language. With the adult ministries team, we then elaborated on the meaning of each letter and wrote down practical ways to live it out as an individual. We also wrote a discussion guide that could be easily used within a mid-size community (social space), small group (personal space), or accountability group (intimate space) setting. You can download the PDF and InDesign files of this pocket guide to modify for your church at danielim.com.

Letter	Description	Example Application Question
Begin with prayer	I will pray for the people in my life and the places that I'm in.	Who do you live, work, and play with that is far from God? Pray that God would create spiritual curiosity in them, and then spend time with them.
Listen	I will listen to and discover the needs of others and the places where God is at work.	In your interactions with others today, take the posture of a learner. Lay down your assumptions, and practice being present.
Eat	I will share meals and spend time with people in my life.	Who can you eat with (or have a coffee with) that is far from God? A coworker over lunch? A neighbor during the day? A friend or family member over the weekend?
Serve	I will respond to the needs of others and help them in practical and impactful ways.	Who can you serve this week? Who do you know that has a practical need? Ask them how you can help them.
Story	I will share the story of Jesus and what he is doing in my life with others.	Start by sharing how God has blessed you and made a difference in your life.

FIGURE 5.7: BLESS CONSTRUCT EXPANDED

This BLESS construct also made its way into our spiritual formation courses, evangelism training, Alpha classes, student ministry, and into Spanish for our Hispanic campus. What amazed me most was how our children's department ran with the concept and created a comic book that helped children understand how to live out the BLESS construct in their lives.

In addition to a construct like BLESS, helping your church practice the spiritual disciplines through a missional lens will also help you normalize mission. In *Habits for Our Holiness,* my friend Philip Nation introduces how to do just that. He believes that the central discipline of the Christian life is love, and that "love is what propels habitual holiness and the desire to follow God into the world for His redeeming mission."[47] As a result, if you practice the disciplines, while disregarding others and God's mission for this world, you miss the entire point. The fact is, the spiritual disciplines lead to mission.

Spiritual disciplines lead to mission.

While reading his book, I developed this chart that outlines and defines each spiritual discipline, while also sharing how it specifically leads to mission (see Figure 5.8). This is a practical construct to equip your church members with the tools to normalize mission in their lives and in community.

Name	Definition	How It Leads to Mission
Worship	Worship is focusing our heart's affection on God, while rejecting everything else.	Worship is an opportunity for the unbelieving world to see a celebration of the gospel.
Bible Study	Bible study is regularly engaging the Scriptures in a way that produces a habitual holiness fueled by God's truth and grace.	Bible study allows us to grow up so that we can reach out, while at the same time, reach out so that we can grow up.
Prayer	Prayer is two-way communication between humans and God, and it's initiated by love.	Prayer informs us of our role in God's mission, and is a way for us to seek for God's Kingdom to reign in the hearts of those living in our community.
Fasting	Fasting is completely or partially eliminating food or drink to spend time in prayer for biblical purposes.	Fasting reveals what's underneath our hearts and motives by showing us the barriers that are preventing us from engaging in the missional task ahead of us.
Fellowship	Fellowship is spending time with others and mutually submitting to one another for disciple making and mission.	Fellowship provides us with the opportunity to work together to share the gospel with others.

Rest	Resting is submitting to God's presence, in order to be sustained and fulfilled.	Resting is a testimony to our world that we are delivered from the need of self-reliance.
Simple Living	Simple living is loving God, rather than the abundance of things.	Simple living declares that our money and possessions do not define our wellbeing, and are merely tools to assist us as we participate in God's Kingdom.
Servanthood	Servanthood is allowing the love of God to motivate our way of life.	Servanthood transforms us into a signpost that points people to the greatest Servant, Jesus.
Submission	Submission is surrendering to God's love, grace, mercy, and his salvation.	Submission allows us to become showpieces of God's grace to the world.
Spiritual Leadership	Spiritual leadership is birthed from God, and is about leading others with discernment.	Spiritual leadership gives us the opportunity to guide others to submit to God, and participate in his mission.
Disciple Making	Disciple making is being intentional and single-minded to help others follow Jesus as the Lord of their lives.	Disciple making is mission.

FIGURE 5.8: SPIRITUAL DISCIPLINES THROUGH A MISSIONAL LENS

Conclusion

Helping you make the micro-shift from training up and releasing *mature disciples* to *missionary disciples* is not only the heart of this chapter, it's my *secret agenda* for you and your church. In this chapter, we laid a foundation for a missional ecclesiology and presented a way to normalize mission in your church. As you move forward and begin to make this micro-shift from maturity to missionary by normalizing mission in your church, beware of these three scenarios:

Constructs without Conviction

What would happen if your church, in its quest to normalize mission and shift from maturity to missionary, focused so heavily on rolling out constructs like the BLESS pocket guide and the missional spiritual disciplines, that you failed to spend enough time laying out the conviction? According to Geiger and Peck, it would result in apathy.[48] Without a John 20:21 conviction, these constructs are mere fads and models that will easily be forgotten when the new program rolls into town. A consistent barrage of new constructs without a solid conviction that we are sent and on mission with God, *wherever* we are and in *whatever* we do for a living, is sure to result in apathy.

Constructs without Culture

Let's imagine the same scenario but with one change. Instead of lacking conviction, your church lacks the culture to normalize mission. This situation would result in exhaustion.[49] If you try to implement either of those two constructs to normalize mission without first establishing a culture of mission, every initiative will feel standalone. Your attempts to help people live as missionaries will feel like just "another-thing-the-church-has-asked-me-to-do," rather than a natural outflow of discipleship. Without a culture of mission, it will be hard for people to see how all of your tools, constructs, and initiatives link together and contribute to the whole, inevitably resulting in exhaustion.

Conviction without Constructs

Wouldn't it have been frustrating if I had only written the first half of this chapter, and left out everything from the sub-header, "From Maturity to Missionary," onwards? That's how your church would feel if all you did was talk about mission, without providing tools for people to actually live it out! Although conviction and culture need to be the starting points to make this micro-shift, you cannot leave out constructs.[50]

Beulah would not have been able to make the micro-shift to a missional culture without the BLESS construct. Let's be honest. Everyone in the church had already heard plenty of sermons about the Great Commission and their calling in this world, but why had they not lived it out? It was because there weren't constructs for them to grab hold of, nor were there internal constructs of communication and prioritization for the staff to organize ministry around.

Let's now move on to section 2, where you will learn some constructs to create, develop, and tweak your church's discipleship pathway.

Reflection Questions

1. What are the pet peeves that drive ministry philosophy and strategy at your church?

2. Are you living on mission in a sustainable manner? After all, "Ministry that does not flow out of a sense of rootedness and a deep understanding of your identity in Christ will always flame out."

3. What are your next steps to normalize mission in your church? How can you apply the conviction, culture, and constructs framework to help you do this?

SECTION II

THE PATH

CHAPTER 6

INTRODUCING CHANGE

"The choice is simple: change or die."

—Thom Rainer

"We were criticized for playing God."[1]

It was a cold, winter, Massachusetts day—December 23, 1954. History was either going to be made or repeated. Richard Herrick, due to a failing kidney, was cadaverous, pale, and hallucinating from severe anemia. He was so out of sorts because of the toxins in his blood that he even "bit a nurse who was trying to change his sheets" and "cursed the medical staff and accused them of sexually assaulting him."[2]

He was dying of kidney disease, and other than undergoing an "experimental" kidney transplant, he had no hope. To be honest, the word *experimental* might have been a bit generous considering the fact that the late Dr. Joseph E. Murray had never successfully performed one on humans. In fact, no one had.

Dr. Murray had first discovered organ transplantation during a nine-month military surgical internship at Valley Forge General Hospital in Pennsylvania. Rather than being sent overseas to serve in World War II, Dr. Murray's supervisor, who just happened to be the Chief of Plastic Surgery, requested that he be kept at the hospital. During the next three years, Dr. Murray performed skin grafts on many soldiers. However, there were some patients that were so severely burned, they literally had no healthy skin left for a graft. So, as a life-saving measure, skin grafts were taken from others to be used as a temporary surface cover.

What happened next fascinated Dr. Murray—these foreign skin grafts were slowly rejected by the soldier's bodies. Somehow, their body was able to distinguish another person's skin from its own, and the grafts did not last. After discussing this with his supervisor, he discovered that "the closer the genetic relationship between the skin donor and the recipient, the slower the dissolution of the graft."[3]

As a result, in 1937, after his supervisor successfully performed a skin graft on a pair of identical twins—and the graft survived permanently—Dr. Murray began studying organ transplantation. He started with dogs and kept swapping kidneys in them until Richard Herrick showed up on his doorstep. Although he learned the surgical technique and discovered how to prevent organ rejection through his experimentation on dogs, he had never done this on a human.

Since Herrick had an identical twin who was willing to give him a kidney, Dr. Murray said that this seemed like it "was the perfect human setup for our laboratory model."[4] So before the surgery took place, while being criticized for "playing God," Dr. Murray decided that it was a good idea to practice his surgical techniques on a cadaver. After all, there really wasn't going to be an extra kidney lying around that he could use if he messed up with the first one.

When the surgery was complete, Dr. Murray recollects that "'there was a collective hush in the operating room' as blood began to flow into the implanted kidney and urine began to flow out of it."[5]

Both the donor and the donee ended up surviving the surgery. Dr. Murray went on to perform kidney transplants on more than a couple dozen pairs of identical twins, and then to a non-identical recipient in 1959. He later even figured out how to use a cadaver kidney for a transplant in 1962. In addition to winning the Nobel Prize in Physiology or Medicine in 1990, he went on to train doctors who have since become some of the best leaders and surgeons in transplantation across the world.[6]

Why Transplants Don't Always Work

Why did the foreign skin grafts get rejected, while the ones using the soldier's own skin worked? Why did the twins have to be identical for that first organ transplant to succeed? Why did it take years before an organ transplant from stranger to stranger worked? And then from a cadaver? I might be way in over my head, but let me try to simplify it for all of us non-doctor types. Our immune system is highly sophisticated and works to defend our body against bad bacteria, viruses, and other foreign materials that may enter it. It works well when fighting against the common cold— not so well when getting a graft or an organ transplant. Unfortunately, our immune system cannot "differentiate between disease-causing microorganisms and the cells of a lifesaving transplant. Both are perceived as foreign, and both are subject to attack by the immune system."[7]

As a result, in order to prevent rejection and ensure a successful transplant, doctors must take several things into consideration. They must, for example, decide whether or not to do blood transfusions, since they sometimes work positively toward the transplant, and other times negatively. Since organs deteriorate rapidly without a blood supply, doctors must also take into account the time in removing the organ from one body and putting it into another. Further, the right dosage of immunosuppression drugs to stop the body from attacking the transplant or graft is critical so that the "blood-cell-forming tissues in the bone marrow are not damaged, which could lead to infections and bleeding."[8] And the list goes on and on.

No wonder change is so hard to implement in our churches. It's like the immune system of our church body knows when we try to transplant foreign ideas. And not only does it detect the new idea, it sees it as bad bacteria, a virus, or foreign material—thus resulting in its rejection. This is why, as we see in the Influences Matrix below (see Figure 6.1), the Copy Cat Church moves from one model to the next, while the Hippie Church never really settles on one at all. Even though the pastor introduces the change initiative as being different and truly better for the church— including being completely different than all the other changes the pastor might have brought in the past—the body detects it as foreign material and often rejects it. This happens because there's a lack of accountability in the

Why is change so hard to implement in our churches?

church's culture. The pastor has not considered all the ways that this change will affect the church and thus has not planned and prepared the different departments and leaders in his church for it.

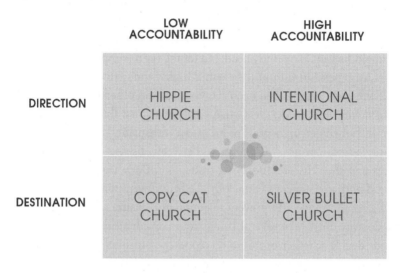

FIGURE 6.1: THE INFLUENCES MATRIX PERSONAS

Now the Silver Bullet and Intentional Churches—both having a high level of accountability—know how change will affect the different systems in the church, ministry areas, and leaders. As a result, when foreign ideas, micro-shifts, vision, strategies, and values are introduced to the church body from a book, conference, or another church, the pastor—as well as the leadership of the church—knows what needs to happen in order to accept the transplant. Instead of disregarding the church's unique personality, history, leadership style, and culture, the pastor and leadership of the church determine the right dosage of change, and the areas to which it needs to be applied, in order to accept and retain the transplant.

Everything Is Connected

I've always been fascinated by foot reflexology because of those colorful charts that I see in the mall. Although I'm only half joking, let's be honest with each other—those charts are definitely eye-catching! It's a fascinating concept to think that applying pressure to specific areas of your feet could result in healing in other parts of your body. Now, I've never done foot reflexology—and to be honest, I'm not quite sure what to think of it—but when my wife was showing early signs of labor at thirty-two weeks, I stayed away from her feet! I don't know if the whole massaging-feet-induces-labor is due to foot reflexology or just an old wives' tale, but I wasn't about to test it!

Our body is a complex system because it's so interconnected. Everything around us in nature is as well. Just think about the way the gravitational pull of the moon and the sun affect the tide. Or the impact of a keystone species[9] disappearing and just how damaging that can be for an ecosystem. For example, in 1969, when Robert T. Paine removed the entire sea star species from a particular tidal plain in the State of Washington, there was a devastating effect on the ecosystem. Since sea stars like to eat mussels, the mussels were able, now that their predator was gone, to take over the entire tidal plain and crowd out the other species.[10]

In the same way, your church is a system, and it's interconnected. So to think that you can introduce change quickly and easily, without it affecting the other areas of your church, is naïve at best. For example, you'll only be disappointed if you decide to introduce the latest evangelism curriculum into your church, in hopes that it will increase your church's evangelistic culture, but subsequently don't take the time to consider how this is going to affect everything else that you're doing. It will not work as advertised. You won't be able to make the micro-shift from a maturity to missionary mind-set, unless you introduce change in the right way. You might as well just claim your thirty-day money-back guarantee before it's too late.

A Failed Attempt Averted?

Let's play this example out. You notice that your church nods their heads when you talk about evangelism and the importance of living on mission, but you're not actually hearing stories of them doing it. So you look online and notice that there's some new curriculum that promises to increase evangelism and normalize it. At first glance, it looks good, but being a bit skeptical, you decide to look deeper. You then find a few testimonials on the website from pastors that you trust, who are leading thriving ministries. But because Sunday is just around the corner, you put it off and get back to preparing for ministry.

Let's fast-forward a few weeks. You're now at a conference and notice a compelling video advertisement where pastors you respect and their congregants are both sharing their testimony regarding the effectiveness of that evangelism curriculum you were just looking at a few weeks ago. So you decide to stop by their booth during one of the breaks. After asking a couple brief questions, you take out your wallet and decide to bite the bullet.

Now let's stop for a moment. Most of us know what happens next. In fact, we threw out a couple scenarios earlier in the chapter when talking about transplants and the Influences Matrix. So, if you were in that pastor's shoes, what would you do differently to ensure that the change effort isn't seen as foreign matter and subsequently rejected by your church body? How would you determine whether or not this idea would fit into your church in the first place? Who would you talk to? How would you make the decision?

Expectations and the Change Process

When an angel told Mary that she was going to give birth to Jesus—the One who was going to save all people from their sins—expectations for the life Jesus was going to live were birthed (Matt. 1:21). When Jesus was baptized and the heavens opened up, the Spirit of God descended upon him like a dove, and a voice came from heaven, "This is my beloved Son, with whom I am well pleased," everyone there formed their own expectations (Matt. 3:16–17). When "Jesus began to go all over Galilee, teaching in their synagogues, preaching the good news of the kingdom, and healing every disease and sickness among the people," everyone ministered to by Jesus developed expectations (Matt. 4:23). When Jesus preached the Sermon on the Mount, "The crowds were astonished at his teaching, because he was teaching them like one who had authority, and not like their scribes," so inevitably they too had expectations (Matt. 7:28–29). When Jesus cast demons out of one man and into a whole herd of pigs that then ran down a steep bank and drowned in the sea, the man who was set free had a completely different set of expectations than the whole town that "begged him to leave their region" (Matt. 8:28–34). When Jesus commissioned twelve disciples and "gave them authority over unclean spirits, to drive them out and to heal every disease and sickness," those twelve had expectations for their future (Matt. 10:1). When Jesus declared that anyone who does "the will of my Father in heaven" is his family, everyone there—including his family—had their expectations altered (Matt. 12:48–50). When Jesus was rejected in Nazareth, his hometown (Matt. 13:54–58), those rejecting him had a different set of expectations than the five thousand who were subsequently fed by Jesus and his disciples (Matt. 14:13–21).

It seemed like the disciples, the crowd, his family, and those he ministered to all had their own set of expectations *for* Jesus and for what they could get *from* him. While the Pharisees, Sadducees, chief priests, and elders of the people all had a different set of expectations as to what they were going to *do* to him (Matt. 26:3–4).

Expectations are like putting on a pair of colored glasses. Regardless of the color, you still see what's in front of you. What changes is the way you see what you see—your perspective. For example, a gray tint will reduce brightness without distorting the other colors much at all. A yellow tint will eliminate all blue, while making everything else sharp and bright.[11] And a rose tint will make everything look attractive.

Just as rose-colored glasses—which characterize young love—prevent one from seeing the flaws of another, the color of your tint actually changes your perspective on what you see. This is exactly what happens when we form expectations. Expectations create the reality we want to see, not necessarily the reality that others see.

Close to the end of Jesus' life, there's this moment when James, John, and their mother approach Jesus with a presumptuous request. The mother asks Jesus to promise that her two sons would sit on the right and left side of Jesus in his kingdom (Matt. 20:20–21). Their expectations had led them to create the reality that they wanted to see, rather than discover the one that Jesus was actually creating. This is why Jesus responded to their request with, "You don't know what you're asking," (Matt. 20:22) and then later on with, "But to sit at my right and left is not mine to give; instead, it is for those for whom it has been prepared by my Father" (Matt. 20:23).

> **Expectations create the reality we want to see, not necessarily the reality that others see.**

James, John, and their mother saw this opportunity as a way to grow in power, or position themselves over and above the other disciples. Their perspective on reality was ruler and ruled, the haves and the have-nots, and the ins and the outs. And because they were now finally a part of the "in" crowd, they wanted to secure their position and climb the "corporate ladder," per se.

But Jesus responds with a radically different perspective on reality:

> Jesus called them over and said, "You know that the rulers of the Gentiles lord it over them, and those in high positions act as tyrants over them. It must not be like that among you. On the contrary, whoever wants to become great among you must be your servant, and whoever wants to be first among you must be your slave; just as the Son of Man did not come to be served, but to serve, and to give his life as a ransom for many." (Matt. 20:25–28)

Although Jesus and his disciples were constantly together, many of his disciples, like John and James, often interpreted reality much differently than Jesus. Now if this could happen to Jesus, who is the greatest leader of all time, let's be honest with each other: It can happen to us as well! In fact, it probably has.

Misinterpreted Expectations

How often have you tried to change something in your church, only to be met by opposition somewhere along the process? By misinterpreted expectations? I love the opening story in Thom Rainer's book, *Who Moved My Pulpit?*

Rainer introduces us to a pastor named Derek who had recently shifted to more of an informal style of preaching in order to better reach Millennials. This eventually led Derek to get rid of the traditional massive wooden pulpit that stood in between him and his congregation. Though there were murmurings the Sunday morning that it was gone, it wasn't until that afternoon that the world began to cave in on itself for Derek. The damage had been done and confidence in Derek had been lost. He felt like it was too late to move the pulpit back. What happened the following Sunday is what really shocked him. Upon entering the auditorium, he noticed something different. Someone had moved the old pulpit back.[12]

Derek carelessly introduced change without considering how this would affect the very people he was called to serve. He didn't realize that his reality stood in contrast to those in his church because everyone had a different set of expectations. In other words, he was blindsided because he didn't think through the ways that this would affect others in the church. Most of all, his change effort didn't stick because he didn't have a clear process to implement change in his church.

Steps for Change

I am thankful for the work of Rainer and what he's done for the church in his book *Who Moved My Pulpit?* He has clearly outlined the process and steps that are required to lead change uniquely in your church. In fact, it reminds me much of John Kotter's eight-step process for leading change in his books, *Leading Change* and *Accelerate*. The difference is that Rainer has contextualized the art and science of change management for the church.

For example, Rainer's first step is to pray. I love this. What use is it to create or establish a sense of urgency if you do not first bring the idea before God? This is not a trite, "Lord, here is my idea, I'm going to do it anyway, so can you please bless it?" Rather, it's an attitude of, "Lord, what are you already doing in my church and in my neighborhood? Does this idea fit with what you are calling us to become and be a part of?"

Who Moved My Pulpit? by Thom Rainer[13]	*Leading Change* by John Kotter[14]	*Accelerate* by John Kotter[15]
1. Stop to Pray	1. Establish a Sense of Urgency	1. Create a Sense of Urgency
2. Confront and Communicate a Sense of Urgency	2. Create the Guiding Coalition	2. Build a Guiding Coalition
3. Build an Eager Coalition	3. Develop a Vision and Strategy	3. Form a Strategic Vision and Initiatives
4. Become a Voice and Vision of Hope	4. Communicate the Change Vision	4. Enlist a Volunteer Army

5. Deal with People Issues	5. Empower Broad-Based Action	5. Enable Action by Removing Barriers
6. Move from an Inward Focus to an Outward Focus	6. Generate Short-Term Wins	6. Generate Short-Term Wins
7. Pick Low-Hanging Fruit	7. Consolidate Gains and Produce More Change	7. Sustain Acceleration
8. Implement and Consolidate Change	8. Anchor New Approaches in the Culture	8. Institute Change

FIGURE 6.2: A COMPARISON OF THREE DIFFERENT CHANGE PROCESSES

I've introduced the three paradigms for leading change in Figure 6.2 because they work. I've used these eight steps—and also a variation of them—personally when introducing small changes, like how to engage newcomers after the service, as well as when introducing big changes, like cutting long-standing programming, developing a new discipleship pathway, and introducing a new environment for community life—the mid-size community.

But here's the thing. While these eight steps are critical, and you likely won't succeed in leading change without them, or some variation of them, how you view change matters even more. When burdened with a new idea, or a desire to change something specifically in your church, definitely start with prayer. But don't move straight to implementation after you say your "Amen."

Now I understand that this is hard to do because of our on-demand, stream-anytime, find-an-answer-to-anything, go-anywhere, and swipe-now-pay-later instant gratification culture. In fact, it's because of this that we often misinterpret a conviction from God as permission to drop everything and engage it, rather than waiting on him for our next steps. However, unless we *introduce* change in a fundamentally different manner than we are doing now, these eight steps will not work.

Buyers beware: You will have to live with change once it's implemented.

It's pretty easy to follow these eight steps for change. They are easy to understand, systematic, and proven. But when introducing change, I'm convinced there should be always be a sticker that says: "Buyers beware: You will have to live with the change once it's implemented." Are you prepared for that? Or will you change your mind and introduce change that reverses the effects of your original change initiative after a couple of months?

Unless your change effort leads you closer to the vision, strategy, and values that God is calling your church to embrace (the topic of the next chapter), you're wasting your time. You're introducing change that will merely be overturned at a later time. You are allowing yourself to settle with mediocrity. After all, isn't good the enemy of great?[16]

Three Steps for Introducing Change

This is precisely why, instead of creating my own version of the eight-step change management process, or elaborating on Rainer's or Kotter's, the rest of this chapter is going to outline a three-step process for *introducing* change. This will help you discern whether or not you even want to *begin* the process of implementing the five micro-shifts in the first section of this book. These three steps will help you evaluate every new or foreign idea to anticipate if it is a good fit for your church, and then determine how exactly it will affect the vision, strategy, and values of your church. Let's start with the first step: performing a SWOT analysis.

Step One: SWOT Analysis

The next time you or one of your team members comes up with a new idea, take some time before presenting it and run it through a SWOT (strengths, weaknesses, opportunities, and threats) analysis (see Figure 6.3). I'd encourage you to do this with each of the micro-shifts that we've covered. This is a great way to systematically think through and discern the broader impact that these ideas and micro-shifts will have on your church, while keeping the unique DNA of your church (your vision, strategy, and values) at the forefront. When you put every new idea through a SWOT analysis, you will discipline yourself and your team to design ministry pro-actively around the strengths and opportunities that this new idea presents for the church, rather than as a reaction to weaknesses and threats from inside or outside the church.

Using the template, start by articulating your new idea in a few sentences. The process of writing it out will begin the clarification process for you. A digital version of this and every other template/audit in this book can be found at danielim.com.

After writing out your new idea, start by filling out the first two quadrants, Strengths and Weaknesses, in the SWOT template. As you'll see here, these quadrants are both related to the idea you're evaluating. What are the strengths and weaknesses of the idea on a conceptual and practical level?

Let's resume our example from before to see how you would process the strengths and weaknesses of this curriculum. You could start by looking at the learning objectives that this evangelism curriculum provides, and then categorize them as strengths or weaknesses. Is this curriculum moving you toward being a maturity church or a missionary church, as we saw in chapter 5? You could also take a look through the content and questions of the curriculum to see whether or not it takes the adult education principles from chapter 3 into consideration. Alternatively, you could look to see whether the curriculum takes a holistic approach to development by offering study questions and application points that are intended to develop any one of the output goals from chapter 2. Basically, your goal in filling out the S and W quadrants is to address *the idea* in and of itself, rather than determine whether or not it'll fit into the context of your church—that's what the O and T quadrants are for.

Once you finish with the S and W quadrants, you can then move onto the next two, which address the opportunities and threats that come with the idea. More specifically, what are the helpful opportunities, and the harmful threats that this idea presents for your church?

Going back to the curriculum example, you could fill out the next two quadrants by thinking through your answers to questions like the following: In the opportunity quadrant, What will the church look like in a year from now if we introduce this successfully? How will this affect our presence in the city? In the threat quadrant, If we introduce this, and it doesn't take off as well as we thought it would, how would the church feel about evangelism a year from now? How would any future initiatives that we bring be perceived?

After putting your new idea through this SWOT analysis, complete the bottom of this template by evaluating whether or not the idea fits with the vision, strategy, and values of your church. Having worked through this template, your idea should feel a bit more concrete and fleshed out. In fact, this analysis might have even tweaked your idea so that it is better contextualized for your church. But unless the idea fits within the existing vision, strategy, and values of your church, I would recommend that you not move ahead with it. That is, unless you are willing to change the vision, strategy, and values of your church to fit this new idea. We'll get into this more in the next chapter.

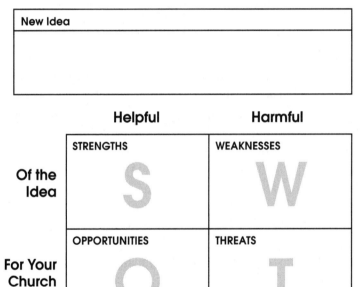

FIGURE 6.3: SWOT ANALYSIS TEMPLATE

Step Two: Conversation Checklist

If, after putting your new idea through the SWOT Analysis Template, you still feel strongly about the benefits that this will bring to your church, the next step is to determine who you need to talk to. The developing a Conversation Checklist will help you determine who this idea is going to affect and will prepare you for the conversations that need to take place in order for the new idea to stick (see Figure 6.4).

In the first two columns, be sure to list every single ministry area in your church and its point leader, as well as the decision makers or power custodians of the church. I've listed most of the common ones that are found in churches today, but feel free to edit this list so that it reflects all the ministry areas of your church. When introducing any change in ministry, it's important to consider how it will affect the influencers in your church, since they will play a crucial role in the success of the idea's implementation, so be sure to list them as well.

Next, in the third column, you will want to systematically think through whether or not your new idea will directly affect, or indirectly be related to any one of the ministry areas. If yes, you will want to describe the connection.

For example, continuing with our curriculum example from above, I would list this idea as having a direct relationship with groups and Sunday school, because that would be our primary delivery system to teach it. I would then mark this curriculum as having an indirect relationship with Sunday worship, since it would be good to preach the main principles from this curriculum, and also integrate it into a few sermon illustrations afterwards. For children and students, I would mark them both as having a direct relationship with the idea, since we could use a modified version of this curriculum in Sunday school for them. Since we are introducing this in groups, Sunday school, and the Sunday worship service, there would be no need to introduce this into the separate men's, women's, or singles ministry. However, I would be sure to mark down the elders as having an indirect relationship with the curriculum. This is because the enduring success of this idea would hinge on whether or not they get involved and live out the principles from this curriculum, even though I don't officially need their approval for any sort of curriculum choice.

CONVERSATION CHECK LIST

Ministry Area	Point Leader	Direct/Indirect Relationship	Time to Meet
Groups/Sunday School Christian Ed. Classes Men's Ministry Women's Ministry Singles Ministry Missions Young Adults Counseling Guest Services Operations Students Children Elders Deacons Worship			
Influencers			

FIGURE 6.4: CONVERSATION CHECKLIST

Step Three: Ministry Area Idea Audit

Next, for every ministry area and influencer that you either marked as having a direct or indirect relationship with the new idea, you need to schedule a time to have a conversation with its respective point leader. When together, the focus of the meeting would be to collaborate on the idea and get their thoughts by doing a SWOT analysis together (see Figure 6.3). Instead of sharing your SWOT analysis with them, do a new one together with each point person. Help them answer each quadrant by thinking through how the idea will affect their ministry area. The SWOT Analysis Template will guide your dialogue with them, while giving them the opportunity to process all the implications of this new idea for their ministry area.

When you are finished, take some time to summarize the conversation by transferring their respective answers to the SWOT columns on the Ministry Area Idea Audit (see Figure 6.5). This will give you a bird's-eye view as to the strengths and weaknesses that this idea presents, as well as the opportunities and threats that the idea poses for the entire church.

If you feel that moving ahead with this idea is best for your church, then finish this audit by writing out your next steps for today, next month, in three months, in six months, and a year from now.

MINISTRY AREA IDEA AUDIT

New Idea				
Ministry Area	Strengths	Weaknesses	Opportunities	Threats

Next Steps				
Today	Next Month	3 Months	6 Months	1 Year

FIGURE 6.5: MINISTRY AREA IDEA AUDIT

Conclusion

"It takes courage to be a change leader in the church. Opposition and resistance often come frequently and fiercely. But too much is at stake to do otherwise. . . . The choice is simple: change or die."[17] Rainer couldn't be more right in his statement here. The fact is, if there's anything constant in ministry and in life, it's change.

Any change you try to implement in your church has one of three fates. 1) It'll never get off the ground because it will be seen as a bacteria, virus, or foreign matter and subsequently be rejected. 2) The change will happen, but because it doesn't fit into your vision, strategy, and values, you will inevitably end up changing things again. 3) The change will move you closer to the vision, strategy, and values that God has called you to embrace because you started with discernment by using the three steps for introducing change.

These steps to discerning whether or not you want to begin the change process are important on a few levels. First of all, they are a practical way to evaluate new ideas that will cause change in the church. Second, they provide a process to evaluate the extent to which those new ideas—take the micro-shifts presented in this book as an example—will work in your church. Third, and most important, this approach ensures that you filter every new idea through the vision, strategy, and values of your church.

But there's one question that's begging to be asked. What are your church's vision, strategy, and values? Unless they capture the DNA of your church, in a manner unique from every other church in your area, you will not be able to successfully implement any lasting change. So it's to this that we now turn.

Reflection Questions

1. Think about a time when you were unable to successfully introduce change into your church. What would you do differently to ensure that the change effort isn't seen as foreign matter and subsequently rejected?

2. Take a new idea that you have, or that's been brought to you, and put it through the three-step process for introducing change.

CHAPTER 7

YOUR VISION, STRATEGY, AND VALUES

*"What do we have to do today to be ready
for an uncertain tomorrow?"*

—Peter Drucker

As a child, I remember flipping through the *Encyclopedia Britannica* set that my parents bought my sisters and I. To this day, I don't know how much they paid for it, nor how they justified spending so much, when we weren't wealthy by any means. I wonder if it was somehow symbolic of the sacrifice that they made to give up everything, leave what was normal and comfortable, and immigrate to a foreign land for the hope of a better future. In any case, they must have had *big* dreams for my sisters and I because they went all out—they bought the 1994 burgundy bonded leather limited anniversary set with gold edging all around it. It was truly a work of art.

Let's be honest. I was probably the one that convinced them to buy it. It was about that time that I was showing promise in my schooling. I was so good at math (and it's not *just* because I am Asian) that I could recite my multiplication tables up to twelve, back and forth in speed rounds. I even entered into a math competition with those older than me.

For my career and personal planning class, I had requested a college prospectus from Harvard, since that was my school of *choice*—as if it were even my choice to go there! Now, that might've been a pipedream for a junior or senior in high school, but I was in elementary school at the time. My life was planned out. I was going to skip a few grades, graduate at the top of my class, go to Harvard for my undergrad and medical school, and then finish out a fellowship at Johns Hopkins. And then, congratulations, I was going to be Dr. Daniel Im—the Neurosurgeon. Although I never became a medical doctor, I did become a "doctor of the soul," as my Hindu doctor friend once said to me.

As I reflect back on that time in my life—as a curious child with an insatiable love for learning—I remember times when I would just open up the encyclopedia and read. My favorite section was the human anatomy, since I wanted to be a doctor. In fact, I vividly remember looking through and being amazed by the layers of complexity that the human body presented.

This section was always several pages long. In fact, it always stuck out from the other pages in the encyclopedia, since each system in the human body was printed on its own plastic, transparent page. If you had one of these old-school encyclopedias in front of you, the first system you'd see would be the integumentary system—the body's outer covering. In other words, you'd see a naked human body with skin, hair, and nails. If you flipped that transparent page over to the next—I apologize for the graphic nature of this next phrase—it would almost be like you were peeling the skin off of a human. You'd be left with the muscular system. If you flipped that page over again, you would see the circulatory system. With every progressive page turn, you would uncover another system that makes up the human body. The nervous system, the lymphatic system, the skeletal system, and so on.

The systems in your church are designed to work together.

Just like there are different layers of systems in the human body, so it is with the church. The systems in your church are designed to work together, like they do in the human body, to help your church function as God intends it to. After all, "God has arranged each one of the parts in the body just as he wanted" (1 Cor. 12:18).

So what exactly are those systems for your church?

Your Guide on the Side

Over the next two chapters, I want to be your guide on the side to help integrate and implement one, a few, or all five of the micro-shifts from the first section. One of the best ways to root these shifts into the life, culture, and rhythms of your church is by weaving them into the way you develop disciples—this is your discipleship pathway.

"Discipleship pathway" is just a fancy phrase for the intentional route, steps, and paths in your church to develop missionary disciples for Kingdom impact. If your church does not have a discipleship pathway, then over the next two chapters, I want to help you uncover what's underneath the skin of your church, so that you can build one that's right for your context.

If your church already has a discipleship pathway, I want to challenge you to consider how the vision, strategy, and values of your church are getting you there. Are they integrated and working with one another? Or are they like the situation we read in 1 Corinthians 12, where each of the body parts are saying that they don't need each other? These next two chapters will offer you ideas on how to integrate any one of the five micro-shifts into the way that you disciple and lead your church.

In other words, if you're planting, replanting, or revitalizing your church, I'm going to help you build and develop a discipleship pathway from scratch. However, if the necessary systems are already set up in your church, but you aren't quite sure they are the right ones or if they're performing at full capacity, then my goal is to help you clarify and tweak them, so that your ministry is unleashed toward greater Kingdom impact.

Let's start by uncovering what the systems in your church are ultimately working toward—your vision. Then we'll turn over the transparent page and take a look at how every system in your church ultimately falls under your core system, which is your strategy. Finally, we'll turn one more transparent page and finish with your values, which are the very things that influence the way your core system/strategy runs. It's important that we start here so we can lay a solid foundation for your discipleship pathway, which is the topic of the next chapter.

Vision

Vision is about the preferred future. It's the ability to conceptualize a picture of a golden tomorrow that does not yet exist. It's about seeing both the difficulties and possibilities so clearly that you can actually visualize a different reality than the one you can see with your eyes. Simply put, vision is about painting the dreams that God has laid on your heart for all to see. In order to discover those God-given dreams, you need to start by considering "everything to be a loss in view of the surpassing value of knowing Christ Jesus my Lord" (Phil. 3:8) so that you can stop wondering "what kind of mission God has for *me*," and instead begin asking, "what kind of me God wants for *His* mission."[1]

For leaders, vision is having such a deep-seated conviction and relentless hope that tomorrow can be different than today, that you view your life, family, priorities, ambitions, gifts, talents, and time as a "living sacrifice, holy and pleasing to God" (Rom. 12:1). This is the vision that the missionary Jim Elliot had when traveling to share the gospel with the Huaorani people of Ecuador, an unreached tribe. He viewed his life with such commitment to the kingdom of God that he once said, "He is no fool who gives what he cannot keep to gain that which he cannot lose."[2]

> **Vision is about painting the dreams that God has laid on your heart for all to see.**

Vision can be so infectious that despite all good *worldly* reasoning, you are willing to live with the very people that killed your husband, so that you can reach them with the gospel, as Elisabeth Elliot did.[3] Vision is not safe. In fact, oftentimes, before vision can be fulfilled, there are periods of suffering, non-response, and apathy—both personally and for those you are leading. But great leaders are tenacious and know that while the days might be long, the years are short, so they can help others envision that golden tomorrow. Elisabeth Elliot puts it well, "Our vision is so limited we can hardly imagine a love that does not show itself in protection from suffering. The love of God is of a different nature altogether. It does not hate tragedy. It never denies reality. It stands in the very teeth of suffering."[4] Great and godly vision has the ability to provide everyone with the strength to endure what may come, in order to see that God-given vision come to life.

Martin Luther King Jr. had that sort of vision, and he was able to so powerfully articulate and inspire others toward that future dream that his speech still rings in the halls of our schools, down the streets, and in our society today.

I have a dream that one day this nation will rise up . . . I have a dream that one day on the red hills of Georgia sons of former slaves and the sons of former slave-owners will be able to sit down together at the table of brotherhood . . . I have a dream that my four little children will one day live in a nation where they will not be judged by the color of their skin but by the content of their character . . .[5]

Can you see it? Can you taste it? Are you ready to jump up out of your seat and move to action? Move to making that dream a reality? That's the power of vision.

Two Components of Vision

Instead of focusing on techniques to wordsmith statements or phrases, I want to help you uncover, discover, and identify *the stuff* of who you are—the core content for your vision, strategy, and values. So let's start with vision.

There are two components of a good vision. The first one is the Big Hairy Audacious Goal (BHAG) as Jim Collins likes to say, the Wildly Important Goal (WIG) as outlined in the *4 Disciplines of Execution*, or the *Big Holy* Audacious Goal as I once heard from a few Christian leaders. Whatever you call it, this is the five-, fifteen-, or thirty-year future you envision for your church.

The second component is a vivid description of what your church, community, city, and this world will look like when you achieve the goal.[6] In other words, it's your answer to the question, "Would anybody notice if your church disappeared tomorrow?" Would they? What would be missing? Who would miss you? What gaps would be created? Take a moment and write down your answer to that question.

_____

_____

_____

_____

_____

The Starting Point of Vision

When creating, or re-creating, your church's vision, the Great Commission (Matt. 28:18–20) and Great Commandment (Matt. 22:36–40) linked together should always be your singular *starting point*. I like how Eric Geiger and Kevin Peck put it:

> The Great Commission is Plan A; Jesus has no Plan B. Discipleship, developing believers who grow over a lifetime, is His method. The full extent of discipleship is the development of disciples who are able to lead and develop others, not merely people who gather together for worship once a week.[7]

Did you notice how I emphasized the phrase, *starting point*? To take the Great Commission and Commandment as is, and directly make it the vision of your church, wouldn't be taking your context into consideration. While a church that goes and makes disciples of all nations, while loving the Lord and their neighbors, is the golden tomorrow that we all need to work toward, it's not specific or contextualized enough to be a contagious vision today.

By no means am I saying that Scripture is not enough or that Jesus didn't get it right. But just imagine if every church's vision in your city was Matthew 28:18–20 and/or Matthew 22:36–40—the only difference being that every church used a different translation of the Scriptures? If that were the case, it would be easy to assume that all the churches were the same; but as you and I well know, every church is unique and distinct.

Since the Great Commission and Commandment, when put together, is God's Plan A, what if you used it as the *starting point* when creating, or re-creating your church's vision? You would then contextualize it to the specific *where* God is taking your church. Let me share a few examples of churches that are doing a great job with this approach:

- **Beulah Alliance Church** (Edmonton, AB, Canada): To reach 1 percent of greater Edmonton for Christ; engaging people to connect with God, grow through community, and serve our world.[8]
- **The Austin Stone Community Church** (Austin, TX): To build a great city, renewed and redeemed by a gospel movement, by being

a church for the city of Austin that labors to advance the gospel throughout the nations.[9]

- **Church of the Beloved** (Chicago, IL, Seattle, WA, and Washington, DC): Our vision is to see the gospel transform people into Spirit-filled disciples, who know they are the beloved of God because of Christ alone.[10]

- **Northwood Church** (Keller, TX): Transformed lives transforming the world.[11]

- **The Summit Church** (Durham, NC): To plant a thousand churches in our generation.[12]

- **Transformation Church** (Indian Land, SC): To be a multi-ethnic, multi-generational mission-shaped community that loves God completely (Upward), ourselves correctly (Inward), and our neighbors compassionately (Outward).[13]

- **Doxa Church** (Bellingham, WA): We hope to see gospel saturation in the Eastside and beyond so every man, woman, and child has a daily encounter with Jesus in word and deed.[14]

- **Redeemer Presbyterian Church** (New York, NY): As a church of Jesus Christ, Redeemer exists to help build a great city for all people through a movement of the gospel that brings personal conversion, community formation, social justice, and cultural renewal to New York City and, through it, to the world.[15]

Each of these churches has captured the unique *stuff* of who they are. They have done this through a vivid description of their future reality that contextualizes their understanding of, and ongoing response to, living out the Great Commission and Commandment. For example, although 1 percent is roughly ten thousand people in Edmonton, Keith Taylor at Beulah has chosen to use the 1 percent language because big numbers don't motivate Edmontonians. In fact, being a blue-collar city, big numbers are often interpreted as presumptuous or aggrandizing, whereas the 1 percent language has a uniquely humble, yet ambitious, goal that people can rally around.

While Northwood Church's vision statement is incredibly short, knowing Bob Roberts and his church, I couldn't think of another phrase that so distinctly and accurately describes who they are and what they're about. They start by helping individuals understand the Great Commandment by discovering their calling in Christ (transformed lives). This flows into equipping and empowering them to live out the Great Commission and transform the world through *Glocal* ministry (global + local).

Recently, while having coffee with David Choi, I was struck by the way that his church, Church of the Beloved, embarks on a twenty-one-day Daniel fast every year. They do this in order to saturate their lives and ministry in prayer and reliance on God. This corporate fast reminds them that they are first the beloved of God (Great Commandment), rather than what they do or who they know. It's out of this rootedness in Christ that they participate in Great Commission ministry; otherwise, their efforts would be fruitless.

Last, when Derwin Gray planted Transformation Church, he intentionally infused a multi-ethnic and multi-generational DNA in the who, what, and where of their church. As a result, they've been able to not only live as a tangible expression of that Revelation 7:9 vision, but also be a reconciling presence in their neighborhoods and their local prison system.

Vision Audit

While it's much easier to copy another church's vision than it is to come up with your own, don't cheat yourself or your church. Just take a look at your fingerprint. God has so uniquely designed humans that even identical twins have different fingerprints![16] So just like you will never meet another person who is *exactly* like you, you will never meet another church that is *exactly* like yours. This is why every church ought to have a unique vision that God is calling them to fulfill.

The best way to determine your church's vision is through the power of questions. I agree with Francis Bacon, "A prudent question is one-half of wisdom." The other half is taking the time to answer it. Peter Drucker says it similarly, "Answers are important; you need answers before you need action. But the most important thing is to ask . . . questions."[17]

Don't cheat yourself or your church.

As a result, divided into four categories, I've written several questions that will help you take the first steps in discovering the unique vision God has for your church—a vision that's rooted in God's Plan A, the Great Commission and Commandment. The questions on this Vision Audit (see

Figure 7.1) are intended to be conversation starters that will help you and your team simplify the complexity of all you do in your church into "a single organizing idea, a basic principle or concept that unifies and guides everything."[18] Jim Collins in *Good to Great and the Social Sectors* calls this the Hedgehog Concept, and my friend Will Mancini in *Church Unique* calls it the Kingdom Concept. Ultimately, your answer to these questions will help differentiate your church from every other church "in how you develop followers of Christ for God's ultimate honor."[19]

You can either answer the following questions in the space below, directly on figure 7, or on the digital version that can be downloaded at danielim.com.

1. Community History

Have there been any natural disasters, riots, battles, or wars in the last hundred years? What are the prime landmarks in your area and how do they shape the community? How was the area where your church is located developed (i.e., lack of housing, gentrification, industry development, etc.)? What are important moments in the history of your area? What reputation does the church have in your area? Have there been any significant pastoral scandals, church splits, or closures recently? Have there been any significant changes in your community over the last ten to twenty years? How has God moved in your community?

_____

_____

_____

_____

_____

2. Community Context

How diverse (ethnically, socioeconomically, and generationally) is your church's community? Who are the haves and have-nots? What are the strengths and weaknesses in the following systems: education, transportation, health care, social services, recreation, housing, and police services? How often do newcomers move into your area? What do people do for fun? What are the recurring community events in your area? What are the people in your community passionate about? What are their hopes and dreams? How many places of worship (any religion) are there in your community? What are the idols in your community? If your church disappeared tomorrow, what gaps would be left vacant in your community? How do you see God moving in your community?

_____

_____

_____

_____

_____

3. Church People

How diverse (ethnically, socioeconomically, generationally, and spiritual maturity) is your church? How many newcomers do you get on a regular basis? How did they find out about the church? Why do people generally transition from being a guest to a member? What motivates people to volunteer? Does your church have an ownership or renter culture? What triggers generosity in finances? Are people discipling and being discipled? What do people see as their primary vocation? Does your church see themselves as missionaries? What is your church passionate about? How do you see God moving in your church?

_____

_____

_____

_____

_____

4. Church Leadership

How do you lead? Do you have team members or hirelings? How similar/dissimilar are you from your leadership team? Who do you look up to? Who are your mentors? What books have influenced you most? What are you passionate about? What do you love to do in ministry? How has God uniquely talented you more than others? In what competencies do your leaders display a high-level of proficiency in? Do you see a pattern? What do you consider a *win* in ministry? How is God moving in your life and in your leadership?

_____

_____

_____

_____

VISION AUDIT

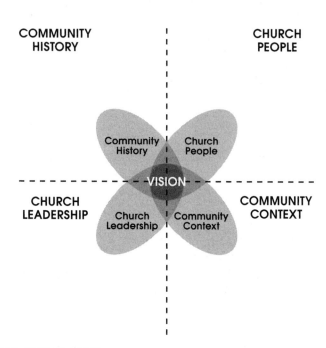

FIGURE 7.1: VISION AUDIT

The next time you gather with your leadership team, staff, decision makers, and/or key volunteers, discuss these four categories of questions and see what they have to say. You can even fill out the Vision Audit together as a team, but make sure you set aside a sufficient amount of time for your team to wrestle through these questions and have healthy dialogue. You don't want to rush this process.

In order to uncover the *stuff* of who you are and what makes your church distinct, you need to listen to diverse perspectives from the various leadership levels in your church. After all, you may think the vision is clear at your level, but those under and above you might see things differently. So ask questions, dialogue, debate, analyze, and synthesize your answers in order to start the journey of discovering the unique vision that God is calling your church to paint.

Strategy[20]

I hate shopping. In fact, when observing the Sabbath, I resist doing anything that doesn't nourish my soul, give me life, or point my family and myself toward Christ—this includes shopping. But I love going to IKEA and Costco. For some reason, I don't feel the same way about these stores as I do about nearly any other shopping center or mall.

Let's take IKEA as an example. What I love about IKEA, other than their cheap breakfasts, bargain priced prints, "as-is" section, and their low prices, is the fact that I don't have a sales person harassing me while I'm looking around! I also love the fact that I can take my furniture home with me, rather than waiting for it to be shipped. I don't mean to sound like an anti-social Scrooge, but shopping for me is about getting the best deal I can, and getting it right away when I need it, without feeling like I'm being convinced to buy something that I don't need.

If you were to compare IKEA to a traditional furniture retailer, you'd notice a big difference. The first strike that traditional furniture retailers have against them is that they are more expensive. Second, they have sales associates that walk around trying to up-sell me to get a greater commission. The next strike is related to the fact that I typically can't take the furniture home with me the day I buy it, since inventory is limited at the store, and they usually have to ship it from a factory. Must I go on?

Strategic Trade-Offs

When you break it down, IKEA and every furniture retailer share the same fifty-thousand-foot vision—*to make furniture great again.* After all, for any business, doesn't the bottom line *ultimately* drive everything? However, when looking at the way every organization nuances or contextualizes their vision, IKEA stands out. Their vision is "to create a better everyday life for the many people."[21] Compare that to nearly every other furniture store I looked up, which used generic words like "high-quality," "great-prices," "friendly people," and "brand name" to describe their vision.

In order to achieve the unique stuff of who they are, every furniture retailer has a strategy. They have things they need to do (strategy), that will get them to the place that they want to go (vision). IKEA is a prime example of an organization that has tailored their strategy to a contextualized vision.

Since they know who they are, what they do, and where they're going, the way they do business stands in stark contrast to every other furniture retailer as exemplified above. Harvard Business School professor, Michael E. Porter, attributes this to the strategic *trade-offs* IKEA has made.

"Strategy," as defined by Porter, "is the creation of a unique and valuable position involving a different set of activities."[22] Strategy is as much about what you choose *not* to do as it is about what you choose to do. When you choose not to do something, you are opening up the opportunity to do something else better—this is what Porter calls a strategic trade-off. For example, IKEA chooses not to have an army of sales associates on the floor, in order to keep their furniture prices low. The trade-off is that I need to grab my own furniture and supplies when I need them.

> **Strategy is as much about what you choose *not* to do as it is about what you choose to do.**

Compare that to a traditional furniture retailer who will deliver the furniture to my house, and sometimes assemble it for me. The trade-off, though, is that I will pay a higher price, since there are more people who need to get paid along the process.

Porter goes on to say that organizations that refuse to make trade-offs and "try to be all things to all customers, in contrast, risk confusion in the trenches as employees attempt to make day-to-day operating decisions without a clear framework."[23] Trying to do everything results in rampant ineffectiveness and mediocrity.

We see this in churches. How often do we start new ministries without shutting others down? Eventually, it gets to the point where there are so many programs to choose from that resources are spread thin, messaging is confusing, and newcomers have no idea what to do or where to go. So they end up doing what's easiest: going back out the door they came in!

Strategy is not about doing anything and everything to get to your vision. It's about first saying no to the good, extra, and peripheral, before you can say yes to the great, focused, and opportune. "Simply put, a trade-off means that more of one thing necessitates less of another."[24] So take a moment and answer this question. What do you need to stop doing, in order to fulfill the vision God has called your church to? You can't simply keep on saying yes to more ministry, opportunities, and programming—no matter how good they might seem—until you first say no to something else.

Strategy as Pathway and Pipeline

Once you have determined the vision of your church, the natural questions that follow are, "What needs to be done to get there?" and "How do we do it?" This is the stuff of strategy. After all, strategy without vision is ineffective. It's powerless. It's inept. It's unproductive.

Since the starting point for every church's vision should be the Great Commission and Commandment, it makes sense to view your discipleship pathway as the strategy that'll get you to the vision. After all, a discipleship pathway is the intentional route that you have set up in your church to develop and form missionary disciples for Kingdom impact. Now while your discipleship pathway will definitely move your church toward your vision, it's really only half of the equation. The other half is your leadership pipeline, which is the process and structure you have put in place to equip leaders. The two go hand in hand—together, they are the framework for your church's strategy. Let me explain.

Strategy without vision is ineffective, powerless, inept, and unproductive.

In order to move toward the vision that God has called your church to, your church needs a strategy. This strategy needs to both form *and* equip your church. It needs to shape their character *and* develop their competencies. In this strategy, your church needs to be transformed *and* learn how to be transforming agents. They need to be developed *and* deployed. And finally, in order to have any movement, your church needs to have fuel *and* an engine. Both are important and both are the heart of your church's strategy.

In other words, your discipleship pathway will form your church into missionary disciples, while your leadership pipeline will equip your church to live as missionary disciples. Your discipleship pathway will shape your people's character, while your leadership pipeline will develop their competencies. Your discipleship pathway will transform hearts, while your leadership pipeline will train transforming agents. Your discipleship pathway will develop, while your leadership pipeline will deploy. Using an analogy, if your church were a car that had to get to a particular endpoint, which would be the vision, the discipleship pathway would be the fuel, and the leadership pipeline would be the engine. Both are equally important and have to rely on each other if the car is going to experience any movement.

Strategy = Core System

In the previous chapter, we discovered why introducing change can be so difficult—it's because everything is connected. Your church is made up of a multitude of systems, like the human body, that *ought to be* working together toward one goal—your vision.

A system is simply defined as "a group of related parts that move or work together."[25] For example, the way you greet newcomers, get people into community, onboard new volunteers, plan out the weekend service, and baptize are all their own systems. To be an Intentional Church, as outlined in the Influences Matrix in chapter 1, your church cannot view all of its systems *independently*. This would be like your eye saying to your kidney, "I don't need you!" Or, the head saying to your heart, "You're useless. I can do this on my own." Rather, every system in your church needs to operate *interdependently* under these two overarching systems: your discipleship pathway and leadership pipeline. Together, these two make up the core system of your church, which is your strategy (see Figure 7.2).

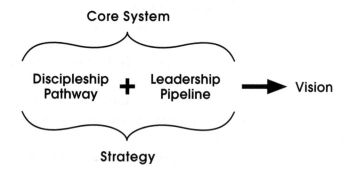

FIGURE 7.2: DISCIPLESHIP PATHWAY AND LEADERSHIP PIPELINE AS STRATEGY AND CORE SYSTEM

Interlude: What Is a Leadership Pipeline?

While chapter 8 will focus entirely on helping you develop half of your strategy or core system (your discipleship pathway), the topic of developing your leadership pipeline—the other half—is so extensive, that it is simply out of scope for this book. However, rather than leave you hanging, I would like to take a moment and offer you a brief summary of two resources to help you understand the concept.

The first one is by my friend Todd Adkins. He has written an invaluable eBook that summarizes the concept for the church; it's called *Developing Your Leadership Pipeline*. In it, he outlines the need for churches to develop their leadership pipeline by sharing research that was conducted with one thousand pastors. In this study, the majority affirmed "the importance of training and development for church leaders and volunteers," but less than "30 percent of churches actually [had] a plan in place to develop their staff members and only 1–in–4 churches [required] leaders and volunteers to attend the training that [was] offered."[26] This is why churches need to develop their leadership pipeline, which is the process and structure to equip leaders in your church!

The second resource is *Designed to Lead* by Eric Geiger and Kevin Peck, which I have already referenced in this book. In it, Geiger and Peck lay out the conviction, culture, and constructs required to establish a leadership pipeline for your church. They reference a two-year project that Todd and I, along with our team at LifeWay Leadership, conducted. We brought in eighteen leadership experts, some leading in the church and some outside of it, from different backgrounds, perspectives, and positions. Over a series of meetings, we wrestled through the idea of leadership development and if there were a core set of competencies that church leaders shared, regardless of position.

As outlined in the book, *The Leadership Code*, researchers discovered that 60 to 70 percent of leadership is transferable from position to position.[27] In other words, up to 70 percent of what makes a leader effective in one organization, role, or position, is transferable to another organization, role, or position.

Over the course of these meetings, we compiled a list of more than 280 leadership competencies. While studying and filtering through this data, we uncovered a pattern. We noticed that there were six broad categories that stood out as the common themes.

1. Discipleship: Theological and spiritual development
2. Vision: A preferred future
3. Strategy: Plan or method for the preferred future
4. Collaboration: Ability to work with others
5. People Development: Contributing to the growth of others
6. Stewardship: Overseeing resources within one's care

Regardless of the ministry area that a leader might serve, every leader needs to be equipped in these six shared core competencies. These competencies can act as a template, guide, and curriculum as you develop leaders through your leadership pipeline. We realize that every ministry area will also have their own specific competencies, like rhythm for a musician, or the ability to ask questions for small group leaders, but we discovered that they all share these six. If you want to learn more about these competencies, you can download a template that has a fuller explanation of each competency at danielim.com.

Strategy Audit

While you may not believe in long-range strategic planning, and while there are definitely many arguments advocating for its ineffectiveness in today's rapidly changing society; the fact is, we often overestimate what we can do in the short-term and underestimate what we can do in the long-term. So instead of long-term strategies, what if we had long-term *vision* with short-term *strategies*?

> **We often overestimate what we can do in the short-term and underestimate what we can do in the long-term.**

Vision acts as a compass for your church, and it will keep you on course and in line with true north, while strategies will move you toward achieving that vision and also keep you coordinated between ministry areas. Vision is better long-term, since the type of golden tomorrow that can be conceptualized ten years from now is much more dynamic than the golden tomorrow of a few hours from now. Strategy, on the other hand, is better short-term, so that you can be flexible enough to pivot when needed. After all, how often does the Lord open up opportunities that were never on your radar but fit perfectly into your church's vision?

The late management and leadership expert Peter Drucker put it well:

> Strategic planning does not deal with future decisions. It deals with the futurity of present decisions. Decisions exist only in the present. The question that faces the strategic decision-maker is not what his organization should do tomorrow. It is, "What do we have to do today to be ready for an uncertain tomorrow?" The question is not what will happen in the future. It is, "What futurity do we have to build into our present thinking and doing, what time spans do we have to consider, and how do we use this information to make a rational decision now?"[28]

Strategy comes down to making the right *trade-offs*. In order to introduce and implement the micro-shifts outlined in this book, as well as the discipleship pathway in the next chapter, you need to first make some trade-offs; you need to determine what your church is going to stop doing.

Stopping is the birthplace of strategy. Like putting the last nail in a coffin, Drucker goes on to say, "Getting rid of yesterday is the decision that most long-range plans in business never tackle—maybe the main reason for their futility."[29] Take a moment and complete the following Strategy Audit (see Figure 7.3), in order to figure out how your church needs to "get rid of yesterday" and start moving toward the vision that God is calling your church to. Do this in much the same manner that you did with the Vision Audit—with your leadership team, staff, decision makers and/or key volunteers.

Stopping is the birthplace of strategy.

You can either answer the following questions directly on this audit, or do it on a digital version that can be downloaded at danielim.com.

1. Stop

What should you stop doing? What are you doing that is ineffective, annoying, or isn't working? What are you doing that's not leading you to your church's vision? Are you doing anything that doesn't relate to your discipleship pathway or leadership pipeline? What can you stop doing today?

_____

_____

_____

_____

_____

2. Start

What should you start doing? Which of the five micro-shifts outlined in this book will move your church toward its vision? What have you not started yet that is related to your discipleship pathway or leadership pipeline? What small change can you make today to get going?

_____

_____

_____

_____

_____

3. Refine

What should you refine and continue doing? What are you doing well that's moving your church toward its vision? How can you refine it today to make it better? How can you better engage your church in your discipleship pathway and leadership pipeline?

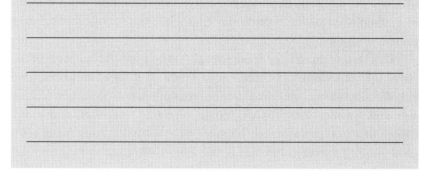

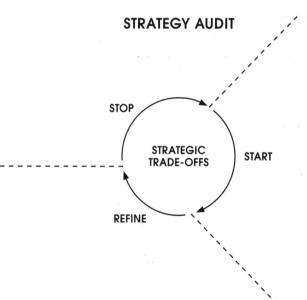

FIGURE 7.3: STRATEGY AUDIT

Performing an audit on your strategy is not a one-and-done matter. With the rapid rate of change in today's world, I would recommend that you do this audit on a regular basis with all your ministry areas. Doing this at least quarterly, if not monthly, will ensure that you are staying on course and moving toward the vision that God is calling your church to. If you are performing this audit on a frequent basis, monthly as an example, then limit the number of items that you will stop, start, and refine to no more than two per category. This way, you can develop actionable items that can be accomplished within a thirty-day time span, instead of overwhelming yourself with too much.

This section on strategy is not intended to be a full treatment on all the ways that your church can fulfill your vision. If it were, we would have talked about setting strategic ends, key result areas, critical success factors, lead and lag measures, SMART goals, reporting, meetings, and more. Rather, this section was merely intended to be a starting point. After all, a good strategy executed today is better than a perfect plan that *may* get executed next week. So be sure to perform this Strategy Audit on a regular basis using the micro-shifts outlined in this book, since they relate specifically to one-half of the broader strategy framework—your discipleship pathway. If you would like to go deeper on strategy and vision, pick up a copy of my friend Will Mancini's book, *God Dreams: 12 Vision Templates for Finding and Focusing Your Church's Future.*

> **A good strategy executed today is better than a perfect plan that *may* get executed next week.**

Values

Before putting my children to bed, we usually spend a few minutes playing LEGO. It always surprises me to see the different ways that my children approach the same task. My first born, Victoria, loves to follow instructions and build structures as she sees on pictures. My middle child, Adelyn, just puts pieces together until she eventually ends up with something creative. And my son, Makarios, loves anything with wheels—so that he can roll over everything his sisters make. Though they are all starting with the same blocks, the end result is different for each of them because of their unique personalities.

And so it is with the church! Though every church shares the same starting point for their vision—the Great Commandment and Commission—the way they approach it is unique. This is because every church has a unique personality—a distinct set of values. As a result, it is precisely the unique values of a church that drive which strategic trade-offs they will make to move toward their vision. This is because the church's values act as the guardrails, riverbanks, and boundaries for their strategy (see Figure 7.4). In other words, values influence the way the core system of your church runs.

For example, a church that has the value, "Kingdom multiplication," is going to make the strategic trade-offs to set aside funds for future church planters, send out members to be a part of church-planting teams, and train staff to be future church planters or campus pastors. In contrast, a church that has "the marginalized matter" as one of their values, will make a different set of strategic trade-offs by allocating their funds for community engagement, training up their members to serve the homeless, and possibly having a strategic partnership with their local food bank.

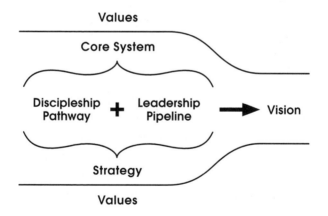

FIGURE 7.4: VALUES AS GUARDRAILS AROUND STRATEGY

Do you see how important it is to identify your church's values? They influence behavior and strategic decision-making. They influence the way your systems operate. They influence the strategic decisions and direction you need to make to get to your vision. They are essentially the personality of your church. To put it another way, your values are the litmus test that determines who will feel comfortable in your church and thrive as a valuable member and leader in it. Values are not what you do; they are what characterize everything you do.[30]

Four Types of Values

Now you might be thinking, just how unique can one church's values be? After all, if the framework for every church's strategy is their discipleship pathway and leadership pipeline, which in turn leads to a contextualized version of the Great Commandment and Commission for their vision, can the values from one church to the next really be that different? The answer is a resounding yes! The problem, though, is that most churches have only uncovered their aspirational or permission-to-play values, rather than their core ones—the real ones that drive strategic decision-making or trade-offs. In *The Advantage*, Patrick Lencioni defines four different types of values: core, aspirational, permission-to-play, and accidental. Let's define and look at examples for each, in order to lay the ground for you to discover or tweak yours.

Values are not what you do; they are what characterize everything you do.

1. CORE VALUES

Core values should not be confused with strategies, cultural norms, or operating practices. "Core values lie at the heart of the organization's identity, do not change over time, and must already exist. In other words, they cannot be contrived."[31] Even if people left your church because of one of your core values, would you still keep it? If the answer is yes, then you can be sure it's a core value. After surveying the values of churches that I know, here is a list of some that I know to be core:

- Life is better together
- We bless those we live, work, and play with
- Come as you are
- Helping people find their way back to God
- Where it's okay not to be okay

2. ASPIRATIONAL VALUES

In contrast to core values, aspirational values are those values that your church thinks they need to have in order to succeed—these are often borrowed from "successful" churches down the road or across the country. These values are aspirational, since your church doesn't yet embody them, but is "aspiring to adopt" them into the church.[32] The tricky thing is that these values can be aspirational to some, but core to others:

- We're not afraid to take risks
- We don't maintain, we multiply
- Lost people matter to God and they matter to us
- God is at work to heal and renew the world
- We want to be winsome people

3. PERMISSION-TO-PLAY VALUES

These values are the bare minimum that you need to function as a biblical, gospel-believing, and gospel-proclaiming church. "Although they are extremely important, permission-to-play values don't serve to clearly define or differentiate an organization from others."[33] As a result, I recommend that these values be articulated in your statement of faith, instead. Here are a few I often encounter:

- The Bible is our sole authority
- Jesus is the center
- Gospel centered
- Serve others
- Build community

4. ACCIDENTAL VALUES

Lastly, accidental values are exactly that—values that have accidently been developed in your church. As a result, they don't often serve the church in a positive manner.[34] If a church is intentional enough to articulate their values in print or on their website, they probably won't include their accidental values. A church's accidental values are the things that subtly influence behavior and strategy, often against the leadership team's wishes. Here are a few examples that churches are prone to:

- Debbie Downer
- Devil's advocate
- Homogeneous
- Timekeeper
- Status quo

The relationship between these four types of values can be easily understood with this diagram of an arrow (see Figure 7.5). Aspirational values are at the tip of the arrow, since they are the ones that your church does not yet have, but are striving toward. Core values are right in the center of the arrow, since they are central to the personality of your church. Permission-to-play values are your entry point into the arrow, since they get you in the game. Accidental values are still a part of the picture, but they are not in the arrow, since they are unintentional and unwanted.

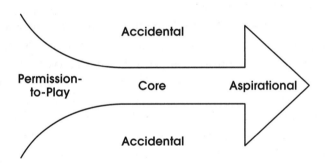

FIGURE 7.5: FOUR TYPES OF VALUES

Values Audit

Your church has a unique set of values because you and every one of your leaders—no matter how much you have in common—are distinct in personality, education, upbringing, and life experiences. As a result, the way you and your leaders view the mission of the church and approach ministry give your church its unique flavor. It's kind of like chili. Although the basic composition of chili is beans, tomatoes, chili powder, and some type of meat (unless you're vegetarian), there are thousands of unique ways to make it.

Isn't that why chili cook-offs are a thing? While one person might add paprika, onions, and cumin, another will add peppers, corn, and three types of beans. The variations seem endless. In fact, you might have two recipes with the exact same ingredients, but the chili will still taste different depending on the amount of time it has simmered and the way each ingredient was cooked.

In the same way, you might have two churches in the same neighborhood with the same vision and strategy, but they will feel completely different because of the unique values of each church.

So why does your church taste the way it does? What was the recipe that made the unique flavor of your church? If you're like most church leaders, you got to where you are through a recipe of prayer, best practices, opportunities, and mistakes that God, in his providence, so graciously redeemed.

This audit will help you uncover what your church's vision is, so you can discover what it will be.

The purpose of this Values Audit is to reverse engineer your existing values and uncover the unique flavor of your church. In fact, I'd recommend that you ask the leaders and influencers in your church to fill out the audit as well. Then you can compare answers and uncover the values that already exist, so that you know which values you need to adopt, abandon, and keep in order to better lead your church toward the vision that God has laid on your heart. This audit will help you uncover what is, so you can discover what will be.

Let's play a game to complete this Values Audit (see Figure 7.6). Write down the very first feeling, thought, image, or idea that comes to mind beside each word. Don't overthink it and keep your answers to one or two words. When you're finished, ask a few others to fill out this audit as well. You can do this for them by simply writing down their answers beside yours. If possible, try to find a senior level leader at your church, a congregant, and a highly invested volunteer for diverse perspectives.

VALUES AUDIT				
	Your Response	_____'s Response	_____'s Response	_____'s Response
Favorite Book				
Favorite Movie				
Worst Music				
Community				
Children				
Newcomers				
Evangelism				
Worship				
Diversity				
Preaching				
Students				
Singles				
Discipleship				
Missions				
Mercy				
Leadership				
Missionary				
Volunteers				
Fellowship				
Innovation				
Multiplication				
Bible				
Groups				
Attendance				
Team				
Prayer				

Culture				
Giving				
Collaboration				
Development				

FIGURE 7.6: VALUES AUDIT

Just like you did with the Vision and Strategy Audit, I want to encourage you to do this with your leadership team, staff, decision makers, and/or key volunteers. Discuss the similarities and differences. Where do you have widespread agreement? These are likely the raw ingredients that make up your church's values. Where are the answers vastly different? You'll likely need to clarify your church's strategy in those areas. This Values Audit is not intended to help you wordsmith the set of values for your church. Rather, it is intended to bring you one step closer to that ever-important step by clarifying what is, so that you can discover what will be.

Seeing the Micro-Shifts as Values

While permission-to-play values should be on your statement of faith and accidental values need to be mitigated against, the values for your church must be a mix of core and aspirational ones. A mix of who you are today and what you want to become. While the Values Audit should have helped you identify the raw ingredients of a few of your current core values, don't forget to include one or two aspirational ones. Based on the five micro-shifts in this book, which ones are you most excited to adopt and integrate into the life of your church? These can form the basis for your aspirational values.

When you articulate the micro-shifts as values, you are setting yourself up for success, since you're embedding them into the systems of your church—across all ministry areas, into your discipleship pathway, and up and down your leadership pipeline. Instead of the micro-shift being seen as a strategic add-on or trade-off, it becomes *the* value that dictates strategy. It becomes both the why and the how for your strategy.

Here's a chart to spark ideas and different creative ways to articulate these five micro-shifts as values (see Figure 7.7). Feel free to adopt, contextualize, or alter any of the following values for your church.

MICRO-SHIFTS AS VALUES		
Micro-Shift	**Value**	**Alternate Wording**
From Destination to Direction	Directional	• Knowing and being known • Belong before you believe • Come as you are • Helping people find their way back to God • Where it's okay to not be okay
From Output to Input	Measurable/ Intentional	• Honoring Christ in all things • Doing more with less • Take it personally • Prioritizing what matters • We want to be winsome people
From Sage to Guide	Experiential	• The trained and equipped • Changed lives • Growing people change • Contributors, not consumers • A way to grow
From Form to Function	Relational	• Life is better together • You can't do life alone • Honoring one another • Peel the onion • Family
From Maturity to Missionary	Missional	• Blessed to be a blessing • Sending out our own • Reproducing the mission in others • Bless those we live, work, and play with • A chance to make a difference

FIGURE 7.7: MICRO-SHIFTS AS VALUES

Conclusion

Recently, while shopping at Costco—and not having anyone harass me to buy something I didn't need—I noticed a new book in the children's section. It was a 3D version of the various systems in the human body! No, it wasn't a pop-up book; it was rather a 1.5-inch thick book that had a miniature plastic human body right in the middle of it. Every page highlighted a different system. For example, if you were looking at the muscular system, when you turned the page, all of the muscles would go with it, and you'd see the circulatory system.[35]

Though this illustration may seem simple, or comical at best, the fact is, there was a time where we didn't know how the various systems in the human body worked. As a result, to treat headaches, "doctors" drilled holes in people's skulls. And to treat fevers, the standard practice was to cut the patient and let them bleed. The same has been true for many churches. To make disciples, many believed that all you had to do was preach the Word and pray because everything else would just take care of itself.

There was only one way for doctors and scientists to leave ignorance behind and begin learning how the various systems in the human body interacted—through autopsies of dead rodents, animals, and humans. The same was true for churches. Fortunately, we don't have to wait until your church dies to figure out why things are the way they are.

Think of the audits in this chapter as surgery. They hurt, they're invasive, they're uncomfortable, there's recovery time, and life isn't always the same afterwards; but it's better than death. Rather than waiting until an extensive and comprehensive post-mortem autopsy to figure out why things didn't work the way they should have, these audits are like a series of day surgeries on your church. With each surgery, you are seeing how things are working, leaving what's healthy, and fixing what's broken. Though the audits may be temporarily inconvenient, the benefits far outweigh the cost. So be sure to complete the audits in this chapter before moving onto the next and final chapter.

Reflection Questions

Fast-forward six months from now. Let's say you implemented the newly created, or refined, vision, strategy, and values in your church, and things went south.

1. What would this disaster look like?

2. What went wrong?

3. What would you have done differently to prevent this from failing?

Now, imagine that six months from now your church embraces its unique, God-given vision and embraces all of your currently aspirational values.

1. What strategic trade-offs did you have to make to get there?

2. Who in your church did you involve to accomplish these goals?

3. How do individual church members, your church as a whole, and your community look different as a result?

CHAPTER 8

YOUR DISCIPLESHIP PATHWAY

"Preserve the core and stimulate progress."
—Jim Collins and Jerry Porras

I hate running. It feels pointless. If you want to get from point A to point B, then drive. If you want to burn some calories, then play a sport or lift weights. If you want to get out and enjoy the fresh air, then hike. Running on hard concrete is bad for you anyway. Doesn't it wear down your joints? Treadmills are even worse. It's like you're a hamster. No matter how hard you run, you never get anywhere. I think there's a proverb for that, isn't there? He that runneth in circles is like a dog that returns to its vomit.

Despite my hatred for running, I signed up for a 10K race. Well, my wife, Christina—who actually also hates running—signed us both up for a 10K. And since misery loves company, we decided to create a discipleship program around it and enlist others in our church to join us.

After nine weeks of training together on a weekly basis, with daily devotionals and exercises in between our large group gatherings, it was finally race day. It was a brisk autumn morning in Montreal, Quebec. The leaves had already begun to change colors, so the landscape was full of rich shades of red, brown, purple, and orange, while the sun was just beginning to emerge over the horizon. Now, despite my ongoing hatred for running, I felt my heart begin to shift—but it was only a *micro-shift*.

The vision for this discipleship program was to tangibly teach the participants how to own their faith, spiritually feed themselves, and develop the disciplines needed to continually grow in Christ, no matter how hard running/life gets. It was based on Philippians 3:13–14—I love how *The Message* paraphrase puts it: "By no means do I count myself an expert in all of this, but I've got my eye on the goal, where God is beckoning us onward—to Jesus. I'm off and running, and I'm not turning back."

So every week we would meet together to stretch, run, and learn. Every aspect of this discipleship program linked what we were doing physically with a spiritual principle. For example, while stretching, we would teach on the importance of prayer. While running, we would memorize Scripture. And while sharing tips on nutrition, we would teach about daily spiritual disciplines.

During the week, the participants would process the theme of the week by digging into the Scriptures through a daily devotional that Christina and I developed. These devotionals were designed, with a scope and sequence, to equip individuals with the tools needed to own their faith. For example, we covered topics like the spiritual disciplines, character, identity in Christ, serving in the body of Christ, spiritual warfare, perseverance, critical thinking, and more.

Then some time during the week, each participant was responsible for a self-run. In this self-run, they had to practice what they learned in the group run, while meditating on and memorizing one of the passages they studied during their devotionals. Afterwards, there would be a time to journal.

I know the program seems intense, but our goal was to prepare the participants, not only for the upcoming race, but for an enduring faith in Christ throughout the rest of their lives. Ultimately, we wanted to teach them a faith that was more about direction, than a destination, as it's written in Hebrews 12:1–2:

> Therefore, since we also have such a large cloud of witnesses surrounding us, let us lay aside every hindrance and the sin that so easily ensnares us. Let us run with endurance the race that lies before us, keeping our eyes on Jesus, the source and perfecter of our faith. For the joy that lay before him, he endured the cross, despising the shame, and sat down at the right hand of the throne of God.

Your Discipleship Pathway as a System of Systems

As outlined in the previous chapter, your discipleship pathway is one half of your strategy or core system—the other half being your leadership pipeline, which we briefly covered last chapter. So as it relates to your discipleship pathway, in order to move toward the vision that God is calling your church to, you need to do one of two things: Either organize all the discipleship-related systems in your church into one broader system—your discipleship pathway—or create one from scratch. This chapter will serve as your guide on the side to help you do either or.

Ultimately, your discipleship pathway is a system of systems that will help you begin accomplishing the vision of your church. Peter Senge, a systems scientist at MIT, puts it well: "Vision without systems thinking ends up painting lovely pictures of the future with no deep understanding of the forces that must be mastered to move from here to there."[1] While Senge might have not had the church in mind when writing this, the "forces" that he refers to can actually be understood as the steps or systems that make up your discipleship pathway.

As we'll unpack in this chapter, there are three systems within a discipleship pathway that will move your church from here to there (see Figure 8.1). When working together, these three systems, which can be categorized as ongoing steps, first steps, and next steps, will help you accomplish the vision God has called you to. Let's start by unpacking the most important system in your discipleship pathway: the ongoing steps.

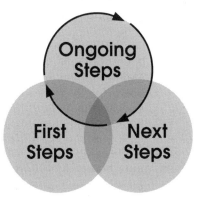

FIGURE 8.1: DISCIPLESHIP PATHWAY AS A SYSTEM OF SYSTEMS

Ongoing Steps

In order to start and be able to finish the 10K, there were things I had to do regularly—ongoing steps I had to take—to prepare my body, so that I would not call a cab or Uber mid-way. For example, I had to watch my calorie intake, stretch, cross-train, complete a self-run, and then run with the group. Not only did the weekly group run keep me accountable to stay disciplined on a daily basis, it was also the place where we would be challenged to run further and faster than we did the week before. After a few weeks, it was apparent who the self-feeders and disciplined ones were, since those who solely relied on the group run for their training would often drop out or only nominally participate.

Here's the thing. Unless every runner regularly practiced the series of ongoing steps that were proven, tested, and sure to prepare him or her for the race, it would not work. No matter how attractive, exciting, or gimmicky the weekly run was, that gathering in and of itself wouldn't mature and condition the runner to be able to complete the race. In other words, personal ownership of the ongoing steps was key.

Personal ownership of the ongoing steps is key.

And let's be clear: The goal for this discipleship program was to not just complete one race and then go back to life as usual. The vision was to train and disciple the participants to be self-feeders—both physically and spiritually—so that they would be equipped to run this race of faith throughout life.

Running the Race of Faith

No wonder running was often used as an illustration for the spiritual life throughout the Scriptures (Act 20:24; 1 Cor. 9:24–27; Gal. 2:2; 5:7; Phil. 2:16; 3:13–14; 1 Tim. 6:11–12; Heb. 12:1–2). The parallels are uncanny. Here are three similarities between running physically and spiritually.

First of all, in order to run this race of faith with perseverance, you need to equip individuals in your church to run without baggage. Just like a runner would never race with a heavy backpack on, it would be wise to disciple others how to regularly lay down their baggage and burdens by confessing their sins (Heb. 12:1).

Second, if you disciple others on ways to keep their eyes forward and on Christ, in the midst of all kinds of distractions, they will run faster and be less likely to be derailed (Heb. 12:2). After all, anytime you look behind or to the side, you lose speed and might trip or get off course (Phil. 3:13). Lastly, running—both physically and spiritually—requires self-discipline and self-feeding (1 Cor. 9:24–27). In other words, just like a runner would never *solely* rely on group runs for his development—as helpful, encouraging, and necessary as they are—individuals in your church cannot *solely* rely on the weekend worship services for their discipleship—as helpful, encouraging, and necessary as they are to their spiritual growth.

Runners need to monitor their calorie intake, stretch, cross-train, and go on multiple self-runs, so that they are ready for the group runs, and any race that they may enter. In the same way, a growing disciple needs to own his development and learn how to spiritually feed himself, rather than solely relying on the preacher to feed him and give him what he needs for that week.

Ownership Matters

After surveying and studying the discipleship pathways of thriving churches across North America for my master's thesis, I discovered that ownership matters. Let me explain.

Most discipleship pathways are typically organized around what the church can do for individuals. This is because churches typically see their discipleship pathway as the ways disciples are formed through the ministries of their church: weekend services, classes, events, groups, and serve opportunities. And while I do not disagree that the church needs to offer environments and opportunities for individuals to get plugged in and grow, I've come to discover that the goal for a discipleship pathway is never to get someone through it; the goal is to get individuals to own it.

> **The goal for a discipleship pathway is never to get someone through it; the goal is to get individuals to own it.**

As long as the church owns the pathway, the only possible response for an individual is consumption, which is really the same thing as that *faux-pas* word in discipleship circles—consumerism. This is like the difference between renting and owning, or being an hourly worker versus a shareholder. When something is ours, a shift happens inside of us, and we tend to approach it in a fundamentally different way.

Hotels understand this, and this is why they spend millions of dollars giving away free gifts to incentivize people to buy a timeshare, or as they now like to call it, "vacation ownership." They know that customer loyalty can only run so deep with a points program, but when a customer invests and buys a piece of a vacation property, their loyalty is guaranteed.

WestJet, one of the two major Canadian airlines, understands this as well. They pride themselves and base their success on the fact that they don't have employees—they have owners. This is not a gimmick or a leadership strategy. Every employee can actually purchase shares of the company, and when they do, WestJet will match those share purchases dollar for dollar. In addition, twice a year, employees get to benefit from the company's success through profit sharing![2] No wonder flying WestJet feels distinctly different than most other airlines I've been on. Ownership works.

While the first and next steps of your discipleship pathway are environments where disciples can be formed through the ministries of your church, they are only ever intended to be temporary experiences. First steps are designed to identify and welcome individuals into the life of your church, while next steps are focused on stretching, enhancing, and refreshing an individual's spiritual life. However, both are short-term and intended to bring individuals back into the center of the pathway—the ongoing steps—where they will learn how to self-feed and become a self-disciplined runner in this race of faith. It's ultimately in the ongoing steps that individuals in your church will learn how to own their faith and this discipleship pathway.

The Ongoing Steps Never End

Discipleship is not accomplished by getting through a set of classes and receiving a certificate. Nor is it achieved by sharing your testimony, getting baptized, and becoming an usher. There's never a point—at least on this side of eternity—where you will "arrive" and be finished. This is because disciples are not widgets—they cannot be mass-produced on an assembly line. Instead, disciples are formed *while moving* in the direction toward

Christ. As outlined in the first micro-shift, from destination to direction, discipleship is "a long obedience in the same direction."[3]

I love how the theologian J. I. Packer puts it. In a systematic theology class that I had with him in seminary, I remember him relating discipleship and the journey of faith to an ever-spiraling tower. The first time around the tower, you touch on the basics of Christology, Pneumatology, Ecclesiology, Bibliology, Hamartiology, Soteriology, Eschatology, and all the other "-ologies." But then, when you go around the tower the second time, the broader topics don't change—you still go over the same "-ologies." The only difference is that you are now higher up the tower and everything you have learned is now feeding into one another. So while the broader topics are the same, you are not learning the same things but are actually going deeper into each subject. This happens again as you go around the tower the third time, and the fourth, and the fifth, and on and on.

The journey of the Christian life is like moving up an ever-spiraling tower. Even when you think you've arrived and have come to the top of the stairs, you see a door. Upon opening that door, what do you see? Another set of stairs to continue the journey. And just so we're clear, the journey to the top is not a journey to salvation, since we are saved by grace through faith (Eph. 2:8). This journey consists of glorifying God (Ps. 63:3; Rom. 16:27; Rev. 4:11), growing in deeper intimacy with him (Matt. 22:37; Ps. 73:28; James 4:8), knowing him and being known (John 8:32; Gal. 4:9; Eph. 3:19; 1 Cor. 8:3), walking in the good works that God has prepared for us (Eph. 2:10), and helping others discover Christ (Matt. 28:18–20), just to name a few.

The Input Goals as Your Ongoing Steps

In chapter 2, we discovered that a disciple is someone who is moving toward Christ. The question that followed then was how to disciple people toward Christ and know whether or not they're progressing and moving up that ever-spiraling tower. Based on the Transformational Discipleship research, we discovered that there were eight output goals, or signs of maturity, for a disciple: Bible engagement, obeying God and denying self, serving God and others, sharing Christ, exercising faith, seeking God, building relationships, and being unashamed (transparency).

However, as we discovered in that chapter, simply knowing what a mature disciple looks like (the eight output goals) is not the same thing as moving people toward Christ. Making the micro-shift from output to input goals is not only the first step to figuring out how to actually move people toward Christ and disciple them; it's actually the way you shift ownership from the church to the individual.

By integrating the input goals centrally into your discipleship pathway as the ongoing steps, you would be discipling everyone to be self-feeders. You would be making the very actions that we know from research result in maturity the ongoing steps for everyone in your church. As a result, these input goals would become the ongoing rhythms, disciplines, habits, or steps for every individual in your church, regardless of their maturity level in Christ. They are essentially synonymous to the proven and tested ongoing steps that runners—both experienced and novice—need to be disciplined to do, in order to stay fit and compete. Let's revisit the key input goals from chapter 2. Consider, as you read, how they can be translated into the ongoing steps for your discipleship pathway

1. Reading the Bible

How can you normalize Bible reading in your church? Where the Sunday sermon or small group gatherings are not the only times the Bible is opened? According to our research, the input goal of reading the Bible on a regular basis was one of the greatest predictors to maturity across all the output goals. In other words, the more frequently an individual reads the Bible, the higher he or she will score in the eight output goals. To put it another way, reading your Bible positively affects your ability to consistently obey God and deny self, serve God and others, share Christ, exercise your faith, seek God, build relationships, and be unashamed about your faith!

How can you normalize Bible reading in your church?

"You are what you eat." While this phrase finds its origins in early nineteenth-century France by a gastronomist named Jean Anthelme Brillat-Savarin, it's equally true for our spiritual lives. As long as individuals in your church are living on a diet of pre-chewed roast beef from the preacher, you will reap what you sow.

I think this is what the apostle Paul was referring to when he said, "Brothers and sisters, I was not able to speak to you as spiritual people but as people of the flesh, as babies in Christ. I gave you milk to drink, not solid food, since you were not yet ready for it. In fact, you are still not ready, because you are still worldly" (1 Cor. 3:1–3).

What was surprising about the research is that it does not even refer to studying the Bible or memorizing it, but merely reading it! While those two were definitely important factors that led to maturity, the input goal that we're talking about here is simply opening up the Scriptures and personally reading them. Anyone can do that. And today, with the plethora of Bible translations and the numerous apps available, we have more access and opportunity than any generation before us to read the Scriptures.

2. WORSHIP SERVICES

Your worship service needs to be viewed as an ongoing step in your discipleship pathway. This is not a separate matter. In fact, for many in your church, Sunday might be the only time they pray, look at the Scriptures, and consider life beyond the here and now. For others, the worship service is the place where they are reminded that they are not what they do, who they know, what they have, or what they've done. It's the place where they are reminded afresh that they are a beloved child of God and are a part of a greater family, called to a different world, and a higher purpose. This is one of the places where they are encouraged to—as it is important for running the race of faith—throw off their baggage and keep their eyes on Christ (Heb. 12:1–2).

According to our research, the more frequently an individual attended a worship service, the higher they scored in the eight output goals. In other words, your maturity level as a disciple is greatly influenced by the frequency that you attend worship services.

Your worship service is an ongoing step because it is the vehicle in which individuals will develop a heart of worship and grow in their affection and love for God. It's like the relationship between weekly group runs and self-runs. Both are important and actually work in a cyclical fashion.

For example, the weekly group run is where you increase your distance, are encouraged to persevere, and are reminded why you're doing this in the first place. Your self-run is then where you put to practice what you learned in the weekly group run, grow in endurance, and see the changes in your life. By keeping up with the self-runs, you are enabled to continually be stretched in the group run, which then spills over into your self-runs, and on and on.

The opposite is true as well. When you miss a weekly group run, it becomes easy to skip out on the self-runs, which then actually lowers your likelihood to go to the next group run. It's cyclical and it's similar to the relationship between weekly worship services and your personal life of worship.

The goal for your worship service is never greater attendance; it's to cultivate a heart of worship and love for God in people's lives. The goal is not the worship service; it's a life of worship. When individuals participate in a worship service, many things can happen. They can be reminded of who they are in Christ, they can be stretched in their faith, they can grow in their love for God, they can be encouraged to persevere through the trials of life, and they can be equipped for mission, among many other things. Then, it's in the everyday stuff of life where they can put to practice what they learned from the worship service and what they are learning through their daily moments with God in the Scriptures. As they continue to be faithful, they will begin noticing fruit in their lives, which will propel them to continue to worship together with others, which then leads them to continue to put it to practice and spend time with God. Do you see the similarities with running?

The goal for your worship service is never greater attendance; it's to cultivate a heart of worship and love for God in people's lives.

The opposite is just as true. When an individual misses a worship service at their church, it's likely that they'll skip out on their daily moments with God—if they were even happening in the first place—which then actually lowers their likelihood to go to another worship service, and on and on. It's cyclical.

3. SMALL CLASSES OR GROUPS

There is no doubt that community is an important component of discipleship. I mean, just take a look at all the "one anothers" in the New

Testament with the early church. So while an argument to include this input goal as one of the ongoing steps is not quite needed, it is important to remember that the biblical function of community is more important than any particular form or model. As we saw in the fourth micro-shift, we must hold our forms loosely and our functions firmly.

In the research, we discovered that the more often an individual attended a small community, like a small group, Bible study, Sunday school, or Adult Bible Fellowship, the higher they scored in the eight output goals. This makes sense because it's in a small community where you can do life together with others, disciple one another toward Christ, and make disciples who make disciples who make disciples. No wonder individuals who were regularly a part of a small community significantly grew in their ability to obey God and deny self, serve God and others, share Christ, exercise faith, seek God, and be unashamed about their faith. Discipleship in close proximity leads to maturity in Christ.

If you remember back to chapter 4, we outlined four different spaces that individuals connect in. It's important to note that the TDA research project did not differentiate between the social and personal spaces. In other words, you were either answering questions about the worship service (the public space), questions about small classes or groups (the social *and* personal space), or questions about one-on-one mentoring or discipling relationships (the intimate space). This is why Adult Bible Fellowships, which are typically the social space like mid-size communities, were an explicit example alongside small groups.

4. Serving God and Others

Upon further research, we discovered an additional factor that had the same sort of effect as the previous three input goals. We discovered that the more normative serving God and others was for an individual, the higher they scored in the other output goals. The reason I did not list this in chapter 2 was because "serving God and others" is technically an output goal that positively affected all other output goals. Rather than getting mired down in technicalities, let's get to the heart of the matter.

Serving God and others impacts spiritual growth. It influences an individual's ability to consistently obey God and deny self, share Christ, exercise faith, seek God, build relationships, and be unashamed about one's faith.

In other words, serving God and others develops *missionary disciples,* as outlined in the fifth micro-shift, from maturity to missionary.

Providing opportunities for individuals to serve God and others is not just a way to "pull off" the weekend service, nor is it about serving at the soup kitchen so we can feel better about ourselves. Serving God and others is about living the life that Christ came to live (Matt. 20:28). This is about helping individuals in your church understand that all of their life is about mission. This starts by helping them understand that their primary vocation is to go and make disciples of all nations, *while* secondarily doing whatever they need to do to get food on the table. It's not the reverse, as it is often viewed.

> Serving God and others is about living the life that Christ came to live.

Preserve the Core and Stimulate Progress

After six years of research, I believe this is the key to building a visionary company: "Preserve the core and stimulate progress."[4] While Jim Collins and Jerry Porras in *Built to Last* were specifically referring to secular organizations, I have found this to be true for churches as well.

In order to move toward the vision God is calling your church to, your discipleship pathway needs to have both fixed and flexible elements to it. The fixed or core element that needs to be preserved is your system of ongoing steps. The ongoing steps are your foundation and base. They are timeless, enduring, and are the very steps that have proven to result in spiritual maturity.

The flexible elements, on the other hand, are where you can experiment and change often. These are your systems of first and next steps. It is here where you can change methods, programs, and curriculums based on the fruit that you are seeing in your context. These are the systems that have a shelf life and need to be interchangeable. But what doesn't change is the overarching purpose for these first and next steps. They are short-term and always need to direct people back into the center of the discipleship pathway—the ongoing steps—where individuals will learn how to self-feed, own their faith, and run this race of faith with endurance.

"By being clear about what is core (and therefore relatively fixed), a [church] can more easily seek variation and movement in all that is not core."[5] In other words, clarity in your ongoing steps will give you and your leadership team/staff the freedom to experiment and try different things in your first and next steps.

According to Collins and Porras, preserving the core and stimulating progress are not just posters on the wall, aspirational values, or the culture of an organization. Rather, highly visionary companies have found a way to create "concrete, tangible mechanisms to *preserve the core* ideology and to *stimulate progress.*"[6] For churches, this concrete, tangible mechanism is the discipleship pathway.

Let's now move onto the two other systems of the discipleship pathway, the next and first steps, to see how they all work together as a system of systems to move people toward Christ.

Next Steps

It was finally race day. As we checked into the race, the race organizers handed me a map and explained the course. They assured me that there were going to be pace setters, signage, and volunteers along the course that would direct me if I got lost. Knowing I wasn't going to lead the pack, I just tossed the map aside. I didn't think it was worth the effort, since I could just follow others.

Rather than using starting blocks, like I was used to during my track and field sprinting days, hundreds and hundreds of runners just congregated around the starting line until the gun was fired. We weren't allowed to have anything in our ears, so while I would've preferred to be listening to a podcast or audiobook, for the next hour, it was just going to be me, my thoughts, and a swarm of runners.

Once the race began, I transformed from a reluctant runner into a man on a mission who was going to finish the race in sixty minutes. Despite the fact that this was my first time running a 10K, I was gunning for a personal record.

Though it was a bit chilly at first, there was something about putting on that bib and passing dozens of runners that caused the adrenaline to soar through my body. I had emerged from the pack and was on pace to hit my goal.

About four kilometers into the race, the pack had thinned considerably. Now I knew the course had some sort of figure eight in it, but since I hadn't paid much attention to the map, I had to make a split-second decision. There were two signs ahead of me: one pointing straight and another pointing right. Since neither were labeled, I just gunned for the right, while picking up my pace. Do you know that moment, when driving on the freeway, when you release your foot off the gas at the beginning of a bend, only to floor it as you're coming out of it? That's how I felt as I turned the bend and gunned forward.

Now all throughout the race, there were always a few people ahead of me and behind me, but once I turned that bend, I suddenly felt alone. I knew I was making good time, but when I saw a sign that said I only had two kilometers left until the finish line, I began to second-guess what had happened. I'm a pretty athletic guy, but it had only been twenty minutes! How could I only have two kilometers left? Was I really on pace to beat the world record?

As you've probably figured out by now, I made the wrong turn. I was supposed to go straight instead of turning right. So I had a choice to make. I was either going to finish the race, set a world record, and then hang up my shoes, or I was going to figure out a way to make this right. Instead of living my life as a lie, I decided to backtrack and make up the distance that I had missed. In other words, I began running the opposite way.

The first few people that passed me didn't even give me a glance—they were focused and were probably the ones gunning for the records. The next few gave me an odd look, and eventually people began laughing at me and asking me why I was running the wrong way. But nothing was going to phase me. I was on a mission. I hadn't trained all these weeks to cheat or give up, so once I made up my distance, I turned back around and pushed to the finish line.

Why Next Steps?

For a runner, races are designed to stretch you. They are a place to set a goal and break it. For many, the competition is invigorating. For others, it's a way to stay disciplined, keep motivated, and have something to work toward. For many runners that I surveyed, it was the sense of community at each race that kept them coming back. Essentially, every runner races for a different reason, but one thing is the same—every race has a start and end point—they are all short-term.

This is how the system of next steps works in your discipleship pathway. They aren't a place where disciples are intended to live, or be a part of in a continuous manner. That's what the system of ongoing steps is for! Like races, next steps are short-term, temporary experiences focused on stretching, enhancing, and refreshing an individual's spiritual life in community.

Unfortunately, in many churches, next steps are not seen as short-term experiences. This is why you'll have some individuals who seem to be at everything your church offers—no wonder they "don't have time" to invest in relationships with non-Christians. In turn, this is also why you'll have others who don't get involved in anything, because everything is pitched as being important. The fact is, if everything is important, nothing is important.

If everything is important, nothing is important.

Although I persevered through the training program, it was the upcoming race that ultimately motivated me to continue running and exercising. In fact, although I still dislike running, nothing works better than a race to keep me disciplined in my ongoing exercise. In the same way, the goal for your discipleship pathway is never to get someone through it—it's to get individuals to own it. As a result, the next steps are designed to motivate and discipline your church to keep running the race of faith with perseverance.

Three Categories of Next Steps

In your discipleship pathway, next steps can be understood as any concentrated, short-term, and temporary experience or learning opportunity designed for fresh insight and growth. They fall under three distinct categories: discover, deepen, and deploy.

1. DISCOVER

In a church that has a directional posture toward discipleship, you will have individuals engaged in the life of your church who feel like they belong, even though they don't profess Christ as their Savior and Lord. This "discover" category of next steps has them in mind. Popular examples are programs like Alpha[7] and Starting Point.[8] Both are focused on providing a safe environment for individuals who are curious about the Christian faith to learn about God, ask life's biggest questions, and discover what it means to have a relationship with him. Here is a table comparing the major topics for both:

Alpha Film Series[9]	Starting Point[10]
1. Is there more to life than this?	1. Start – Who is Jesus?
2. Who is Jesus?	2. Problem – We are sinners
3. Why did Jesus die?	3. Trust – God moved toward humanity
4. How can I have faith?	4. Rules – Rules assume a relationship
5. Why and how do I pray?	5. Jesus – Jesus is the solution
6. Why and how should I read the Bible?	6. Grace – The impact of grace
7. How does God guide us?	7. Faith – The power of faith
8. Who is the Holy Spirit?	8. Invitation – We are designed for a purpose
9. What does the Holy Spirit do?	
10. How can I be filled with the Holy Spirit?	
11. How can I make the most of the rest of my life?	
12. How can I resist evil?	
13. Why and how should I tell others?	
14. Does God heal today?	
15. What about the church?	

FIGURE 8.2: EXAMPLES OF DISCOVER NEXT STEPS

2. Deepen

The "deepen" category of next steps are designed to do exactly that—provide opportunities for individuals to deepen their faith. These can be short-term classes, seminars, conferences, or studies, but there must be a clear beginning and end date. The goal is not to hop from one "deepen" next step to another. In fact, "deepen" next steps are best experienced when individuals, who are in an ongoing group, participate in it together.

For example, a small group who has recently finished their study can take a break from their regular meetings to participate in a "deepen" evangelism seminar or class together. Once that's over, they can then resume their regular group meetings, or possibly multiply into new groups with others whom they have met and built a relationship with through the seminar or class. As you can see, these "deepen" next steps are also great opportunities for individuals who are not connected in community to get plugged in.

It's important to frame these "deepen" next steps as short-term experiences, lest an individual thinks they have arrived and are finished with discipleship upon completion. This is why I advise churches to take the numbering sequence off of their foundational set of classes. For individuals in your church, a numbered set of "deepen" next steps subtly makes the goal more about completion than competency. This is because of how we have been conditioned through our 101–401 educational system, as I explained in chapter 1. As a result, a numbered approach creates an accidental value toward a destination mind-set, rather than a directional one.

When you strip the numbering sequence off your "deepen" next steps, the focus shifts to the topic. This is most conducive to retention and transformation since adults learn best—as outlined in the third micro-shift, from sage to guide—when they see the relevance of the lesson to their life, and if they can immediately apply the knowledge in some way.

Consequently, if your "deepen" next steps are numbered, many will complete the sequence just for the sake of finishing it. However, if the numbering is stripped off, and the "deepen" next steps are offered at different times and intervals of the year, while your overall attendance might be lower, you will attract and teach those who need it most, when they can apply it best. Which would you rather have—better statistics or application of the knowledge?

While I would encourage you to look at how churches like The Village Church,[11] The Summit Church,[12] Redeemer Presbyterian Church,[13] Saddleback Church,[14] Church of the Highlands,[15] The Austin Stone Community Church,[16] Holy Trinity Brompton,[17] and others, are creating opportunities for individuals to take their next steps to deepen their faith. Let me share two specific examples with you.

When I was pastoring at Beulah Alliance Church, I led our adult ministry team through a design process to create an adult-education oriented set of "deepen" next-step seminars. These short-term seminars, which we called "The Essentials," were rooted in the principles outlined in the third micro-shift, from sage to guide (see Figure 8.3). In addition to the unengaged coming to these seminars, small groups and mid-size communities were invited to participate as well. The seminars were never comprehensive, since the goal was to connect individuals into a group afterwards, so that they could continue learning in community. As a result, while options ranged from a one-session, two-hour seminar to a Friday night–Saturday afternoon seminar, we always provided curriculum suggestions, and connected people into groups afterwards so they could continue to dig deeper into the topic. Here were the four seminars that the team and I designed together.

The Essentials
The Essential Practices: Learning about the spiritual disciplines and how to become a self-feeder
The Essential Story: Understanding the story of God and how to communicate it (evangelism)
The Essential Character: Identifying your strengths, growing in character, and finding a place to serve
The Essential Life: Discovering freedom in Christ and your identity in him

FIGURE 8.3: OUTLINE OF THE FOUR ESSENTIALS

The Disciples Path[18] is the other example that I'd like to highlight (see Figure 8.4). This was created by disciple-makers for disciple-makers. Fourteen disciple-making church leaders were invited by LifeWay to think through all the ways disciples needed to be formed so they could make other disciples. The result is a scope and sequence that is progressive, disciplined, relational, and replicable. The curriculum comes in two formats: a short-term, six-volume experience where each volume is five or six sessions, or a longer-term, four-volume experience where each volume is thirteen sessions. While the Disciples Path is more of a curriculum for a group than a "deepen" next-step seminar, here are a few creative ways you can utilize the short-term version as a "deepen" next step.

With the short-term version, you can create six "deepen" next-step seminars using the six volumes. Each seminar would cover the broad topic, or first session, of each volume in a one-night, two-hour experience. Then, if individuals were not a part of a group, they could form or join one to continue studying the material in the following weeks. If they came as a group, they would leave equipped with their study material for the following weeks.

There are many ways to offer these six "deepen" next step seminars to your church. You could offer them once a month, so that each seminar would be offered twice in a calendar year, or, if you had enough teachers and rooms, you could offer, on a quarterly basis, all six seminars on the same day. Whatever you choose to do, the point is to never offer them successively six weeks in a row. Otherwise, you would be teaching your church that these "deepen" next-step seminars were the end goal, rather than the means to living out the ongoing steps in your discipleship pathway.

Disciples Path (Short-Term Six-Volume Experience)

The Beginning: First Steps as a Disciple	The Way: More Intimate with Jesus
1. What Just Happened to Me?	1. Defining "Disciple"
2. The Centrality of Christ	2. Jesus Calls Disciples
3. Time with Jesus	3. Jesus Teaches His Disciples
4. The Church	4. Jesus Equips His Disciples
5. The Mission	5. Jesus Sends His Disciples

The Call: Your New Identity	The Truth: Exploring Doctrinal Truths
1. Who Is Jesus?	1. The Doctrine of God
2. What Did Jesus Do?	2. The Doctrine of Man
3. Following Jesus	3. The Person and Work of Christ
4. The Priorities of a Disciple	4. The Kingdom of God
5. The Cost of a Disciple	5. The Doctrine of the Holy Spirit
6. The Fruit of a Disciple	6. The Doctrine of the Church
The Life: Essential Disciplines	**The Mission: Joining God's Work**
1. Immersed in the Word	1. Christ Came to Us
2. Connected through Prayer	2. Christ Came with a Mission
3. Living in Community	3. Christ Came to Die
4. Being Filled with the Spirit	4. We Die with Christ
5. Serving One Another	5. We Go with Christ
6. Sharing Your Faith	6. We Go Together with Christ

FIGURE 8.4: IN-DEPTH SESSION OUTLINE FOR DISCIPLES PATH

You can create "deepen" next-step seminars leveraging any curriculum. The key is to put the curriculum up against the eight output goals to make sure that it is comprehensive and moves individuals toward Christlikeness. You can use the following audit to evaluate whichever curriculum you would like to leverage (see Figure 8.5). Just be sure to list every session in the curriculum you are evaluating, and mark off which of the output goals it addresses.

CURRICULUM AUDIT

Name of Curriculum:	Bible Engagement	Obeying God and Denying Self	Serving God and Others	Sharing Christ	Exercising Faith	Seeking God	Building Relationships	Unashamed (Transparency)
Session 1:								
Session 2:								
Session 3:								

FIGURE 8.5: CURRICULUM AUDIT

3. DEPLOY

This last category of next steps is all about empowering and deploying individuals into service and ministry. If you haven't already created a "deepen" next-step class or seminar focused on helping individuals discover their spiritual gifts, strengths, and passion for ministry, you can do that here, while simultaneously helping them find a place to serve. It's important to understand that the "deploy" next step is a short-term, action-oriented service opportunity. It's intended to attract individuals who have a bent toward action and using their hands, over and above sitting in a classroom. It's short-term because the goal is to give people a taste for service, so that they can make it a regular rhythm and begin living out the ongoing step of serving God and others.

For example, a serve fair at your church, where individuals can learn about different opportunities to serve, could be categorized as a "deploy" next step. So could packing a shoebox for Operation Christmas Child, giving to a relief fund when a natural disaster has struck, weeding and mulching your local school's property, and serving at the local homeless shelter. A short-term mission trip, internship, or residency could also be considered as "deploy" next steps, since they are short-term experiences giving individuals a taste for full-time paid or bivocational ministry.

Handoffs

Next steps are only successful when they lead individuals back to the ongoing steps. This is why handoffs are critical. Just like relay races are won and lost in the baton handoffs, unless the three categories of next steps are all short-term, temporary experiences that handoff individuals back into the ongoing steps, the race is lost.

Next steps are only successful when they lead individuals back to the ongoing steps.

In the churches that Thom Rainer and Eric Geiger studied for their landmark book, *Simple Church,* they discovered that vibrant churches "have a simple process that produces movement, a process that facilitates the handoffs. The programs in these churches are tools used to promote movement. The leaders focus on what happens in between the programs as much as they do the programs."[19]

This is why the next steps in a discipleship pathway and the first steps, as we'll now see, are all focused on promoting movement to the center of the pathway—the ongoing steps. After all, it's ultimately in the ongoing steps that individuals in your church will learn how to own their faith and this discipleship pathway.

First Steps

After biting the bullet and signing up for that 10K race, not only did I have to develop this curriculum to train our church how to run in such a way as to finish well—both physically and spiritually—but I had to take my first steps. I had to buy myself a pair of white short shorts—like the one the man playing Eric Liddell wore in the 1981 version of *Chariots of Fire* . . . Alright, all joking aside. I did have to buy a new pair of running shoes and learn the basics of running.

Here's the thing. A runner who doesn't start well may not finish well. They may get injured, sidetracked, or discouraged, and not know how to bounce back, reengage, or recover. This is why you cannot neglect or assume your first steps as a runner. And this is precisely why you should also pay attention when getting the map for the race! The same is true for newcomers to your church.

Newcomers who dive right into the ongoing or next-steps portion of your discipleship pathway are not your concern. They will have either come with a friend who is already on your discipleship pathway, have a specific need or question that one of your next steps are addressing, or already understand the importance of being a self-feeder. They will get plugged in just as long as your website is up-to-date, church calendar is easily accessible, and it's apparent who they should contact to learn more or get registered.

The newcomers that you do need to pay attention to are the ones who arrive and look wide-eyed because they're trying to figure out where to go and who to talk to, since they are taking everything in for the first time. You should also be aware of the professional church shoppers, who have mastered the art of, "fake it 'til you make it," and will typically slip in and out of your worship services without talking to anyone. And don't forget about the CEO (Christmas, Easter, and Other) newcomers either, as they are often only a first step away from engagement.

If newcomers leave your church, how will you disciple them?

All three of these newcomer personas are prone to slip out the back door of your church and never return unless you engage them with the first steps of your discipleship pathway. And here's the thing: This is not just an issue for the Guest Services department! If they leave your church, how will you disciple them?

First-Time Audit

The system of first steps in your discipleship pathway needs to be designed to identify and welcome individuals into the life of your church. So instead of thinking about this process as a separate ministry or system, view it as a part of your discipleship pathway—as its entry door or first step.

What a difference this makes! Now, instead of viewing your newcomers class or connection cards as mere details or necessary evils, they now take on new prominence. In order to help individuals move toward Christ, you need to first know who they are, and in turn, they need to know who you are—thus, the importance of first steps.

One of the best things you can do to identify and map out the system of first steps for your discipleship pathway is to take a weekend off and visit another church. Do this together with your leadership team, or split yourselves up and visit different churches. By visiting another church and completing the following First-Time Audit, you will *feel* what newcomers feel when they visit your church (see Figure 8.6). This will provide you with a solid starting point to develop a system of first steps that works for your church.

If you want to take it to the next level, ask a few friends of friends (so that they're not biased and so that you can't get mad at them) to secretly visit your church and complete this First-Time Audit. It will only serve to help you define and refine the first steps for your discipleship pathway.

FIRST-TIME AUDIT			
	What do you see/hear/smell?	What seems important?	What's missing/confusing?
Website			
Google and Apple Maps			
Road Entrance			
Parking			
Building Entrance			
Lobby			
Information/Welcome Center			
Signage			
Restrooms			
Children's Area			
Student's Area			
Classrooms			
Auditorium			
Service Order			

Music			
Announcements			
Connection Card, Bulletin, Brochures			
Sermon			
Other			
SUMMARY FEEDBACK			
How many times were you greeted? By whom? How did it feel? What did you learn?			
As a newcomer, do you know what your next steps are to get plugged in? Elaborate.			
Other Comments			

FIGURE 8.6: FIRST-TIME AUDIT

The ABCs of First Steps

In order to identify, welcome, and begin discipling newcomers, you need to map out your system of first steps. The ABCs of first steps is a simple way to understand and structure the first steps of your discipleship pathway: **A**ctions, **B**iases, and **C**lasses.

1. ACTIONS

When a newcomer walks into your church the first few times, what are the actions that you, your leadership team, and your volunteers are doing to identify and welcome them? What are the actions you can do, repeat, and measure, so that you are setting up newcomers with the best opportunity possible to take their first steps in your discipleship pathway?

First of all, you need to know how to identify a newcomer. While the professional church shoppers and the CEO newcomers will tend to have their body language under control, most newcomers won't—they'll walk in the doors of your church building and look all around like a deer in headlights. This is why it's important that you train all of your volunteers, especially your greeters and leadership team, to spot newcomers and welcome them.

In exchange for their contact information, it's great to give them a gift that is too big to put in their purse or "murse," for guys. Not only does this demonstrate generosity and appreciation for visiting, but this oddly sized or oversized gift will serve as a visible marker for the rest of your volunteers and leadership team to be able to identify and welcome these newcomers as well. A coffee mug or an oversized yellow envelope both work well.

Once you have the contact information for a newcomer, be sure to create a system for follow up so that newcomers know they were noticed, are loved, and belong. This is where a church management system, or a shared digital spreadsheet will come in handy. You want to make sure to identify who the newcomers were and whether or not they experienced your follow-up system. It's critical that this information is shared among the appropriate leaders, since there are many different ways to identify newcomers.

For example, a newcomer could have filled out a connection card with a greeter at the information/welcome center or in the worship service. Alternatively, they could have checked their children into the kids' or student ministry. They might have given for the first time. Or they could have texted or emailed your church for more information. Regardless of how a newcomer was identified, it's important that all contact systems are talking to one another, so that you can put every newcomer through your follow-up system.

Remember, in the ABCs of first steps, A is for Actions, so your follow-up system needs to focus on actions that your church can do, rather than actions that the newcomer may or may not do. There is no one perfect follow-up system, but here is an example of a simple one to get you started, based on your church's preferred style of communication (see Figure 8.7).

MODE OF COMMUNICATION				
Traditional	**Digital Hybrid**	**Mobile First**	**Date**	**Content**
Phone Call/ Voicemail	Email	Text Message	Week 1 - Sunday	Thank them for coming
Mail	Phone Call/ Voicemail	Email	Week 1 - Wednesday	Share information on the current/ upcoming sermon series for adults; and if they have children, share the teaching schedule for the kids or student ministry
Phone Call/ Voicemail	Email	Text	Week 1 - Saturday	Invite them to the newcomers class if they haven't already attended
Mail	Email	Email	Week 2 - Wednesday	Share the vision of your church and the ongoing steps of your discipleship pathway
Mail	Email	Text	Week 3 - Wednesday	Invite them to the upcoming next step opportunities in your discipleship pathway

FIGURE 8.7: SAMPLE FOLLOW-UP SYSTEM FOR NEWCOMERS

2. BIAS

Every action has a bias—your actions toward newcomers are no exception. So instead of letting your unconscious biases come out in the way you interact with newcomers, or giving free rein to your leaders and volunteers to do the same, be proactive. Set the culture you want all of your leaders and volunteers to embody toward newcomers. Here are three examples of biases and how they can shape your system of first steps: personal, fun, and the second mile.

A personal bias is all about keeping your eyes open and being aware— it's about sweating the small stuff and noticing. There's so much noise today with the proliferation of junk mail, email, and text messaging that anything personalized always stands out. For example, if you were to get a letter, e-mail, or text message from a church that you visited for the first time, you would expect it to be templated and canned.

If it were a letter, what if it were hand written? If it were an email, what if it looked like a personalized message, rather than a graphically designed email template? What if, in the content of the message, there was a reference to something you had talked about with one of the church volunteers on Sunday? Wouldn't this catch your eye?

Personalization stands out, so train your leaders and volunteers to not only answer questions, but also have conversations with newcomers. Make sure there's a space on your connection card demarked, "For Internal Use Only," and then train your leaders and volunteers to jot down anything personal that came up during the conversation—it can be anything from a prayer request, to a comment about the weather, or how they found the church. You can then use this to add a personal touch to your follow-up communication.

Personalization stands out.

A bias for fun is another example that can uniquely shape your culture as you engage with and welcome newcomers to your church. Although we sent a man to the moon, developed more than a dozen cures for deadly diseases, and invented the Internet, the one thing that humanity seemingly could not accomplish was getting the Chicago Cubs to win a World Series. Well, that was true up until the bottom of the tenth inning on November 2, 2016.

After coming back from a three to one deficit in the World Series, the Cubs scrapped their way to Game 7. When the Cubs headed to the eighth inning with a 6–3 lead, they seemed to be in control. But this was one for the ages . . . the Cleveland Indians just had to go ahead and tie the game in the ninth. After a brief rain delay, the Cubs, with bases loaded at the top of the tenth, managed to get two runs. Now ahead 8–6, the Cubs were only three outs away from breaking their curse and winning the World Series. Although the Indians managed to get one run, they were shut down, and history was made.

The next day, Community Christian Church in Chicago, and their Lead Pastor Dave Ferguson, posted an image on social media that garnered more than eleven hundred reactions and five hundred shares. It was a picture of the Cubs logo with this on top: "FYI, if you made any promises during the bottom of the 10th." Their website on the bottom indicated that they had ten locations across Chicago. Now that's fun and memorable.

Going the second mile is another example of a bias. This is all about doing one more thing, or going above and beyond. For example, when it's winter in Canada, one of the things that people have to deal with is their heavy winter coats, mitts, scarves, hats, and boots. If you have young children, not only do you have to hold all of their winter gear in addition to yours, but you also have to deal with the fact that children tend to want to take it all off immediately upon entering the building. Trust me, I know. I had to deal with this many times when I lived in Edmonton, Alberta.

A greeter that goes the second mile would not only volunteer to hang up all of the family's jackets and winter gear—so that the parent could check their children into the kids' ministry—but they would also go outside and help the children get out of the car!

This reminds me of a story I heard about a valet attendant at the Ritz-Carlton, a world-renowned luxury hotel chain, who saw an empty blue Powerade bottle in a guest's car. Instead of leaving it as is, which is usually the code and conduct for a valet, the attendant threw the empty bottle away and put a brand new one in the cup holder for the guest. While this was definitely a risky move for a valet, this employee owned the Ritz-Carlton bias toward creating "unique, memorable and personal experiences for [their] guests."[20] They went the second mile, and the guest noticed.

3. Classes

Rather than giving newcomers a list of your classes, groups, and events to pick and choose from—much like you would do at a Japanese, all-you-can-eat, Sushi restaurant—you need to offer newcomers pointed, intentional options. This last point is all about focus.

While you may or may not decide to include your baptism and membership class as a first step (it could also be categorized as a next step), the one class that is nonnegotiable is your newcomers class. This is the one place that you need to communicate and work to get all newcomers to attend. This is *the* first step for all newcomers. In the ABCs of first steps, actions are what you, your leaders, and your volunteers do. Biases are the way the actions are done. But classes are what your newcomers do.

So on the communication card, point people to your newcomers class. Instruct all leaders and volunteers to invite guests to the newcomers class. Highlight this in your bulletin and in your announcements—speaking directly to all newcomers. And make sure your follow-up system points people to your newcomers class as their first step.

When individuals arrive at your newcomers class, keep it simple. Share your vision, strategy, and values, as outlined in chapter 7. While talking about your strategy, be sure to share the way your discipleship pathway works. At the end, take time for questions, and finish off your class by helping individuals get started on their ongoing or next steps.

If you're the lead pastor of your church, don't miss this opportunity to engage newcomers with your church's vision. You only get one chance to make a first impression, so don't delegate vision casting to a staff member or volunteer. I've seen newcomers classes double and triple in size when it was communicated that the lead pastor was going to be there, so make time for this ministry.

Don't delegate vision casting.

Now I'm not saying that you need to organize it, set it up, or even be there the whole time. Whether your church is fifty or five thousand, the lead pastor should not own this ministry. You need a dedicated leader to run this class and your Guest Services ministry. However, the lead pastor being there to cast the vision of the church and answer questions will make all the difference.

First Steps Matter

While it may seem anticlimactic to end this chapter talking about newcomers—especially after we've talked about micro-shifts, strategies, and a system for discipleship—let's not forget the importance of first steps. Unless you close the back door, you will always have individuals slipping out just as fast as they came. In fact, if you're not careful, the longer your back door remains open, the greater the chance that your front door will close. After all, don't you find we are more prone to talk about bad experiences than good?

Just think about this for a moment. What if we started celebrating the first steps for newcomers, just like we celebrate when toddlers take their first steps? Unless you can first identify and welcome newcomers, you will never be able to disciple them.

Conclusion

The Battle of Trafalgar on October 21, 1805, is often remembered as the decisive battle that—if it went as planned for the thirty-six-year-old Napoleon's Franco-Spanish fleet—would have changed the course of history and allowed the possibility for a full-on land invasion on Britain. By all accounts, Admiral Villeneuve, Commander of Napoleon's Franco-Spanish fleet, had the upper hand. He had thirty-three ships, compared to Admiral Nelson's twenty-seven British vessels. And with the way that naval battles were often fought at that time—lining up parallel to one another while firing volley after volley until one fleet would surrender—this was the ideal time for attack. This was the moment for Villeneuve to put an end to the lofty British navy and begin his assault against Britain—the odds were in his favor.[21]

There was just one problem: Admiral Nelson didn't follow "the rules." At dawn, instead of lining up in a parallel fashion to Villeneuve's ships, his fleet formed into two columns and charged full-speed toward the enemy line. While this offered Villeneuve an opportune, yet brief chance to begin firing without any risk of return volley, it posed a greater issue. If Nelson's ships successfully punched through Villeneuve's line, how was Villeneuve going to communicate with and command his ships toward action? How would his ships see his flag signaling? How would he control the battle? What would his ships do?

Nelson's unconventional strategy worked. Despite heavy fire that killed and injured men on the upper deck, he led the HMS *Victory* into victory by being the first to punch through the enemy line. The HMS *Victory* fired so powerfully that it killed or wounded over two hundred men on the French flagship—rendering the ship useless. With the British ships in between his, and with his crew decimated, Villeneuve was unable to continue signaling commands to the other ships. The result was widespread chaos, which eventually led to their surrender.[22]

In *Team of Teams: New Rules of Engagement for a Complex World*, General Stanley McChrystal, in his study and reflection on this battle, aptly contrasts the two sides and suggests that the lesson of this battle is often misunderstood. Nelson did not win the battle because he had a better strategic plan than Villeneuve. This wasn't a matter of outsmarting the opponent, having secret intel, or staying one step ahead. In fact, Nelson's strategy wasn't even original to him—it had been used many times before in the British navy! Rather, the key to victory was in making the microshift from command-and-control to empowered ownership. The victory ultimately "lay in his managerial style and the culture he had cultivated among his forces."[23]

Napoleon was a man of power. He had cultivated a culture of command-and-control where he had even forbidden his Admiral Villeneuve "to tell his captains at any stage what the grand strategy for defeating England might be."[24] Compare that to Nelson's empowering leadership style that emphasized "the role of the individual captains" and taught "that individual commanders should act on their own initiative once the mêlée had developed."[25]

Since Villeneuve's captains didn't know the strategy, they had to rely on him to signal the battle plan, tactic by tactic, one step at a time. They were not empowered to act on their own, since they did not even know what the plan was. Contrast that to Nelson, who shared the strategy with his captains, and ultimately trained and empowered them to own the process once the battle began. In fact, he had empowered others so well that, even though he died during the battle, the British were able to achieve victory!

The same is true for discipleship. As a church leader, your goal is not to create disciples who have to rely on you to feed them, develop them, and lead them. Instead, your task and your God-given privilege is to train and empower disciples who are self-feeders, who can then help others become disciples who are self-feeders, and on and on. Ultimately, the goal for your discipleship pathway is not to create disciples, but disciple-makers.

The goal for your discipleship pathway is not to create disciples, but disciple-makers.

Reflection Questions

Take a moment to write out your answers to the following questions. Be sure to schedule time with your leadership team so you can also wrestle through these concepts together.

1. What are the ongoing steps for your discipleship pathway?

2. What are the next steps for your discipleship pathway?

3. What are the first steps for your discipleship pathway?

Reach out to me on Twitter, Facebook, or email. I'd love to hear about your process and help along the way. You can find my contact information at danielim.com.

EPILOGUE

"Whoever is faithful in very little is also faithful in much."

—Jesus

Michael Jackson's "Thriller," Bruce Springsteen's "Born in the USA," Tina Turner's "What's Love Got to Do with It," Cyndi Lauper's "Time After Time," and Leonard Cohen's "Hallelujah." The list of these songs reminds me of that game, "One of these things is not like the other." Other than the fact that they were all released in 1984—"pop's greatest year" according to *Rolling Stone*—they have little in common.[1]

When Leonard Cohen brought "Hallelujah" to his record label—the same label that put out "Thriller" and "Born in the USA"—the president of the label, Walter Yetnikoff, didn't even blink. He said to Cohen, "What is this? This isn't pop music. We're not releasing it. This is a disaster."[2]

He called the song "Hallelujah" a disaster.

Just let that sink in a bit. The song that has since been covered more than 640 times by artists like U2, Bob Dylan, Jeff Buckley, Justin Timberlake, Celine Dion, Bon Jovi, and Pentatonix was a "disaster."[3]

To be fair, if you listened to Cohen's original version of "Hallelujah" in 1984 on the album *Various Positions*, you would've probably made the same call as Yetnikoff. This is literally one of the worst renditions (in my opinion!) of the song I've ever heard—even though it's the original. First of all, it doesn't sound like the "Hallelujah" that I'm used to hearing on films like *Shrek,* shows like *Scrubs,* and singing competitions like *The Voice.* Nor is Cohen using the same lyrics that I'm used to hearing—they're similar, but still different.

So what happened? While the backstory of this song's rise to fame is fascinating, the fact is, it was no silver bullet. The song had to undergo one small shift after another to turn it into what it is today—one of the world's most recognized songs that is still earning accolades and making its way onto billboard charts, more than thirty years later.[4]

Bob Dylan and Leonard Cohen's chance meeting in a Paris café in the mid-eighties offers us a look into the micro-shifts that made this song into a macro-hit. Cohen recounts the meeting with Dylan: "Dylan and I were having coffee the day after his concert in Paris a few years ago . . . and he asked me how long it took to write ['Hallelujah']. And I told him a couple of years. I lied actually. It was more than a couple of years . . . Then I praised a song of his, 'I and I,' and asked him how long it had taken and he said, 'Fifteen minutes.'"[5]

It took Cohen five years, eighty verses, two notebooks, and banging his head on the floor in his underwear in the Royalton Hotel in New York to come up with the final four verses that he ended up recording.[6] And that's not even the version of the song that is so often covered today!

The genius of "Hallelujah" lies not in a silver bullet, fifteen-minute composition, but in the small shifts that have made it into the song it is today. Malcolm Gladwell, on his podcast, *Revisionist History*, puts it well: "Think about how many incredible twists and turns that song takes before it gets recognized as a work of genius."[7]

Let's take a brief look at the twists, turns, and shifts that this song had to undergo, in order to be the "Hallelujah" that we know it to be today.

Cohen, after releasing the first version of the song in 1984 that was apparently a "disaster," went back to the drawing board and tweaked it. He revised the song, slowed it down, added three new verses, and then recorded it again in 1988. As Cohen continued to tweak and perform the song, John Kale of The Velvet Underground heard it, loved it, and asked Cohen if he could cover it. So after receiving over fifteen pages of faxed lyrics from Cohen, Kale chose three verses, changed the feel of the song, and recorded it in 1991. Three years later, Jeff Buckley, after hearing the song while cat-sitting, decided to perform it at a dive bar which then led to him getting signed by the record executive that just happened to be there. After Buckley recorded his one and only album in 1994, people didn't even pay attention to the song until he tragically drowned in Memphis in 1997.[8]

So more than a decade later after being originally written, the song was finally noticed and began to take off. What's fascinating, though, is that the version of the song that took off isn't even Cohen's original version. It's not even his modified version. It's Buckley's version of Kale's version of Cohen's version.[9]

How do you think that made Leonard Cohen feel? That *someone else's* rendition of his original song was being played everywhere?

Well, it's simple. He had two choices. He could boycott the song, call his lawyers, and try to shut down the movement; or he could shift his perspective and see this as a blessing, rather than a curse. As an opportunity, rather than an obstacle. As proof that sometimes the greatest impact in life comes through one small shift at a time.

So don't worry about the credit. In fact, don't try to be a hero. The legacy of your church does not depend on you. God was already doing his work in the hearts of those in your church before you met them, and he will continue after you leave. So stop feeling the pressure to bring the silver bullet.

Instead, choose faithfulness (Luke 16:10). Make one small shift at a time. And pray, "Your kingdom come. Your will be done on earth as it is in heaven" (Matt. 6:10–11).

ACKNOWLEDGMENTS

"From him the whole body, fitted and knit together by every supporting ligament, promotes the growth of the body for building up itself in love by the proper working of each individual part." (Eph 4:16)

I see myself as a ligament in the body of Christ.

For some reason, ever since I was a child, God has used me as a bridge and a connector between individuals, groups, ministries, churches, and cultures. And for that, I'm deeply grateful because of the number of individuals and ministries that I've been blessed to work with.

As a result, everywhere that I've served, and everyone that I've partnered together with in ministry, have indelibly impacted my thinking, being, and doing. So here's my attempt at acknowledging those who have directly impacted the content of this book.

Thank you Appa and Umma for sticking with me. For praying for me. For enduring my tumultuous teenage years. And for supporting me as I discerned my calling to ministry. I am who I am today because of you.

And to all who pastored me—particularly Sung Jin Lee and Mike Lee. Sung Jin, thanks for forcing me to go to that youth retreat—it was truly a turning point in my life. And thanks, Mike, for giving me room to lead and teaching me the ways of spiritual discernment. I'm forever grateful.

To Donna Downes, thank you for believing in me and teaching me the ways of adult education and missiologically-oriented leadership. This book, in its earliest form, is a result of that Global Leadership class that you taught. And to my cohort, Kairos, those were formative years in my development as a leader. I think of you guys often.

To Lorenzo DellaForesta, you were an answer to prayer, and I'm grateful that I can call you friend. Much of the way that I think about ministry and cultural engagement is a result of your influence. To Joel Zantingh, thanks for schooling me in squash; the best years are ahead of us.

To my leaders in Korea, remember those times of study, prayer, and worship in my apartment? Oh, how God moved! And oh how God is still moving.

To Keith Taylor, thanks for your constant encouragement and permission to lead, test, and refine the concepts in this book at Beulah. To Darren Herbold, Darcy Coutts, and Elroy Peters, thanks for taking a chance on me. To Darren Degraaf, my eyes are open. To Neil Truong, Sarah Hunter, Angie La Favor, Bonnie Hodge, Allen Powles, Michael Wilson, Tim Doherty, Mike Millward, Scott Jespersen, and Maynor Motta, it was fun designing and dreaming together. To all of our pioneering mid-size community leaders, I'm grateful that you created MSCs that were a sign, instrument, and foretaste for the kingdom of God. And to Beulah and the C&MA, you have a special place in my heart.

To Ed Stetzer, Eric Geiger, Earl Roberson, Brad Waggoner, and Dr. Rainer, thank you for entrusting me with the privilege to serve pastors, planters, and multipliers all over. To Rick Howerton, thanks for inviting me to The Lobby and introducing me to LifeWay—remember that call we had about mid-size communities while you were driving through the hills of Kentucky? To Micah Fries, thanks for baptizing me in the ways of the SBC. To Philip Nation, thanks for giving me the confidence to move ahead with this manuscript. And to Scott McConnell, Lizette Beard, and Casey Oliver, thank you for your insight with the TDA research and unpacking it for me and the readers of this book via the regression analysis!

To Jeremy Maxfield, I still hate that you left me, but those times chipping ice, hanging out at the pool, and over the fire pit with our families are some of my fondest memories in Nashville. Thanks for keeping me accountable, real, and honest, and for giving me the encouragement to finish this.

To Todd Adkins, whaaaat? Thanks for helping me refine the quadrants, charts, graphs, and concepts in this book. Your management style has allowed me to thrive, innovate, and strategize at LifeWay. I'm grateful that we can serve together and that I can call you my friend.

To Len Taylor, Scott Matthews, Aaron Loy, and the elders at The Fellowship, thank you for allowing me to exercise my love for preaching on a regular basis. To my LIFEgroup, you guys are like family to Christina and me. Thank you for welcoming us in.

To Taylor Combs, Devin Maddox, Jennifer Lyell, Dave Schroeder, and the team at B&H Publishing, thanks for believing in me and this book's message. My heart is to serve churches and the pastors that are leading them, so thank you for refining this message and helping get it out.

To my sisters, Gina, Tina, and Elly, we've come a long way and now look at all our children! Can you imagine what they're going to be like when they're teenagers? If they're anything like we were, we need to get on our knees and pray. And to my brothers-in-law, aka golfing buddies, I'll beat you one of these days.

To mom and dad Hu, the love and support that you've shown Christina and me is beyond words. Thank you for always being there for us . . . and for all the books. And to Michael and Liz, I'm grateful to call you family and fellow coworkers in Christ.

To my children, Victoria, Adelyn, and Makarios, I'm proud to be your Father, but my heart's cry is to call you fellow brothers and sisters in Christ, and coworkers for the kingdom. I pray that your kingdom impact would outshine your mother's and mine.

To the love of my life, Christina. Thank you for letting me write in the evenings and on Saturday mornings. You made this book possible . . . period. All that I have is yours, and there's no one I'd rather do life and ministry with than you. Thanks for putting up with my stubbornness and painting those cabinets. Here's to greater years of ministry ahead.

And finally, to King Jesus. Without you, I am nothing. Thank you for this opportunity to serve the Church by writing. It's all for your glory, honor, and praise.

ABOUT THE AUTHOR

 Daniel Im is the founder of NewChurches.com and the director of Church Multiplication for LifeWay Christian Resources. He is a teaching pastor at The Fellowship, a multisite church in Nashville. He is the coauthor of *Planting Missional Churches: Your Guide to Starting Churches that Multiply* (Second Edition) with Ed Stetzer. He also hosts the New Churches Q&A Podcast.

Daniel has a M.A. in Global Leadership from Fuller Theological Seminary and has served and pastored in church plants and multisite churches ranging from one hundred people to fifty thousand people in Vancouver, Ottawa, Montreal, Korea, Edmonton, and Nashville. He is passionate about the local church and loves to be a part of creating systems, strategies, tools, and resources to help new churches get planted and campuses get started, and to catalyze churches toward multiplication. With his experience in both church planting and multisite ministry, Daniel will provide you with insight to help you take that next step.

NOTES

Foreword

1. Mason Currey, *Daily Rituals: How Artists Work* (New York: Knopf Doubleday Publishing Group, 2013).

Introduction

1. http://www.cbc.ca/radio/thisisthat/texas-sugar-water-bring-your-kids-to-work-day-newfoundland-apology-no-gambling-casino-1.2843567/texas-town-adds-sugar-to-water-supply-to-encourage-residents-to-drink-more-water-1.2843568

2. http://news.nationalgeographic.com/news/2006/06/060609-gorges-dam.html

3. https://www.nasa.gov/centers/goddard/news/topstory/2003/0210rotation.html

4. http://www.jpl.nasa.gov/news/news.php?feature=716

5. http://news.nationalgeographic.com/news/2006/06/060609-gorges-dam_2.html

6. http://www.aerospace.org/education/stem-outreach/space-primer/a-brief-history-of-space-exploration/

7. https://www.nasa.gov/pdf/566250main_SHUTTLE%20ERA%20FACTS_040412.pdf

8. http://gizmodo.com/why-did-nasa-end-the-space-shuttle-program-1721140493

9. http://www.aerospace.org/education/stem-outreach/space-primer/a-brief-history-of-space-exploration/

10. https://www.nasa.gov/centers/kennedy/about/information/shuttle_faq.html

11. http://www.history.com/topics/challenger-disaster

12. https://www.britannica.com/biography/Ivan-Pavlov

Chapter 1

1. http://www.forbes.com/sites/lewishowes/2012/07/17/20-business-quotes-and-lessons-from-walt-disney/#2336c3061f56

2. This was at the Praxis 2015 Conference with the V3 Church Planting Movement.

3. This is the author's paraphrase on the following quote from *The Art of War,*

> "If you know the enemy and know yourself, you need not fear the result of a hundred battles. If you know yourself but not the enemy, for every victory gained you will also suffer a defeat. If you know neither the enemy nor yourself, you will succumb in every battle." Sun Tzu, *The Art of War,* trans. Lionel Giles (England: Allandale Online Publishing, 2000), 11.

4. http://www.strengthsfinder.com/

5. http://www.kolbe.com/

6. Howard Shultz, *Onward: How Starbucks Fought for Its Life without Losing Its Soul* (New York: Rodale Books, 2011), 13, emphasis added.

7. According to Paul G. Hiebert, in addition to bounded and centered sets, there is a third and possibly fourth type of category—fuzzy sets of one type and fuzzy sets of two types. For the sake of simplicity, I am only focusing on bounded and centered sets. For more information on fuzzy sets, read Paul G. Hiebert, "Sets and Fuzzy Sets: Variations in Category Formation" (unpublished paper, Fuller Seminary).

8. Paul G. Hiebert, "Conversion, Culture and Cognitive Categories," *Gospel in Context* 1(4) (1978): 24–29.

9. Ibid., 28.

10. Eugene Peterson, *A Long Obedience in the Same Direction: Discipleship in an Instant Society* (Downers Grove, IL: InterVarsity Press, 1980).

11. Phone call with Dr. Robert Coleman, August 26, 2016.

12. C. S. Lewis, *Mere Christianity* (New York: HarperSanFrancisco, 2001), 208.

Chapter 2

1. Allen Tough, *Adult's Learning Projects: A Fresh Approach to Theory and Practice in Adult Learning* (Toronto: Ontario Institute for Studies in Education, 1971).

2. Kelly Kajewski and Valerie Madsen, *Demystifying 70:20:10 White Paper* (Victoria: Deakin University, 2012).

3. Brad J. Waggoner, *The Shape of Faith to Come: Spiritual Formation and the Future of Discipleship* (Nashville: B&H Publishing Group, 2008), Location 198 Kindle Edition.

4. The following is the full list of interviewees, and their titles at the time of the interview, who participated in the first phase of the Transformational Discipleship Project: Jerry Acosta (evangelism coordinator with the Venezuelan National Baptist Convention), Francisco Aular (pastor in Canada and founder of the Latin American Baptist Discipleship Movement), Henry Blackaby (president of Blackaby Ministries and author of *Experiencing God*), Luis "Gary" Cesar (senior pastor of First Baptist Church Satellite), Marigene Chamberlain (professor at Samford University and former member of General Board of Discipleship, The United Methodist Church), Neil Cole (founder and director of Church Multiplication Associates), Robert Coleman (author of *Master Plan of Discipleship*), Hector Hugo Arias Contreras (leader at the Chilean Baptist Convention), Earl Creps (professor of leadership and spiritual renewal at Assemblies of God Theological Seminary and author of *Off-Road Disciplines*), Edgard Castano Diaz (senior pastor of Central Baptist Church, Bogota, Columbia, and former president of the Colombian Evangelical Council), Jon Ferguson (teaching pastor, Community Christian Church), Angel Mena Garcia (pastor and denominational leader with the Assemblies of God in Panama), Alton Garrision (assistant general superintendent, Assemblies of God), Billie Hanks (founder of Operation Multiplication), Alan Hirsch (founder of Forge), T. W. Hunt (author of *The Mind of Christ* and *The Doctrine of Prayer*), Mary Kassian (professor at The Southern Baptist Theological Seminary and author of *In My Father's House*), Larry Lee (executive secretary of Youth and Leadership Development of National Evangelical Christian Fellowship Malaysia), Aubrey Malphurs (founder of The Malphurs Group, professor at Dallas Theological Seminary, and author of *Advanced Strategic Planning* and *Strategic Disciple Making*), Robertson McQuilkin (president emeritus of Columbia International University), Jaime Riquelme Miranda (pastor and leader of the Chilean Ministers Alliance), Alexander Montero (director of Venezuelan National Baptist Convention), Steve Murrell (founding pastor of Victory Fellowship, Manila), Waldemar Morales Roca (director of Guatemala Baptist Seminary), Leonard Sweet (professor at Drew University and author of *The Gospel According to Starbucks*), Natan Velazquez (pastor of Emmanuel Baptist Church, Caracas, Venezuela), Victor Villanueva (leader at the Mexico National Baptist Convention and professor at Yucatan Autonomous University), Don Whitney (professor of biblical spirituality at The Southern Baptist Theological Seminary and author of *Spiritual Disciplines for the Christian Life*).

5. The telephone survey was conducted August 17–24, 2011. The calling list was randomly drawn from a list of all Protestant churches. Up to six calls were made to reach a sampled phone number. Each interview was conducted with the senior pastor, minister, or priest of the church called. Responses were weighted to reflect the geographic distribution of Protestant churches. The sample provides 95 percent confidence that the sampling error does not exceed +3.2 percent. Margins of error are higher in sub-groups. For more on the methodology, see http://tda.lifeway.com/what-is-it/our-methodology/.

6. Eric Geiger, Michael Kelly, and Philip Nation, *Transformational Discipleship: How People Really Grow* (Nashville: B&H Publishing Group, 2012), 15.

7. The online survey on Protestant church laity in the United States and Canada was conducted October 14–22, 2011 with a total number of 4,016 respondents. Of the total number of respondents, 2,930 completed the survey in the United States, and 1,086 in Canada. A representative sample of American and Canadian adults who attended a Protestant church at least once a month or more was surveyed. Respondents could respond in English, Spanish, or French. The sample provides 95 percent confidence that the sampling error does not exceed +1.8 percent. Margins of error are higher in sub-groups.

8. Geiger, Kelly, and Nation, *Transformational Discipleship*, 59.

9. Dallas Willard, *The Great Omission: Reclaiming Jesus' Essential Teachings on Discipleship* (New York: HarperCollins e-books, 2006), Location 193 Kindle Edition.

10. Robert Coleman, interview by Scott McConnell, August 10, 2011, Phase 1 qualitative interviews for the Transformational Discipleship project.

11. Dietrich Bonhoeffer, *The Cost of Discipleship* (London: SCM Press, 2001), 17.

12. Willard, *The Great Omission*, Location 248 Kindle Edition.

13. Henry Blackaby, interview by Philip Nation, Phase 1 qualitative interviews for the Transformational Discipleship project.

14. Steve Murrell, interview by Philip Nation, June 16, 2011, Phase 1 qualitative interviews for the Transformational Discipleship project.

15. Greg Ogden, *Transforming Discipleship: Making Disciples a Few at a Time* (Downers Grove, IL: InterVarsity Press, 2003), Location 178 Kindle Edition.

16. Henry Blackaby, interview by Philip Nation, Phase 1 qualitative interviews for the Transformational Discipleship project.

17. These descriptions are quoted directly from a TDA Survey Report. You can take the TDA as an individual, small group, ministry area, or church at http://tda.lifeway.com/.

18. Richard J. Foster, *Prayer: Finding the Heart's True Home* (New York: HarperSanFrancisco, 1992), 144.

19. LifeWay Research, "Transformational Church Discipleship Regression Analysis" (unpublished research document, Nashville, 2011).

20. Richard Koch, *The 80/20 Principle: The Secret to Achieving More with Less* (New York: Crown Business, 2008), 10–11.

21. Joseph Grenny et al., *Influencer: The New Science of Leading Change, Second Edition* (McGraw-Hill Education, 2013), 35.

22. LifeWay Research, "Highest Attendance Days" (Nashville, 2011); http://lifewayresearch.com/wp-content/uploads/2012/05/lifeway-research-highest-attendance-days-may-2012.pdf.

23. https://www.southwest.com/html/about-southwest/index.html

24. https://community.southwest.com/t5/Southwest-Stories/Southwest-Airlines-Gets-It-With-Our-Culture/ba-p/36414

25. https://www.southwest.com/html/about-southwest/index.html

26. John Wooden, *Wooden: A Lifetime of Observations and Reflections On and Off the Court* (New York: McGraw-Hill, 1997), 143.

Chapter 3

1. Robert Coleman, interview by Scott McConnell, August 10, 2011, Phase 1 qualitative interviews for the Transformational Discipleship project.

2. Phone call with Dr. Robert Coleman, August 26, 2016.

3. Phone call with Dr. Robert Coleman, August 26, 2016.

4. Jonathan Bergman and Aaron Sams, *Flip Your Classroom: Reach Every Student in Every Class Every Day* (Eugene, OR: International Society for Technology in Education World, 2012), 3–4.

5. Ibid., 4.

6. Ibid., 5.

7. http://schoolsofthought.blogs.cnn.com/2012/01/18/my-view-flipped-classrooms-give-every-student-a-chance-to-succeed/

8. Ibid.

9. Malcolm S. Knowles, Elwood F. Holton, and Richard A. Swanson, *The Adult Learner: The Definitive Classic in Adult Education and Human Resource Development, Seventh Edition* (Burlington: Elsevier, 2011), Location 5923 Kindle Edition.

10. http://www.nytimes.com/2007/01/15/business/media/15everywhere.html

11. Knowles, Holton, and Swanson, *The Adult Learner*, Location 748 Kindle Edition.

12. https://www.wired.com/2014/09/cinema-is-evolving/

13. http://www.telegraph.co.uk/science/2016/03/12/humans-have-shorter-attention-span-than-goldfish-thanks-to-smart/

Chapter 4

1. The stories in this chapter, particularly with Angela and Chris, and Jason and Melissa, are based on real situations from the churches that I've pastored in. I have changed their names and insignificant factors in their story to protect their identities.

2. Lesslie Newbigin, *Foolishness to the Greeks: The Gospel and Western Culture* (Grand Rapids, MI: William B. Eerdmans Publishing Company, 1986), Location 1582 Kindle Edition.

3. George Eldon Ladd, *A Theology of the New Testament* (Grand Rapids, MI: William. B. Eerdmans Publishing Company, 1993), 109.

4. http://www.desiringgod.org/messages/is-the-kingdom-present-or-future

5. Timothy Keller, *Center Church: Doing Balanced, Gospel-Centered Ministry in Your City* (Grand Rapids, MI: Zondervan, 2012), 34.

6. Lesslie Newbigin, *The Gospel in a Pluralist Society* (Grand Rapids, MI: William B. Eerdmans Publishing Company, 1989), 232.

7. Tim Chester and Steve Timmis, *Total Church: A Radical Reshaping around Gospel and Community* (Wheaton, IL: Crossway Books, 2008), 58.

8. http://www.archdaily.com/544355/spotlight-louis-sullivan

9. http://academics.triton.edu/faculty/fheitzman/tallofficebuilding.html

10. Ed Stetzer and Daniel Im, *Planting Missional Churches: Your Guide to Starting Churches that Multiply* (Nashville: B&H Publishing Group, 2016), 346.

11. Edward T. Hall, *The Hidden Dimension* (New York: Anchor, 1990), 114.

12. Ibid., 117–24.

13. Joseph Myers, *The Search to Belong: Rethinking Intimacy, Community, and Small Groups* (Grand Rapids, MI: Zondervan, 2003), 20.

14. Erwin Raphael McManus, *Soul Cravings* (Nashville: Thomas Nelson, 2006), Intimacy Entry 14.

15. Myers, *The Search to Belong*, 52.

16. Bob Hopkins and Mike Breen, *Clusters: Creative Mid-Sized Missional Communities* (UK: 3DM Publications, 2007), 36.

17. http://wearesoma.com/

18. http://thev3movement.org/

19. https://austinstone.org/

20. http://thecrowdedhouse.org/

21. https://www.guildfordbaptist.org/

22. http://www.christchurchwoking.org/

23. http://www.enc.uk.net/

Chapter 5

1. http://www.getannoyed.com/

2. http://newyork.cbslocal.com/2016/10/10/pet-peeve-week/

3. Hans Kung, *The Church* (New York: Image, 1967), 59-65.

4. http://faculty.georgetown.edu/jod/augustine/quote.html

5. William G. Rusch, "The Nature and Purpose of the Church: Some Reflections," *International Review of Mission Vol. XC* 358:236, 2001.

6. Lesslie Newbigin, *The Household of God* (New York: Friendship Press, 1954), 19.

7. Charles Van Engen, *God's Missionary People: Rethinking the Purpose of the Local Church* (Grand Rapids, MI: Baker Books, 1991), 17.

8. Lesslie Newbigin, *The Open Secret: An Introduction to the Theology of Mission* (Grand Rapids, MI: William B. Eerdmans Publishing Company, 1995), 56.

9. Ibid., 64.

10. John Stott, *Man with a Message* (London: Longmans, 1954), 163–64.

11. http://bookofconcord.org/augsburgconfession.php

12. John Calvin, *Institutes of the Christian Religion*, trans. F. L. Battles (Philadelphia, PA: Westminster, 1977), IV.i.xii, 1025–26.

13. Rick Warren, *The Purpose Driven Church* (Grand Rapids, MI: Zondervan, 1995), 103–107.

14. Mark Shaw, *10 Great Ideas from Church History* (Downers Grove, IL: InterVarsity Press, 1997).

15. Millard J. Erickson, *Christian Theology Second Edition* (Grand Rapids, MI: Baker Academic, 1998), 1061–69.

16. http://www.sbc.net/bfm2000/bfm2000.asp

17. Mark Dever, *9 Marks of a Healthy Church* (Wheaton, IL: Crossway Books, 2004), 28–31.

18. Justo L. González, *The Story of Christianity: The Early Church to the Present Day* (Peabody: Prince Press, 2007), 165.

19. http://www.theopedia.com/nicene-creed

20. Van Engen, *God's Missionary People*, 68.

21. Ibid., 69.

22. "Catholic." Merriam-Webster.com. Accessed October 21, 2016. http://www.merriam-webster.com/dictionary/catholic.

23. Van Engen, *God's Missionary People*, 70.

24. Ed Stetzer and Daniel Im, *Planting Missional Churches: Your Guide to Starting Churches that Multiply* (Nashville: B&H Publishing Group, 2016), 21.

25. Christopher J. H. Wright, *The Mission of God: Unlocking the Bible's Grand Narrative* (Downers Grove, IL: IVP Academic, 2006), 24.

26. http://www.christianitytoday.com/edstetzer/2007/august/monday-is-for
-missiology-3.html

27. Stetzer and Im, *Planting Missional Churches*, 19.

28. http://cities.barna.org/america-more-post-christian-than-two-years-ago/

29. https://www.barna.com/research/post-christian-cities-america-2017/

30. Tim Keller, *Center Church: Doing Balanced, Gospel-Centered Ministry in Your City* (Grand Rapids, MI: Zondervan, 2012), 274.

31. Ibid., 272.

32. Lesslie Newbigin, *The Gospel in a Pluralist Society* (Grand Rapids, MI: William B. Eerdmans Publishing Company, 1989), 232.

33. www.NewChurches.com/CPLF

34. http://www.spurgeon.org/s_and_t/srmn1873.php

35. Ibid.

36. You can learn more about the research and download a free copy of both The State of Church Planting in the U.S., and The State of Church Planting in Canada reports at NewChurches.com.

37. You can download a free digital copy of this book at NewChurches.com.

38. Eric Geiger and Kevin Peck, *Designed to Lead: The Church and Leadership Development* (Nashville: B&H Publishing Group, 2016), 14–15.

39. Ibid., 15.

40. David J. Bosch, *Transforming Mission: Paradigm Shifts in Theology of Mission* (New York: Orbis Books, 2006), 390.

41. Dietrich Bonhoeffer, *Letters and Papers from Prison*. The Enlarged Edition. (London: SCM Press, 1971), 382.

42. Geiger and Peck, *Designed to Lead*, 15.

43. Ibid.

44. http://communitychristian.org/

45. http://www.somatacoma.org/how-we-live/

46. https://timchester.wordpress.com/2009/01/28/the-rythms-of-a
-missional-church/

47. Philip Nation, *Habits for Our Holiness* (Chicago, IL: Moody Publishers, 2016), 25.

48. Geiger and Peck, *Designed to Lead*, 17.

49. Ibid.

50. Ibid.

Chapter 6

1. http://www.nytimes.com/2012/11/28/health/dr-joseph-e-murray-transplant
-doctor-and-nobel-winner-dies-at-93.html?_r=0

2. http://www.health.harvard.edu/blog/remembering-dr-joseph-murray-a
-surgeon-who-changed-the-world-of-medicine-201211285590

3. https://www.nobelprize.org/nobel_prizes/medicine/laureates/1990/murray
-bio.html

4. http://www.liveonny.org/uploaded_files/tinymce/files/interview_joseph_
murray.pdf

5. http://www.nytimes.com/2012/11/28/health/dr-joseph-e-murray-trans-
plant-doctor-and-nobel-winner-dies-at-93.html?_r=0

6. Ibid.

7. *Encyclopædia Britannica Online*, s. v. "transplant", accessed October 25,
2016, https://www.britannica.com/topic/transplant-surgery/Special-legal-and
-ethical-problems.

8. Ibid.

9. "A keystone species is a plant or animal that plays a unique and crucial
role in the way an ecosystem functions. Without keystone species, the ecosystem
would be dramatically different or cease to exist altogether." http://nationalgeo-
graphic.org/encyclopedia/keystone-species/

10. http://nationalgeographic.org/encyclopedia/keystone-species/

11. http://science.howstuffworks.com/innovation/everyday-innovations
/sunglass5.htm

12. Thom Rainer, *Who Moved My Pulpit? Leading Change in the Church*
(Nashville: B&H Publishing Group, 2016), 5–9.

13. Rainer, *Who Moved My Pulpit?*

14. John P. Kotter, *Leading Change* (Boston, MA: Harvard Business Review
Press, 1996).

15. John P. Kotter, *Accelerate: Building Strategic Agility for a Faster-Moving
World* (Boston, MA: Harvard Business Review Press, 2014).

16. Jim Collins, *Good to Great: Why Some Companies Make the Leap . . . and
Others Don't* (New York: HarperCollins Publishers Inc., 2001), 1.

17. Rainer, *Who Moved My Pulpit?*, 52.

Chapter 7

1. Christopher J. H. Wright, *The Mission of God: Unlocking the Bible's Grand
Narrative* (Downers Grove, IL: IVP Academic, 2006), 534.

2. Elisabeth Elliot, *Shadow of the Almighty: The Life and Testament of Jim
Elliot* (New York: Harper & Brothers, 1957), 247.

3. http://www.elisabethelliot.org/about.html

4. Elisabeth Elliot, *Passion and Purity: Learning to Bring Your Love Life Under
Christ's Control* (Grand Rapids, MI: Baker Book House Company, 2002), 85.

5. https://kinginstitute.stanford.edu/king-papers/documents/i-have-dream
-address-delivered-march-washington-jobs-and-freedom

6. Jim Collins and Jerry Porras, *Built to Last: Successful Habits of Visionary Companies* (New York: HarperCollins Publishers, 2002), Kindle Edition Location 5284.

7. Eric Geiger and Kevin Peck, *Designed to Lead: The Church and Leadership Development* (Nashville: B&H Publishing), 3.

8. https://beulah.ca

9. http://austinstone.org/

10. http://www.thebelovedchurch.org/

11. http://northwoodchurch.org/

12. http://www.summitrdu.com/

13. http://www.transformationchurch.tc/

14. http://doxa-church.com/

15. http://www.redeemer.com/

16. http://www.nytimes.com/2009/10/06/science/06qna.html

17. Peter F. Drucker et al., *Peter Drucker's Five Most Important Questions: Enduring Wisdom for Today's Leaders* (New Jersey, John Wiley & Sons, Inc., 2015), 90.

18. Jim Collins, *Good to Great: Why Some Companies Make the Leap . . . and Others Don't* (New York: HarperCollins Publishers, 2001), 91.

19. Will Mancini, *Church Unique: How Missional Leaders Cast Vision, Capture Culture, and Create Movement* (San Francisco, CA: Jossey-Bass, 2008), 84.

20. The question that the reader might be asking himself or herself is why I am using the word *strategy*, rather than *mission*. Or, why *mission* is absent from this chapter. Well, it's as the saying goes, "There are more ways than one to skin a cat." Here are three examples of different ways to understand the identity or core DNA of an organization. Peter Drucker has his five essential questions: What is our mission? Who is our customer? What does the customer value? What are our results? and What is our plan? Patrick Lencioni has his six questions: Why do we exist? How do we behave? What do we do? How will we succeed? What is most important, right now? and Who must do what? Will Mancini has his five questions: What are we doing? Why are we doing it? How are we doing it? When are we successful? and Where is God taking us?

My hope in this chapter is to simplify the process and help the reader get to the heart of where their church is going, what it must do to get there, and how it will go about it. I want to bring the reader far enough down the road so that they could begin designing a discipleship pathway in the final chapter. In light of this, I have found many church leaders often confuse vision with mission, or mission with strategy. As a result, many churches have actually abandoned either their vision or mission statement, and have instead opted for one clear statement that describes where they're going.

So if you're wondering where "mission" has gone in this chapter, here's the answer. It's partly in the section on vision, and it's partly in the section on strategy. I have not gotten rid of it altogether. I have, instead, simplified the concept for the average church and in light of the scope of this book.

21. http://www.ikea.com/ms/en_CA/the_ikea_story/working_at_ikea/our _vision.html

22. Michael E. Porter, "What Is Strategy?" Harvard Business Review, November-December 1996, 8.

23. Ibid., 10.

24. Ibid., 9.

25. http://www.merriam-webster.com/dictionary/system

26. Todd Adkins, *Developing Your Leadership Pipeline* (Nashville: LifeWay Leadership, 2016), 3.

27. Dave Ulrich, Norm Smallwood, and Kate Sweetman, *The Leadership Code: Five Rules to Lead By* (Boston, MA: Harvard Business School Publishing, 2009), Kindle Edition Location 190.

28. Peter F. Drucker, *Management: Tasks, Responsibilities, Practices* (New York: Harper and Row, Publishers, Inc., 1985), 125.

29. Ibid., 126.

30. Mancini, *Church Unique*, 129.

31. Patrick Lencioni, *The Advantage: Why Organizational Health Trumps Everything Else in Business* (San Francisco, CA: Jossey-Bass, 2012), 93.

32. Ibid., 94.

33. Ibid., 96.

34. Ibid., 97.

35. If you can't imagine this, just look up *Uncover the Human Body* on Amazon for a similar example.

Chapter 8

1. Peter M. Senge, *The Fifth Discipline: The Art and Practice of the Learning Organization* (New York: Crown Business, 2010), 11.

2. https://www.westjet.com/en-ca/about-us/jobs/ownership-benefits

3. Eugene Peterson, *A Long Obedience in the Same Direction: Discipleship in an Instant Society* (Downers Grove, IL: InterVarsity Press, 1980).

4. James C. Collins and Jerry I. Porras, *Built to Last: Successful Habits of Visionary Companies* (New York: HarperCollins, 2002), Kindle Edition Location 2153.

5. Ibid., 2102.

6. Ibid., 2112.

7. http://alpha.org

8. http://startingpoint.com/

9. https://run.alpha.org/

10. http://startingpoint.com/leader/

11. http://www.thevillagechurch.net/

12. http://www.summitrdu.com/

13. http://www.redeemer.com/

14. http://saddleback.com/

15. https://www.churchofthehighlands.com/

16. http://austinstone.org/

17. https://www.htb.org/

18. http://www.lifeway.com/disciplespath

19. Thom S. Rainer and Eric Geiger, *Simple Church: Returning to God's Process for Making Disciples* (Nashville: B&H Publishing Group, 2006), 73.

20. http://www.ritzcarlton.com/en/about/gold-standards

21. http://www.bbc.co.uk/history/british/empire_seapower/trafalgar_01.shtml

22. Ibid.

23. Stanley McChrystal with Tantum Collins, David Silverman, and Chris Fussell, *Team of Teams: New Rules of Engagement for a Complex World* (New York: Penguin Publishing Group, 2015), 31.

24. Ibid., 30.

25. Ibid.

Epilogue

1. http://www.rollingstone.com/music/lists/100-best-singles-of-1984-pops-greatest-year-20140917

2. Alan Light, *The Holy or the Broken: Leonard Cohen, Jeff Buckley, and the Unlikely Ascent of "Hallelujah"* (New York: Atria Paperback, 2012), 31.

3. http://www.leonardcohenfiles.com/covers-b.pdf

4. http://www.forbes.com/sites/hughmcintyre/2016/11/23/leonard-cohens-hallelujah-has-made-it-onto-the-hot-100-with-7-different-artists/.

5. Light, *The Holy or the Broken*, 2.

6. Ibid., 3.

7. Malcolm Gladwell, "Hallelujah," *Revisionist History,* podcast audio, accessed July 27, 2016, http://revisionisthistory.com/episodes/07-hallelujah.

8. http://web.archive.org/web/20080404002642/www.clapclap.org/2007/04/hallelujah.html.

9. Gladwell, "Hallelujah."

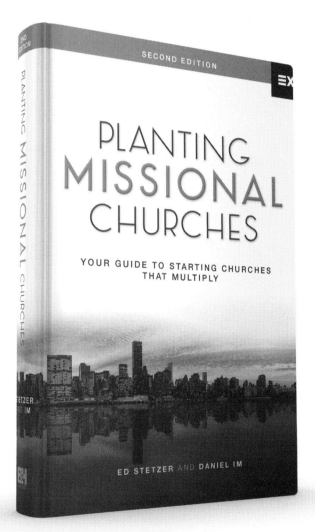